3⁰⁰
STEFANO
8/2/90

Between France and New France

Life Aboard the Tall Sailing Ships

by Gilles Proulx

Published by Dundurn Press Limited
in co-operation with Parks Canada
and the Canadian Government Publishing
Centre, Supply and Services Canada

Dundurn Press Limited
Toronto and Charlottetown
1984

Copyright © **Minister of Supply and Services Canada – 1984**
Catalogue number – RG62-129/1984E

All rights reserved. No part of this publication may be reproduced, stored in a retrieval system, or transmitted in any form or by any means, electronic, mechanical, photocopying, recording, or otherwise (except brief passages for purposes of review) without the prior written permission of the Minister of Supply and Services Canada.

The publication of this book was made possible through the assistance of Parks Canada and the Canadian Government Publishing Centre, Supply and Services Canada. The publisher also wishes to acknowledge the ongoing support of the Canada Council and the Ontario Arts Council.

J. Kirk Howard, Publisher

Copy editor: Blaine R. Beemer
Design and Production: Ron and Ron Design Photography
Typesetting: Q Composition Incorporated
Printing and Binding: Marquis Printing, Canada

Dundurn Press Limited
P.O. Box 245, Station F,
Toronto, Canada
M4Y 2L5

Canadian Cataloguing in Publication Data
Proulx, Gilles
  Between France and New France

Translation of: Entre France et Nouvelle-France.
Published in collaboration with Parks Canada.
Includes index.
Bibliography: p.
ISBN 0-919670-81-4 (bound). – ISBN 0-919670-80-6 (pbk.).

1. Sailing – North Atlantic Ocean – History – 18th century. 2. Ocean travel – North Atlantic Ocean – History – 18th century. 3. Sailing ships – France – History: 18th century. 4. Sailing ships – Canada – History – 18th century. 5. Seafaring life – North Atlantic Ocean – History – 18th century. 6. Canada – History – To 1763 (New France).
I. Parks Canada.
II. Title.
VK18.P7613 1984   910′.091631   C84-099216-5

Between France and New France

Life Aboard the Tall Sailing Ships

by Gilles Proulx

Acknowledgements

This book is based on research undertaken to develop Battle of the Ristigouche National Historic Park and broaden our understanding of the maritime background to the 1760 event. Thanks to the support of Parks Canada and my colleagues, the results of this research are now available to a wider public.

In gathering information from various archives in Canada, France and Great Britain, I was greatly aided by the co-operation and advice of staff members of the following institutions: the Archives nationales and the Bibliothèque nationale in Paris, the Archives maritimes de Paris (Vincennes), the Archives maritimes de Rochefort, the Bordeaux and La Rochelle departmental archives, the Musée de la Marine in Paris, the National Maritime museum in Greenwich, the Public Record Office in London, the archives of the Monastère de l'Hôtel-Dieu in Quebec City, the Musée de Sainte-Anne-de-Beaupré and the Public Archives of Canada.

I am particularly grateful to professors Lucien Campeau of the University of Montreal and Jacques Mathieu of Laval University, as well as to my Parks Canada colleagues – Michel P. de Courval, Marc Lafrance and Louis R. Richer – who agreed to read my manuscript and suggested a number of corrections. I would also like to mention the help of Professor James Pritchard of Queen's University and of Réal Boissonnault of Parks Canada; these gentlemen graciously provided many references. Sincere thanks also go to Noëlla Gauthier and Judith Labbé, who had the difficult task of transcribing my manuscript.

Finally, I am greatly indebted to my wife, Cécile Bilodeau, for her understanding.

G.P.

Contents

List of Illustrations 10
Preface 12
Abbreviations and Monetary Unit 12
Introduction 13

Maritime Traffic and Outfit of Vessels
    The French navy 17
    The merchant marine 21
    Maritime traffic 25
    Operations of the French royal navy 32
    Port activities 42

The Atlantic Course
    Courses and markers 47
    Speed and distances 54
    Climate and averages 59
    Dangers and safety measures 71
    Travelling up the St. Lawrence 76

The People and their Occupations
    The crew 81
    The passengers 87
    Crew members' duties 93

Life Aboard Ship
    Routine and sleeping quarters 100
    Diet 106
    Illness and medical treatment 111
    Religious practice 117
    Insubordination and discipline 123
    Recreation 125

Conclusion 129
Appendices 132
Notes 153
Bibliography 167
Index of Tables 170
Index of Names 171

List of Illustrations

1. King's vessels 19
2. The *Alcide* 22
3. The *Aréthuse* 23
4. The *Chameau* 30
5. Rig of merchant vessels 31
6. Careened vessel 34
7. Stem of the *Machault* 35
8. Pulleys from the *Machault* 38
9. Deadeye of the *Machault* 39
10. View of the *Prudent* and the *Bienfaisant* 40
11. Courses followed by the King's frigate *Diane* 48
12. "West-Indische Paskaert", Pieter Goos 50
13. New scaled-down chart of the Spanish Seas, Gerard Van Keulen 55
14. Capture of the *Alcide* and the *Lys* in 1755 56
15. Map of the eastern portion of New France, or Canada, Nicolas Bellin 60
16. View of the town of Louisbourg 62
17. Part of the St. Lawrence River with the passage through the traverse and nearby islands, Nicolas Bellin 63
18. Plan of the drydock in the port of Louisbourg 65
19. "A general view of Quebec from Point Levy", Richard Short 66
20. View of the port of Rochefort 68
21. View of the port of La Rochelle 69
22. View of the port of Bordeaux 70
23. Sea astrolabe 74
24. Hadley's octant 75
25. View of the port of Brest 88
26. Men-of-war sailing from the Toulon roadstead 91
27. Planes from the *Machault* 94
28. Chinese porcelain bowl from the *Machault* 96
29. Rafts used during the siege of Quebec City 98

30. View of cross-section of a three-decker man-of-war 105
31. Model of a 50-gun man-of-war... 116
32. Votive offering 119
33. Pewter tableservice from the *Machault* 120
34. Pump from the *Machault* 122
35. Pump's piston from the *Machault* 126

Preface

Between France and New France is a study of life aboard the sailing vessels that plied the North Atlantic during the heyday of the French colonial effort in North America. It analyses four major aspects of these early trans-Atlantic crossings and examines maritime communications in the age of sail.

The volume of traffic and the types of vessels are evidence of the roles of the French state and the private shipowners in defending New France and furnishing it with supplies. At the mercy of fickle winds, these ships followed a course where uncertainty prevailed, both in the duration of the crossings and in the risk of accidents. This challenge demanded a sustained effort from both the crews manning the vessels – to carry out their back-breaking work – and the crowded passengers in their care to co-exist despite the diversity of social backgrounds. The physical and psychological living conditions aboard ship afforded few luxuries to either the crews or the passengers in an environment of restrictions.

All the traces of these sailors' lives seem to have vanished as quickly as the wakes of the ships that bore them across the seas, and the history of trans-Atlantic communications is no doubt the poorer for this loss. Fortunately, the captains and the passengers had the time to record their impressions of the voyages, and from their diaries and letters I have drawn this portrait of life aboard ship.

Abbreviations

ADM	Admiralty
AM	Archives maritimes
AN	Archives nationales
CHR	Canadian Historical Review
HCA	High Court of Admiralty
MG	Manuscript Group
NF	New France
NMC	National Map Collection
PAC	Public Archives of Canada
PRO	Public Record Office
PUF	Presses universitaires de France
PUL	Presses de l'Université Laval

Monetary unit

The monetary unit used in this text is the *livre*. It contained 20 *sols*, and there were 12 *deniers* in a sol. The livre was worth some 20 to 23 times less than the English pound in the first half of the eighteenth century.

Introduction

From 1534 to 1760, from Jacques Cartier to François Chénard de la Giraudais, thousands of fishing, commercial, and war vessels sailed across the Atlantic Ocean between France and New France. In chronicling the history of New France, many historians have examined the political, economic, social, and cultural relationships that existed between the colony and the mother country. There has been little study, however, of the maritime setting of this relationship, that is, the world of sailing vessels and their crews and passengers. In recent years, historians have turned their attention to the study of material civilization. This trend, and the resulting speculations about daily life in past societies, have raised questions regarding the nature of maritime communications between France and New France. We can learn much about these two societies from their actions – the many decisions, preparations, and endeavours, and the determination required to succeed in crossing the Atlantic. The growth of New France owes much of its dynamism to the ways in which the French planned and carried out the challenge of crossing the ocean.

Between France and New France is a study of trans-Atlantic communications during the period of France's colonization of America, particularly the eighteenth century. It reconstructs the lives of the men who set out to conquer the Atlantic to earn their daily bread, or who were compelled to cross it to reach the colonies. Few historians of New France have neglected to mention the enormity of the problems a sea voyage could pose during the sailing era. It cannot be denied that the Atlantic Ocean curbed the development of New France; yet, it also represented a link between the mother country and a young colony clamouring for settlers. It is the nature of this unifying role that I should like to elaborate on in this study. To do so, two complementary steps are necessary.

It would be impossible to understand the life of the crew of an eighteenth-century sailing vessel, or that of its passengers, without knowing something of the setting for their activities. It is therefore necessary to begin by first describing the vessels, and secondly, by estimating the volume of maritime traffic between France and New France. This approach should make it possible to identify the types of sailing vessels found most often on the trans-Atlantic route, and sometimes to specify their cargo, which could often influence life aboard ship.

I chose the twelve years preceding the conquest of New France for estimating the volume of traffic. This period, although brief, was very significant, considering the development achieved by the colony. Moreover, the lack of port registers, wherein the arrivals and departures of sailing ships at Quebec City would have been recorded, precludes the establishment of valid statistics for the entire period of French rule in Canada. Despite the legendary gaps in documentation on the history of New France, however, it is possible to advance figures for short timespans that, although they may not be absolute values, at least indicate trends. By limiting my work to six years of peacetime compared to six years of war, I was able to discover the numbers and types of merchant vessels and to estimate their dimensions.

During the Seven Years' War, a considerable number of French warships came to the aid of New France, but this volume decreased as the war dragged on. From various statistics emerge details of France's state policy. For example, the historian Guy Frégault has strongly denounced France for abandoning its colony during the war. Did this desertion result from the effective English blockade, or was it a tragic consequence of the illness that ravaged and immobilized the French *en route* to Louisbourg in 1757? Perhaps France's expeditions to New France reveal instead a strategy that gave more importance to the territories acquired than to protecting sea routes. These questions emphasize the importance of this investigation of maritime traffic.

The physical aspects of trans-Atlantic travel varied according to the means of transportation, and it is this subject I should like to explore first. What types of vessels were used? What were their dimensions and principal features? What differences were there between warships and merchant vessels? These questions draw in the details of outfitting. An expedition to New France must have represented a substantial financial investment for the shipowners.

Rigging and loading a vessel entailed yet another series of activities. And once the sails were set, what course would the captain follow? He would undoubtedly have many obstacles to overcome, often with the aid of only rudimentary techniques, before he reached the St. Lawrence River. This external perspective allows the description of the sailing vessel, its route, and navigation policies.

The handling of these vessels required crew members to climb the ropes, crawl along yards, or set about repairing sails. How big were these crews, and how much were they paid to carry out all these duties? In the between-decks of the vessels were passengers, both civilian and military, bound for New France or returning home. What were their living arrangements on board and what material comforts were available to them? Could they take their ease as they wished? The duration of a trans-Atlantic journey was as unpredictable as its outcome. If provisions stowed aboard were insufficient to feed both sailors and passengers, the spectre of disease would haunt the ship. And how were individuals representing all the regions and social strata in France to co-exist in the close quarters of a sailing vessel? Viewed from within, people either frequented one another's company, or avoided all contact; they confronted one another or co-operated. The isolation of a ship at sea created a self-contained world. Others have written that the sea was the only factor uniting civilizations in modern times. Did it succeed then in breaking down social barriers?

The richest sources for this study were personal accounts of voyages. I began by consulting more than 90 log-books kept by captains and pilots on their trans-Atlantic journeys. About 50 of these record trips to Acadia or Louisbourg; the remainder record passages to Quebec City. They all provide technical data on the courses followed, the distances covered daily and the direction of the winds, and they also included the most noteworthy events, such as damage suffered during a storm or deaths on board. In addition, I consulted about 20 personal diaries of sea journeys, most kept by military officers or members of religious orders, letters written by Saint-Vallier, Frontenac, Talon, Lévis, Montcalm, and Duquesne, recording their impressions of a voyage.

The legal procedures followed by the British Admiralty upon the capture of French vessels bound for New France during the War of the Austrian Succession and the Seven Years' War provide another fascinating source of information. In addition to reports from the interrogation of high-ranking officers describing the circumstances of capture, there are a number of papers seized on boarded vessels. These include personal letters, bills of lading and quite frequently a range of legal documents such as clearances, letters of marque, and port dues receipts. The sometimes quite detailed cargo manifests could be useful for studies on commercial transactions. For my purposes, however, the most interesting of the seized papers are the crew lists, which reveal the names, ages, salaries, and origins of the officers and crewmen serving on the captured vessels. I studied 47 crew lists, which gave me a clearer impression of the eighteenth-century French sailor hired for ocean voyages. Unfortunately, these papers are almost solely concerned with ships sailing to Louisbourg; papers taken from vessels headed toward Quebec City still remain in the London archives of the Public Record Office. My own rapid inventory of those papers revealed files of documents on 71 sailing vessels, including 65 merchant ships captured while *en route* to Quebec City during the Seven Years' War alone. The personal accounts and the seized papers are replete with details on the crewmen and their daily life aboard sailing vessels.

The correspondence between the minister of the Marine and the authorities in the ports and colonies is also valuable, particularly for information on the physical characteristics of the vessels and on maritime traffic in general. The legal procedures at the Quebec city tribunals also provide a great deal of information on the difficulties encountered by the crews during their travels. This information includes captains' statements regarding damages to the ships and records of the losses suffered during their voyages between France and New France. These sources, some of which are included in the appendices, make up the bulk of the material used in my search for answers to the many questions on the subject of early trans-Atlantic communications.

Chapter One

Maritime Traffic and Outfit of Vessels

In the North Atlantic, the French sailing fleet featured two categories of outfit – the king's vessels and the merchant marine. Each was comprised of five types of vessels. For purposes of war or transport, the king or the state would commission men-of-war (*vaisseaux*), frigates, flutes, corvettes, and barges. The merchant marine (the private shipowners) would outfit frigates, full-scale ships (*navires*), brigantines, schooners, and bateaux. The size of the king's vessels was usually expressed in terms of the number of guns carried. In the merchant service, all documents established the capacity of merchantmen and fishing boats in tons.

The French navy

The man-of-war was a three-masted vessel rigged with square sails. A royal regulation, adopted as far back as 1670, distinguished five classes of such vessels.[1] The first and second classes included three-deckers capable of carrying between 56 and 120 guns. Only these men-of-war carried guns of 24-pound calibre or higher (figure 1).[2] The third-class man-of-war had two decks and carried between 40 and 50 guns (figure 2). The calibre of these guns were rarely more than 18 pounds. These belonging to the fourth and fifth classes were also two-deckers; the fourth-class vessel could be fitted out with 30 to 40 guns and the fifth-class with 18 to 28. Table 1 lists the dimensions of men-of-war according to their different classes. They ranged from 110 to 163 feet in length, from 27 to 44 feet in breadth, and from 14 to 20 feet in depth, measured from the top of the keel to the midship beam.[3] In practice, as shown in part two of the table, the actual dimensions of certain vessels that came to Canada departed very little from the theoretical data. Master shipbuilders, therefore, produced vessels faithful to the specifications.

Table 1 Dimensions of Royal Vessels and Merchantmen

Type/capacity	Length (feet)	Breadth (feet)	Depth (feet)
Men-of-war according to the code of 1670			
First class	163.0	44.0	20.3
Second class 1st category	150.0	41.5	19.0
Second class 2nd category	146.0	40.0	18.2
Third class 1st category	140.0	38.0	17.5
Third class 2nd category	136.0	37.0	16.5
Fourth class	120.0	32.5	14.5
First class	110.0	27.5	14.0
Vessels coming to or built in New France			
Tonnant – 80-gun man-of-war	170.0	46.0	22.0
Héros – 74-gun man-of-war	163.0	43.0	20.6
Algonquin – 72-gun man-of-war	160.0	44.0	22.0
Dauphin Royal – 70-gun man-of-war	154.0	43.0	20.0
Alcide – 64-gun man-of-war	(159.0)	(44.10$^1/_2$)	(18.2$^1/_2$)
Rubis – 50-gun man-of-war	131.0	34.3(44.10$^1/_2$)	16.6
Chameau – flute	(152.6)	(34.3)	(15.3)
Aréthuse – 36-gun frigate	(132.2)	(34.5$^1/_2$)	(10.0)
Comète – 30-gun frigate	120.0(126.3$^3/_4$)	31.8(34.3)	16.3(10.0)
Hermione – 26-gun frigate	128.0(130.10)	33.6(37.6$^1/_2$)	18.0(13.5)
Chézine – ship of 430 tons burden	115.0(119.6)	27.10(30.2$^1/_2$)	12.10(12.0$^1/_2$)
Triomphant – ship of 192 tons burden	66.0	24.3	12.0
S. Gilles – ship of 143 tons burden	61.0	22.3	10.5
S. Joseph – brigantine of 90 tons burden	53.0	19.0	9.0
S. Michel – Schooner of 58 tons burden	46.0	17.0	7.5
S. Louis – bateau	42.0	16.5	7.5

(Note: numbers in parentheses are in the longer English feet)

The frigate, whether the king's or privately owned, was also a three-masted, square-rigged vessel (figure 3). As a rule, it carried between 24 and 36 guns, measured 110 to 125 feet in length, and had a beam of 32 feet.[4] By its dimensions and the number of guns it carried, the frigate compared with fourth- and fifth-class men-of-war. It was lighter and more streamlined, however, and thus faster in good weather. In addition, the merchant frigate had only one deck. Whereas 36-gun frigates could carry 12-pound calibre guns, those with 24 to 30 guns were rarely of more than eight- or nine-pound calibre. A rare exception was the *Hermione*, a 26-gun frigate captured by the English in 1757, whose guns were 12-pound calibre.[5] Compared with their English counterparts, French frigates were not strong enough to support high-calibre guns because of the wider spacing between the ribs. Lightness and strength were not synonymous on these frigates.

1. King's vessels. (*Robert Short*, Spoils of War, Portraits of the French and Spanish ships taken by Lord Anson, Captain Buckle and Sir E. Hawke in the year 1747 *Harry Margary, Lympne Castle, 1977.*) This plate shows three French men-of-war captured by the English during the battle of Cape Finisterre in northwest Spain in May 1747. All three are 50-gun vessels: the *Jason*, commanded by Bécart; the *Rubis*, by Macarty; and the *Diamant*, by Hocquart. The *Jason*, built in 1723–24, completed four voyages to New France between 1725 and 1739, including a 1737 passage to Quebec City. The *Rubis*, built at Le Havre in 1728, completed ten voyages to New France including nine as far as Quebec City. It was sailing to the shipyard at Quebec City for repairs during the Cape Finisterre battle. The *Diamant* was built in Toulon between 1730 and 1733. There is no evidence that it ever sailed to New France. (*See Appendix A.*)

Table 2 Draughts of Ships[10]

Name	Type, Capacity	Forward draught	Stern draught
Ardent	man-of-war, 64 guns	18 ft. 7 in.	20 ft. 7 in.
S. Laurent	man-of-war, 62 guns	17 ft. 7 in.	19 ft. 2 in
Rubis	man-of-war, 50 guns	16 ft. 9 in.	18 ft. 1 in.
Jason	man-of-war, 48 guns	16 ft. 6 in.	19 ft. 0 in.
Canada	flute	13 ft. 0 in.	14 ft. 4 in.
Diane	frigate, 30 guns	13 ft. 7 in.	15 ft. 6 in.
Friponne	frigate	13 ft. 7 in.	14 ft. 6 in.
Aréthuse	frigate	14 ft. 0 in.	14 ft. 6 in.

The flute was strictly a cargo or transport vessel, although it was capable of carrying several guns. It was a flat-bottomed, rather massive vessel; it has even been described as a right-angled parallelepiped.[6] Each flute usually carried from 8 to 30 guns whose calibre did not exceed twelve pounds.[7] The drawing of the flute *Chameau* shows five port-holes only (figure 4). Most flutes had a large cargo port in the stern to facilitate the loading of long pieces of construction timber or other materials, as in the case of flutes that came to Canada.

Frigates and flutes had a smaller depth than did men-of-war, and their draughts were naturally shallower. As a result, frigates did not sail in the direction of the wind and had a strong tendency to go off course in bad weather. This nautical defect became critical when a vessel was being pursued; the advantage was with the vessel that could sail closer to the wind.[8] As shown in Table 2, the draughts of royal vessels varied from 13 to 21 feet (figure 7). "It should be noted that the king's vessels, which ordinarily draw twenty feet of water, cannot come within two or three leagues of shore as a rule, even in ocean waters, because there is not twenty feet of water all along the coast."[9] This information was of paramount importance to a captain navigating a waterway of shallow or unknown depths, such as the St. Lawrence. In these waters, flutes and frigates were preferable to men-of-war.

There was also the corvette, a small frigate capable of carrying between 10 and 22 guns. Rigged with a lateen sail on the bowsprit and square sails on the other masts, the corvette served as a messenger ship on trans-Atlantic crossings.[11]

Flutes transported men and goods, whereas the lighter and better-armed frigates carried the mail or escorted other vessels. If the men-of-war were fitted out for fighting, they joined battle or they did escort duty. When fitted out for transport they carried only 22 or 24 guns and transported troops or goods to the colonies. In 1755, the 74-gun man-of-war *Entreprenant*, armed with only 24 guns, carried troops to Quebec City:

"Originally, we had removed all of the first battery from each vessel in order to leave the between-decks absolutely free to house the troops, but as Monsieur du Bois de la Mothe seemed to want each flute to have at least two guns in its first battery in order to use them through the portholes of the *Saint-Barbe* in case of retreat . . ."[12]

To unload the men-of-war, captains could use barges, which were flat, broad-beamed craft designed for this kind of work.[13] The barge was used in particular in 1755 to transport soldiers from the men-of-war anchored at Ile aux Coudres to Quebec City. The 74-gun vessels that were part of the expedition would not sail as far as Quebec City because of the risks in river navigation.[14]

Each type of sailing vessel in the French navy had different nautical attributes and a specific function, either as a transport, escort, or mail-carrying vessel. In other respects, the classification established by statute in 1670 was not just a theory of maritime architecture. Throughout the next century, these models specified the construction details of sailing vessels called on to cross the Atlantic.

The merchant marine

The sailing vessels fitted out by private owners included frigates, ships, brigantines, schooners, and bateaux. The frigates were used either for privateering or for escort vessels when the king did not have enough of his own. For example, in 1758, supplier Joseph Cadet acquired two frigates to protect his trading ships. In 1760, one of these frigates, the *Machault*, escorted the last expedition sent to Canada. The *Machault*, which had been built in 1757, was originally armed to raid enemy commerce.[1] Frigates, therefore, were primarily warships, with a capacity of 550 to 800 tons. The term "ship" (*navire*) was used solely in reference to three-masted vessels of 100 to 500 tons burden.[2] They were used for fishing and trading; when necessary, the king would charter ships to transport troops and reimburse shipowners for their expenses. All of these sailing vessels could carry guns if necessary.

The brigantine, schooner and bateau were distinguished from one another primarily by their rig (figure 5). The brigantine had only two masts, with the foremast square-rigged and a fore-and-aft rig on the mainmast.[3] In the eighteenth century, the 29 brigantines documented had tonnages of between 46 and 150, and averaged 87. The 30 schooners registered were between 20 and 120 tons, and averaged 61. The schooner was a two-masted vessel and was lateen-rigged fore and aft.[4] The 31 bateaux documented had an average tonnage of 55, and had only one mast.[5]

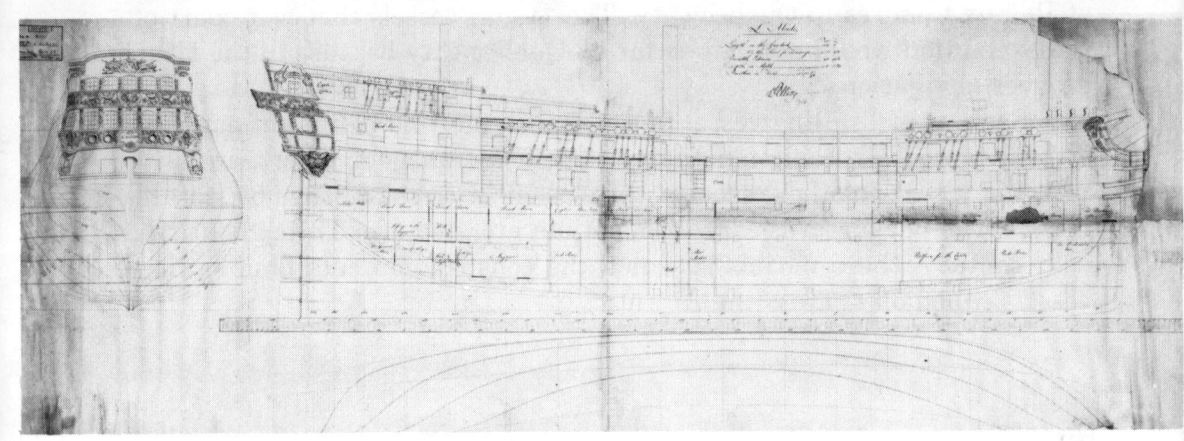

2. The *Alcide*. (*National Maritime Museum, London, Ships Plans Collection, Foreign Warships, Nos. 6001, 6001a.*) The *Alcide*, a 64-gun man-of-war, was captured on 8 June 1755 after 45 minutes of battle. Commissioned as a war vessel, it was escorting troop transport vessels to Canada when the English attacked. These Navy Board plans indicate the placement of the main facilities on board a 64-gun man-of-war, the type of vessel most frequently found during the Seven Years' War on the route between France and New France. *PAC, MG2B4, vol. 68, pp. 211-21.*

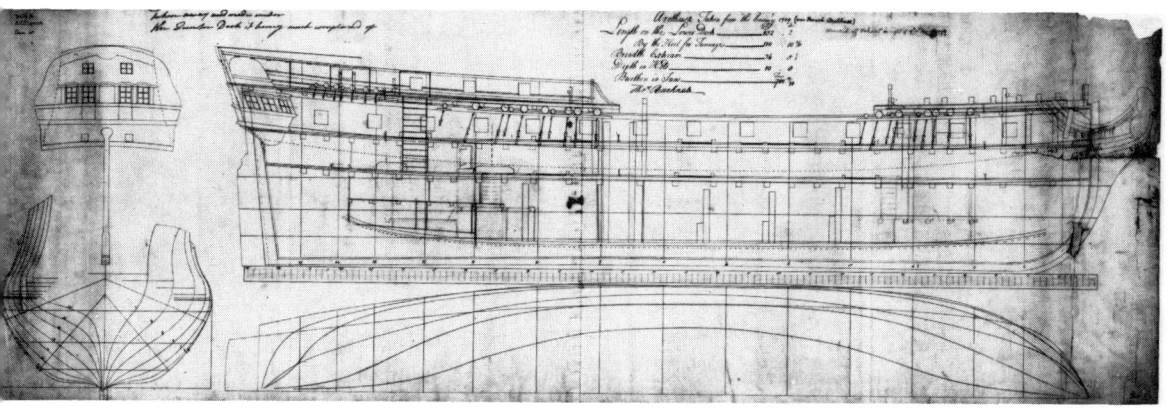

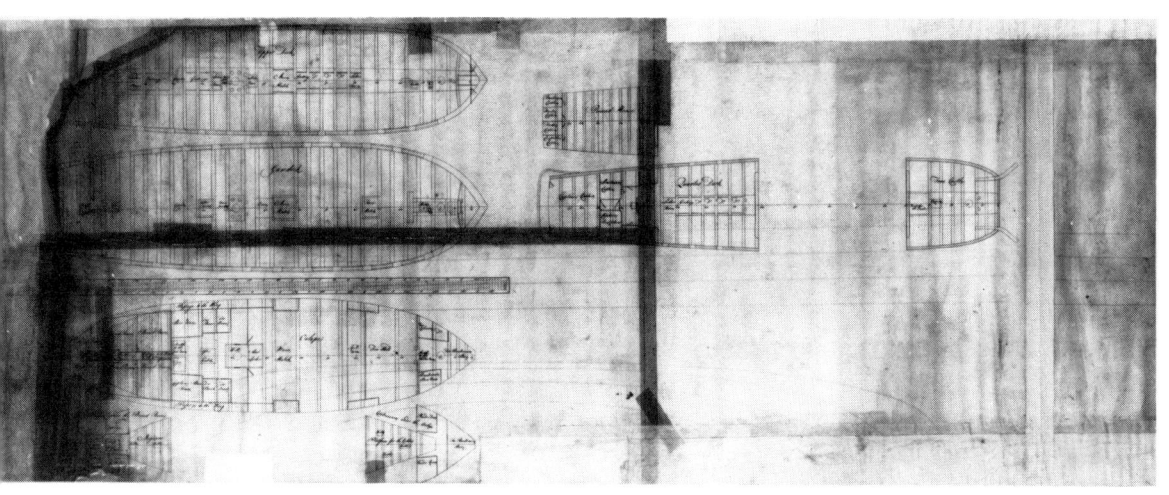

3. The *Aréthuse*. (*National Maritime Museum, London, Ships Plans Collection, Foreign Warships, nos. 2414A, 2414B.*) The *Aréthuse*, a 36-gun frigate, whose guns ranged from 4 to 12 calibre, was anchored in the port of Louisbourg during the seige in 1758. Under the command of Jean Vauquelin, the frigate succeeded in

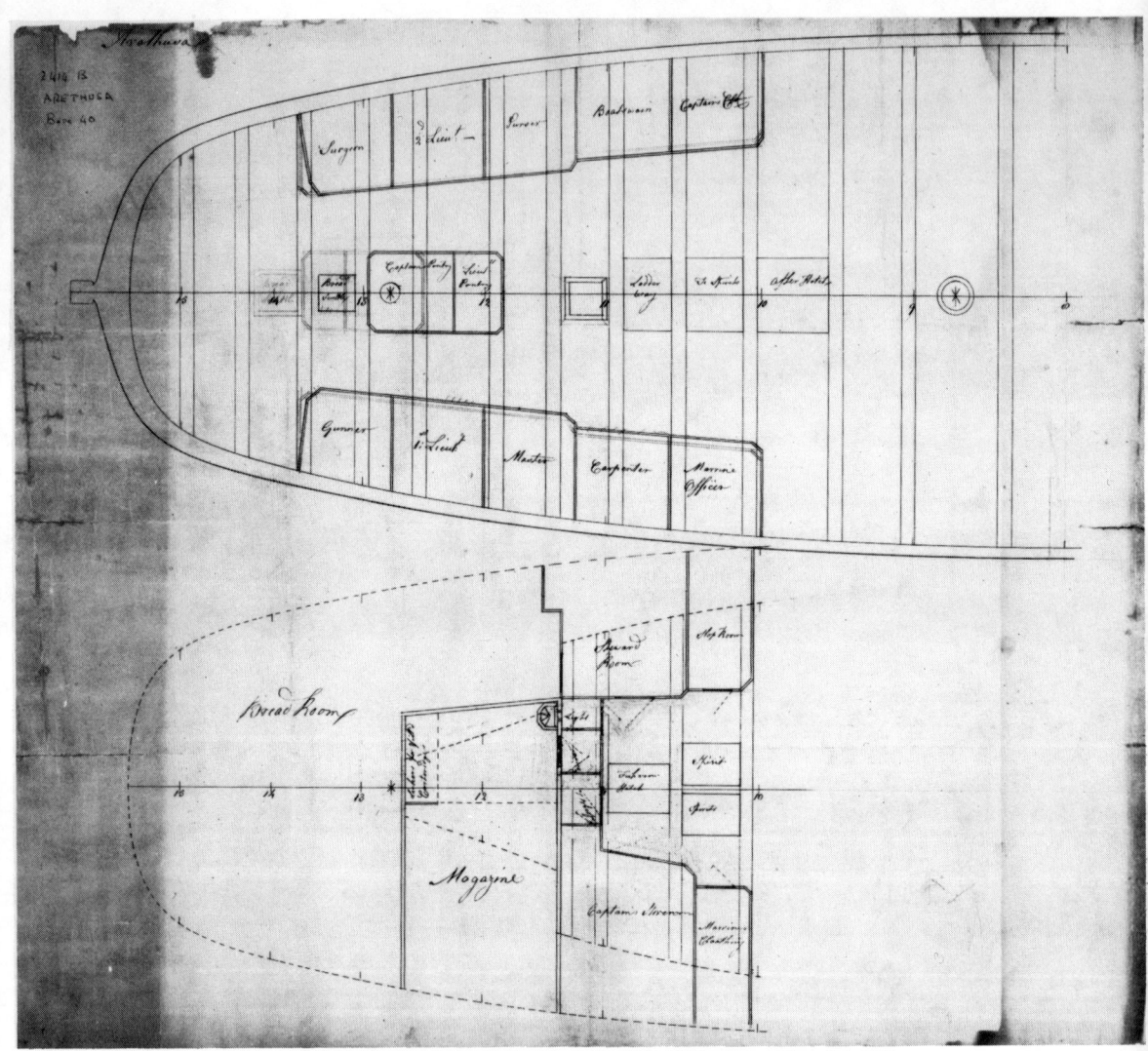

crossing enemy lines to reach France at the moment Louisbourg fell. Frigates were noted for their speed, and this quality no doubt served the captain well on this occasion. On 18 May 1759, however, the Aréthuse was taken by the English during a battle off the coast of France. (*J.S. McLennan*, Louisbourg from its foundation to its fall. *Sydney, Fortress Press,* 1969, pp. 274–75.)

Some references to snows and doggers appear also in the documentation. They were trading vessels with a tonnage similar to that of ships, but their rigs differed. The snow had sails identical to those of ships, but had only two masts. The dogger, also a two-masted vessel, was rigged with a mizzenmast and a mainmast.[6] Neither of these two types of vessels frequented the route between France and New France.

Table 1 indicates the dimensions of the different types of merchantmen. The examples given, with one exception, refer to sailing vessels built in Canada and whose capacity approached the average tonnages observed on the North Atlantic. Tables 3 and 5 indicate that two thirds of the vessels plying the ocean between La Rochelle and New France at the end of the French regime were of less than 200 tons burden. Moreover, for the period from 1755 to 1760, the average tonnage of vessels involved in trade between France and Canada was 219 tons burden. The dimensions compiled in Table 1, therefore, accurately indicate the size of the vessels used most frequently in trans-Atlantic communications.

The sailing vessels with a capacity of less than 200 tons were all less than 75 feet long in the keel, and it was into this rather limited space that passengers and crew, goods and supplies had to be crowded. In the category of ships of more than 200 tons burden, only the dimensions of the *Chézine*, a vessel of 430 tons burden, are known. The *Chézine* was 115 feet long and $27^{1}/_{2}$ feet wide; the hold was 12 feet, 10 inches deep and the between-decks was four feet high.[7] These dimensions are comparable to those of a fifth-class vessel, although the *Chézine* was armed with about 20 six-pound guns. The vessel's limited width and the narrow opening of the port-holes made the manoeuvring of the guns difficult, however. With the capacity of bateaux and schooners averaging 55 and 61 tons respectively, these two smaller types of vessel were seldom used for trans-Atlantic travel. Their tonnage was less than that of vessels regularly involved in commerce between La Rochelle and new France (Table 3), and they were reserved primarily for coastal trade in the Gulf of St. Lawrence.

Unlike the vessels of the French navy, the merchant ships did not have a specific role. Occasionally, political necessity required the shipowners to equip them with guns, in which case they were identifiable only by their tonnage and their rigging. The small tonnage of these vessels is surprising; perhaps what they lacked in size was made up for by their numbers.

Maritime traffic

Of all the vessels whose principal features I have described, which ones came to New France most frequently? From which French ports did they

Table 3 Merchantmen Sailing Between La Rochelle and New France, 1748–1759

Year	1748	1749	1750	1751	1752	1753	1754	1755	1756	1757	1758	1759	Total
70-99 tons	1	3	5	4	2	1	3	4	4	6	0	0	33
100-149 tons	1	2	0	5	4	4	5	5	5	6	2	0	39
150-199 tons	1	0	4	3	1	2	3	2	2	2	2	0	22
200-249 tons	1	1	1	1	1	0	0	1	1	2	2	0	11
250-299 tons	0	0	0	2	0	2	0	2	1	2	2	1	12
300-349 tons	0	2	2	0	2	1	0	0	2	1	1	0	10
350-399 tons	0	1	2	1	2	2	0	1	2	0	0	0	12
400-449 tons	0	0	0	1	2	3	0	1	0	0	0	0	7
500+ tons	0	0	0	0	2	0	1	1	0	0	0	0	4
Total	4	9	14	17	16	15	12	17	17	19	9	1	150

sail and what did they carry? From 1748 to 1759, 150 vessels bound for Louisbourg and Quebec City were fitted out at La Rochelle (Table 3).[1] The classification of these merchant vessels according to their capacity indicates the types and the dimensions of the vessels that undertook trans-Atlantic crossings. Half of those listed were of less than 150 tons burden, so trading was carried on for the most part with relatively small sailing ships.

La Rochelle was not the only port that fitted out ships sailing to New France, however. Upon arriving in Canada in 1755, War Commissioner Doreil wrote: "The first vessels arriving here from France and the majority of ships from French ports come from Bordeaux. . . . Many also sail out of La Rochelle. . . . There is usually a ship from Le Havre, one from Nantes, one from Marseilles and one or two from Bayonne."[2]

According to information from sailing lists in French ports, 176 commercial vessels were fitted out for Quebec City between 1749 and 1754 (Table 4),[3] six years of relative peace. During the next six years, 207 vessels sailed from French ports, also destined for Quebec City (Table 5).[4] In 1758, there were 56 registered departures for Quebec City, and commercial trade reached its peak. It would seem that traffic was slightly higher during wartime. It is impossible to determine how many of the vessels that sailed for Quebec City during the Seven Years' War actually reached their destination. The historian Guy Frégault maintains that in 1757, 51 vessels reached Quebec City, but he does not specify that they had sailed from French ports.[5] Since trade with the West Indies was virtually nil during that year, some of the vessels might have been coasting vessels from Louisbourg.[6] The English were especially active in the North Atlantic during 1757; they seized 21 sailing vessels *en route* from France to Louisbourg. Of the 55 vessels destined for Quebec City, 51 were unable to escape English surveillance.

Table 4 Commercial Traffic Between France and New France, 1749–1754

	Bordeaux (port lists)		Bordeaux (Pritchard's figures)		La Rochelle (port lists)		La Rochelle (Pritchard's figures)		Other ports (port lists)	
Year	New France	Quebec	Quebec	Tonnage	New France	Quebec	Quebec	Tonnage	New France	Quebec
1749	16	12	13	2,540	28	13	10	1,607	1	1
1750	22	16	12	2,130	17	12	11	1,903	9	1
1751	14	8	6	1,185	9	9	9	1,532	0	0
1752	28	21	19	3,869	22	16	9	1,744	3	3
1753	29	17	12	2,195	20	12	10	2,234	9	4
1754	32	21	20	2,715	19	8	9	1,168	13	2
Total	141	95	82	14,634	115	70	58	10,184	35	11

Table 5 Commercial Traffic Between France and Canada, 1755–1760

	La Rochelle			Bordeaux			Other ports			Total		
Year	Number of ships	Tonnage	Average tonnage	Number of ships	Tonnage	Average tonnage	Number of ships	Tonnage	Average tonnage	Number of ships	Tonnage	Average tonnage
1755	8	1,402	175	32	5,215	163	5	640	128	45	7,297	162
1756	10	1,886	189	11	2,330	212	0	0	0	21	4,216	201
1757	14	1,988	142	30	8,605	287	11	540	49	55	11,133	202
1758	7	1,290	184	38	9,300	245	11	2,850	259	56	13,440	240
1759	1	280	280	20	5,820	291	3	652	217	24	6,752	281
1760	0	0	0	6	2,424	404	0	0	0	6	2,424	404
Total	40	6,844	171	137	33,694	246	30	4,682	207	207	45,262	219

The war did not reduce commercial traffic on the whole; however, the statistics for the individual ports are less clear. Departures from La Rochelle fell from 70 for the period 1749–1754 to 40 for the war years of 1755–1760. But for the same periods, departures from Bordeaux increased from 95 to 137. There were 291 departures of commercial sailing vessels destined for New France from 1749 to 1754, and at least 220 departures from 1755 to 1760.[7] The 220 departures indicated in Table 6 do not include departures for Louisbourg from ports other than La Rochelle and Bordeaux. For the years 1749–1754, departures for New France from these two ports represented 12 per cent of the total. There is no indication that there was any substantial increase in departures during the next six years, especially since departures for Quebec City from ports other than La Rochelle and Bordeaux were only 15 per cent of the total. In all probability, traffic was slightly lighter in wartime.

From 1749–1754, the number of departures of French commercial sailing vessels reached approximately 420 annually.[8] This figure includes departures for Santo Domingo, Martinique, and North America, as well as for the slave trade, but does not include fishing vessels. The Guyenne chamber of commerce estimated that 60 ships left for New France during peacetime, or approximately 14 per cent of the departures.[9] According to the figures in Table 4, the departures for New France represent only 12 per cent of the total. Thus, commercial traffic between France and New France was only 12 to 14 per cent of all French commercial traffic with the colonies. France's commercial interest in its colony of New France seems to have been rather limited, and the war did little to improve it, although this is not indicated by the variations in maritime traffic. Historians studying France's foreign commerce, however, have noted the steady increase throughout the eighteenth century, and have pointed out that general trade levelled, and even declined, because of the Seven Years' War. Trade with New France was no exception.

Even if traffic did remain relatively similar in wartime as in peacetime, the same did not apply to the quantity of merchandise transported. According to historian James Pritchard, the war years from 1755 to 1760 saw a considerable increase in the volume of merchandise exported to Canada.[10] Tables 4 and 5 indicate that there was an increase of about 15,000 tons for the ports of La Rochelle and Bordeaux from 1755 to 1760, compared with the six previous years. In fact, the increase applies only to Bordeaux, because La Rochelle's total tonnage actually declined by approximately 30 per cent.

From 1749 to 1755, ships sailing from La Rochelle carried an average of 175 tons burden, whereas those sailing from Bordeaux carried an average of 178 tons burden. During the war years following, the average tonnage of ships sailing from La Rochelle remained stable at 171 tons burden, but the cargo of Bordeaux ships rose to 246 tons. The port of Bordeaux thus played an important role in the traffic of ships sailing for New France.

Tables 4, 5, and 6 show that Bordeaux was actively involved in trade between France and New France from 1749 to 1760. Before the war, approximately half the vessels that sailed for New France were fitted out there. At that time, Bordeaux sailing vessels carried the same average tonnage as ships from other French ports. After 1755, however, two-thirds of the ships bound for New France were fitted out at Bordeaux, and the average tonnage was 50 tons more than that of vessels from other ports. Thus, Doreil's comments about Bordeaux were accurate. What factors led to Bordeaux's domination, especially to the increase in tonnage during the war? Before the Seven Years' War, Bordeaux was responsible for approximately 40 per cent of all commercial traffic to Africa and the Americas, or 166 of the 420 departures.[11] Bordeaux's importance in colonial trade in general explains its major involvement in maritime traffic with New France in particular.

Bordeaux owed its commercial domination to its wine production and its rural agriculture. It exported wine to England, from which it imported tobacco and salt-pork. Some of these imports were then exported to the West Indies, to which Bordeaux also shipped flour from the interior or from coastal trade with Britanny. Perishables were a prime, if not an essential, element of Bordeaux's trade with the colonies. They represented approximately three-quarters of the value of the cargoes shipped during the first half of the eighteenth century.[12] As only 15 per cent of France's commercial trade was with New France, most of Bordeaux's colonial trade was with the West Indies, which traded its industrial products for European foods. Barrels of flour and pork-quarters were heavy and cumbersome and required vessels capable of carrying heavy tonnage in order to realize some profit. Because of its exports to the West Indies, Bordeaux was in an excellent position to import heavy cargoes of sugar and coffee from the islands.

Canadian authors Frégault and Reid attribute Bordeaux's domination in trade with New France to the bonds that existed between the Gradis family of Bordeaux and the corrupt Bigot, Bréard, and Cadet clique.[13] In 1755, Gradis exported 500,000 livres worth of goods to Canada; in 1758, the figure was 2.3 million livres. French historians Butel and Pariset also concluded that the Gradis firm played an important role in the 1750s, because of contracts in Canada or orders passed on by those who controlled trade there.[14] In fact, the ties between Gradis and Bigot would seem to have played quite a subordinate part in Bordeaux's dominance of trade with New France, and, by extension, in the increased tonnage of vessels sailing to Canada.

James Pritchard, in his study of commercial activities in New France, noted that food products shipped from Bordeaux to Quebec between 1755 and 1760 represented 70 per cent of the total cargo.[15] Consequently, cargo shipped from Bordeaux to Canada compared favourably in volume with that shipped to the West Indies from the beginning of the eighteenth century. According to the Guyenne chamber of commerce, French exports to New France were, except during wartime, composed of alcohol, manufactured goods, and luxury items. France's commercial policy, noted by every historian interested in trade between France and New France, determined that manufactured goods be exported to Canada. In describing the triangular route of Bordeaux's ships, Butel explained that sailing vessels transported manufactured goods, such as textiles and draperies from Agenais, to Louisbourg and Quebec City, where they took on wood and cod for the West Indies. From the West Indies, they sailed back to Bordeaux with their holds loaded with sugar and coffee.[16] Although it has been impossible to obtain precise statistics on the cargoes destined for New France, the figures obtained indicate that the cargoes exported from

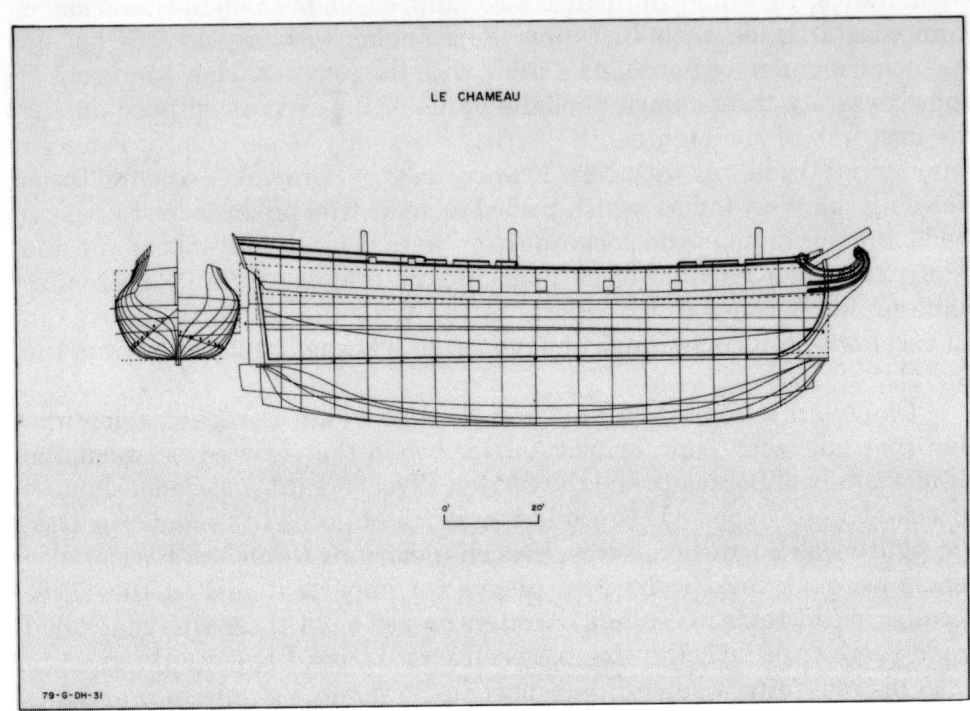

4. The *Chameau*. (*Chapman*, Architecture Navalis Mercatoria, pl. LII [52].) Built in Holland, this flute was launched in 1716. It was 152$\frac{1}{2}$ feet long, 34$\frac{1}{4}$ feet wide, and 15$\frac{1}{4}$ feet deep, or 143, 32, and 14$\frac{1}{3}$ *pieds*, respectively. The *Chameau* was on its seventh voyage to Canada when it was wrecked on the shores of Isle Royale at the end of August 1725. (*See Appendix A.*)

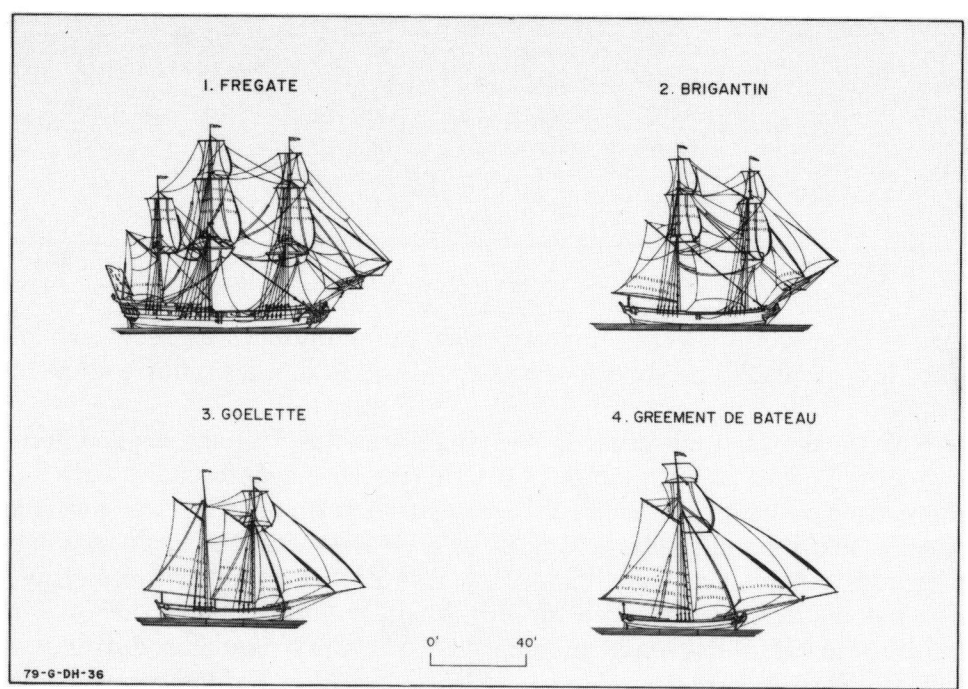

5. Rig of merchant vessels. (*Chapman*, Architecture Navalis Mercatoria, pl. LXII [62].) Example 1 is a frigate with a ship's rig. Both types of vessel were used for trade between France and New France. The other illustrations show the rig of the three other types of vessel used for trans-Atlantic and coastal trade.

Table 6 Commercial Traffic Between La Rochelle and Bordeaux and New France, 1755–1760

Year	Bordeaux Number of ships	Tonnage	Average tonnage	La Rochelle Number of ships	Tonnage	Average tonnage
1755	41	6,238	152	17	3,255	191
1756	11	2,330	212	17	3,081	181
1757	40	10,055	251	19	2,793	147
1758	39	9,700	249	9	1,740	193
1759	20	5,820	291	1	280	280
1760	6	2,424	404	0	0	0
Total	157	36,567	233	63	11,149	177

France in peacetime were composed mostly of manufactured goods, which were less cumbersome than foodstuffs and which did not require ships of heavy tonnage.

With the war and its accompanying hardships, Canada needed flour and salt. Bordeaux was asked to provide these goods, because with its commercial network it was in the best position to supply what was needed. Also, Bordeaux had the largest number of vessels with the large tonnage required to transport flour. Financing was needed to outfit these ships. The shipowners, who wanted to be financially secure, chose the Gradis family and other Bordeaux merchants.[17] Perhaps friendship did play a role in maritime relations, such as those between Bordeaux and New France, but it was not the only factor.

Research into commercial traffic shows that, in general, trade between France and New France was carried out using vessels of small dimensions. The ships' capacity could be increased according to the space required by the goods being transported, but this flexibility did not facilitate life on board. There were also repercussions on the activities in the port, since it was then necessary to use other outfitters and different port facilities. As a result, commercial traffic pointed to a certain specialization for French ports. The increased volume of the traffic until 1758 was an indication of France's interest in New France, but the variations in volume seem to have been closely linked to the protection provided by the French navy.

Operations of the French Royal Navy

Between 1755 and 1760, no fewer than 69 vessels commissioned by the king made a total of 93 voyages bound for Quebec City and Louisbourg (Table 7).[1]

Table 7 King's Vessels in New France, 1755–1760

Type	Vessels Quebec City	Vessels Louisbourg	Voyages Quebec City	Voyages Louisbourg
80 guns	0	13	0	3
74–70 guns	3	10	3	12
64 guns	9	14	11	16
50 guns	3	4	3	5
Frigate	8	13	10	15
Corvette	0	2	0	2
Barge	2	2	2	2
Flute	1	6	2	7
Total	26	54	31	62

Type	Captured Outward	Captured Homeward	Other losses At Louisbourg And Quebec City	Shipwrecked	Diverted
80 guns	0	0	0	0	0
74–70 guns	0	0	0	0	0
64 guns	3	2	4	0	2
50 guns	1	0	0	1	0
Frigate	0	2	4	0	1
Corvette	0	0	1	0	0
Barge	0	0	0	0	0
Flute	1	0	1	1	0
Total	5	4	10	2	3

Of this number, at least 10 were unable to reach their destination, having been either diverted to the West Indies, shipwrecked, or captured *en route*. If we add other units of the French Royal Navy that were captured or destroyed in North American waters, the losses total 25 vessels. Apart from the *Léopard*, which was demolished in Quebec City in 1756 because of its decrepit condition, sailing vessels were destroyed so that they could be used to blockade the entrance to the port of Louisbourg during the siege of 1758.[2] It is somewhat surprising that two thirds of the vessels, and of the voyages, had Louisbourg as their destination. In terms of manpower strength, this post was considerably less important than those in Canada. The high volume of traffic bound for Louisbourg, however, underscores the importance of possession of this strategic fortress and its role in safeguarding French interests in North America.

Most of the sailing ships that were equipped with the greatest number of guns and therefore superior in tonnage and size were dispatched to Louisbourg. The choice of this destination for the large vessels was an indication of the hazards of navigation on the St. Lawrence River. Cap-

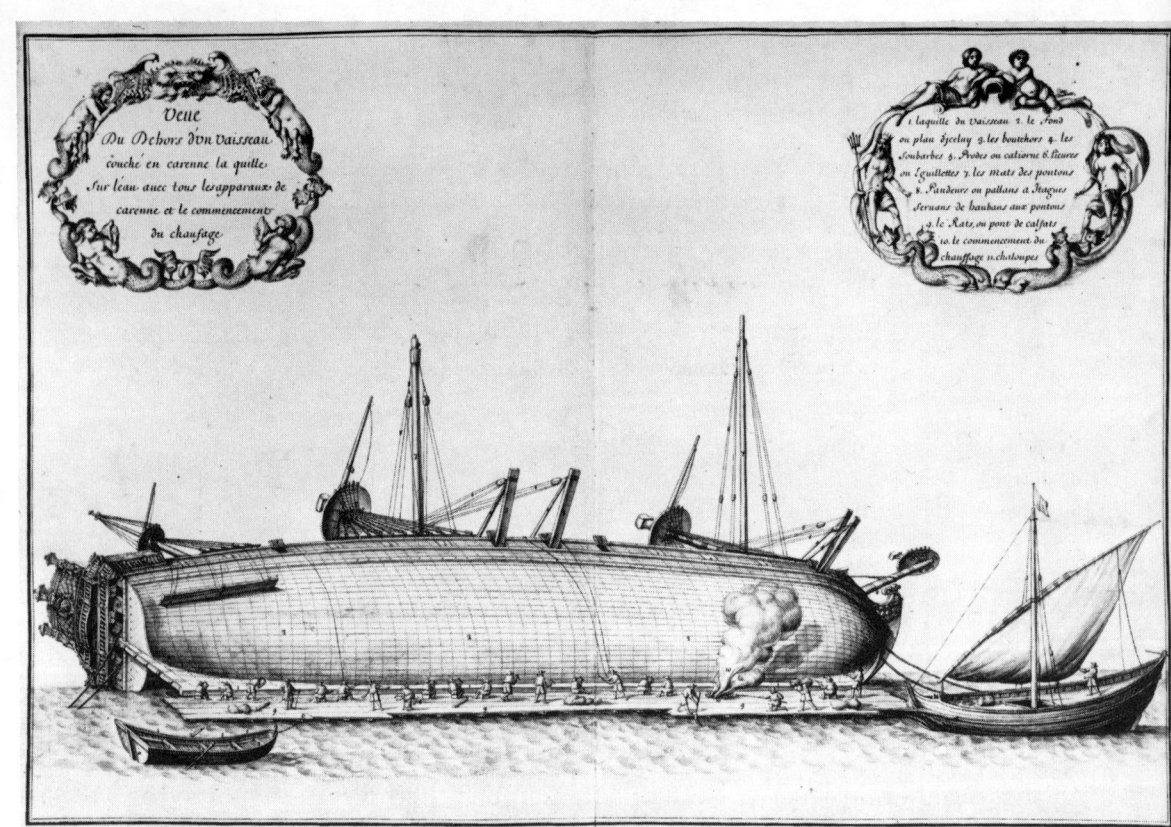

6. Careened vessel. (*Atlas de Colbert, France, Service hydrographique de la Marine, man. 140, Cliché Giraudon, no. LA 154952.*) This sketch of a careened vessel gives some indication of the extent of the work required to fit out a sailing vessel for ocean voyages.

7. Stem of the *Machault*. (*Parks Canada*.) This 26-gun privateer, built in 1757 at Bayonne, was scuttled in the Ristigouche estuary on 8 July 1760. The roman numerals etched in the piece of wood indicate the ship's draught. Underwater explorations conducted by Parks Canada between 1968 and 1972 discovered the remains of the *Machault's* hull, as well as many artifacts that had gone down with the ship.

tains did not dare venture too far inland with deep-draught vessels. More than half of the sailing ships listed appear to have been fitted out as transport vessels and were employed to carry troops and war supplies. The others were escort vessels or served as hospital ships. Throughout the war, France did not send naval forces or squadrons into North American waters.[3] It concentrated on transporting reinforcements to the colonies, rather than maintaining a maritime route. Undoubtedly, this strategy was not the most enlightened one.

From 1755 to 1758, the French Royal Navy transported nearly 6,000 troops from France to Louisbourg and Canada, whereas merchant ships brought some 2,000 recruits for the *Compagnies franches de la Marine*. In 1755, a fleet of 16 vessels and frigates reached Louisbourg and Quebec City. Only three vessels and three frigates sailed up the St. Lawrence with troops in 1756, but in 1757 three divisions of six, nine and twelve vessels respectively set sail for Louisbourg. The next year there was a clear change of policy: the French royal navy's presence was no longer so obvious. The authorities then sent a division of 12 vessels to Louisbourg, but few reached their destination (figure 10).

France seemed to rely more and more on private interests to protect the commerce of its nationals. In fact, in 1759 and 1760, private frigates belonging to the troops' commissary (supply officer), a Canadian named Joseph Cadet, provided protection for the last two commercial voyages to New France.[4] In 1759, about 20 ships, escorted by the frigates *Machault* and *Maréchal de Senneterre*, succeeded in sailing up the St. Lawrence before the English arrived to lay siege to Quebec City. Two royal frigates, the *Atalante* and the *Pomone*, were following closely behind. But the following year, the *Machault*, caught in an ambush deep in Chaleur Bay, fought the last naval battle in North American waters before Montreal's surrender. Short of ammunition and facing certain defeat, the *Machault* sank itself.

Even when fitted out as transport vessels, the men-of-war, by their very presence, provided commercial traffic with some protection during the first years of war. So, after 1757, when the number of royal naval vessels fell to two or three, the volume of commercial traffic also dropped off considerably. The movement of French naval vessels in the waters of New France between 1755 and 1760 was, by all accounts, rare. In fact, throughout the eighteenth century and during the years of peace, only one or two vessels a year arrived at Quebec City and Louisbourg. Most often, these were flutes or 50-gun men-of-war.[5] In 1743, the colonial authorities in Canada called for the dispatch of flutes, instead of men-of-war, and lighter vessels. Apart from the troop transport ships in the Duc d'Anville and the La Jonquière squadrons in 1746 and 1747, flutes and frigates then came to Canada until 1755.[6]

The high number of French vessels in North American waters during the Seven Years' War is somewhat astonishing given the commercial importance of New France. In 1757, the French Royal Navy numbered 165 units, the largest of which included 64 men-of-war carrying between 50 and 80 guns, 36 frigates, 15 corvettes and 7 flutes.[7] Of this number, 23 men-of-war and frigates, or close to one quarter of the most powerful warships in the French navy, were to be found at Quebec City and Louisbourg in that year. Certainly, the French naval presence in North American waters declined steadily in the years that followed, but until autumn 1757 the mother country appears to have been mindful of its responsibilities toward New France. France did not willingly abandon its North American colony. If the assistance provided was not as substantial as the colonists might have wished, that should be viewed more as the result of a long-term policy that had not enabled the French navy to expand. In 1757, the navy boasted 64 men-of-war; by 1758 it had been reduced to 58; and in 1763 it had but 43 and this was in spite of the fact that construction had started on 17 vessels in 1757.[8]

Under these conditions, it proved very difficult for France to provide support for its colony. Moreover, the rather effective blockade that the English established along the French coastline, beginning at the end of 1755, made it increasingly difficult for French ships to put to sea.

The construction sites of 53 of the 69 royal vessels that plied North American waters from 1755 to 1760 have been identified: 24 were built at Brest, 14 at Rochefort, 11 at Toulon, 2 at Le Havre, and 2 – the *Abénaquise* and the *Algonquin* – at Quebec City. Most of these were launched between 1748 and 1752. The oldest was the *Espérance*, which was built at Toulon in 1722 and made its last voyage to Louisbourg in 1755. The *Abénaquise*, a 36-gun frigate launched from Quebec City in 1756, was captured by the English in 1757. Re-baptized the *Aurora*, she continued her career until 1763. Before she set sail again after her capture, the *Abénaquise* was carefully examined by shipbuilders in England. Thereafter, her hull was a model for the construction of two types of English frigates.[9] In this way, the English paid homage to Canadian shipbuilders.

Most of the vessels were of fairly recent construction and, in this respect, they fulfilled the wishes of Governor Duquesne who, in 1752, had called for the use of new vessels for the long and arduous trans-Atlantic crossings.[10] Duquesne had arrived in Canada in 1752 aboard the *Seine*, a flute built in 1718. He had little appreciation for the limited comfort of the old vessel. The predominance of ships built at Brest is no doubt explained in part by the fact that from 1755 to 1758, all troopships destined for New France set sail from that port. From 1713 to 1754, the majority of vessels arriving at Quebec City and commissioned at Rochefort or La Rochelle had been built at Rochefort or Toulon.

Although the efficient administration of the colony in peacetime required only a minimal presence of the French navy, the traffic of royal vessels soon became considerable in wartime, an indication of France's interest in its colony. Only a lack of foresight in policies made it necessary

8. Pulleys made of elm and gayac wood from the *Machault*. (*Parks Canada*.)

9. Deadeye made of elm belonging to the *Machault*, used to tighten the shrouds. (*Parks Canada.*)

10. View of the *Prudent* (74 guns) and the *Bienfaisant* (64 guns). *National Maritime Museum, London, Public Visual Index, no. 1770.* These two men-of-war were

part of a division of 12 ships sent to Louisbourg in 1758. At the end of July, they were caught in an ambush in the port and destroyed by fire.

to turn to private enterprise to alleviate the deficiencies of the royal navy. The warships' primary role was diverted to the transporting of troops. Replacing guns with men contributed to the insecurity of the seas, and also no doubt profoundly affected the living conditions aboard ship.

Port activities

Whether constructed in Brest or in Rochefort, and whether young or old, all sailing ships had to undergo a major refit before each voyage. Thus, when the king ordered an expedition or when a shipowner decided to trade with the colonies, and the choice of captain and vessel had been made, careening would begin (figure 6). This operation, which would start once the vessel's ballast had been removed, consisted of heaving it down using cables running through pulleys attached to the heads of the lower masts and capstans on the ground. Once the vessel was on its side, workmen replaced rotten planks, stopped up the seams or cracks with oakum, and poured on pitch and hot tar to waterproof the hull. The procedure was then repeated for the other side. Sometimes this work had to be redone at different ports of call, with refits so extensive as to involve replacing sections of the keel. This was the case in Louisbourg in 1726 when carpenters had to replace more than 40 feet of the keel on the frigate *Néréide*, which had struck a rock on entering the harbour.[1] Thirty-one years later, also at Louisbourg, the *Tonnant*, an 80-gun man-of-war, had to be careened after a severe storm.[2] Heaving down an 80-gun man-of-war in a colonial port, which was no doubt poorly equipped (figure 18), must have been a formidable task indeed.

After the careening, the vessels were refloated so that other workmen could continue the preparations for departure. These included scraping and repainting the surface portion of the hull and then loading old iron, stones, and gravel for ballast. Experience determined the quantity of ballast required. Provisions and cargo were a natural form of ballast, so when casks of wine or drinking water had been consumed, the casks were refilled with sea water to maintain the vessel's equilibrium. To ballast a 30-gun frigate, such as the *Diane* in 1755, 41 barrels of iron and 75 barrels of stone were required. This weight was supplemented by 83 casks of fresh water.

In 1755, however, the captain of the *Diane* complained, "no matter how careful I am to have the water and wine casks refilled as they run empty, the frigate handles poorly under sail and I will be forced at the first sign of good weather to stow some of the guns of the first battery in the hold for smooth sailing".[3] It was not enough just to stack ballast barrels in the bottom of the hold: it was just as important to ensure that they were distributed evenly, for the speed of the sailing ship as well as its behaviour in the water depended on it.

The lack of deep-water port facilities meant that all men-of-war and most merchant ships had to be loaded or unloaded using lighters and barges in France and longboats, schooners, and bateaux in New France.[4] Cargo was taken out to the men-of-war or ships, hoisted on board with the help of tackle, and lowered into the hold and the between-decks through hatchways. In flutes, the large cargo port in the stern facilitated loading. As the captain of the *Chameau* observed in 1720, there were occasional drawbacks to this loading procedure in a roadstead such as the one at Quebec City, where gusting winds were frequent in the autumn, the loading season:

> Indeed, I had no sooner made a chute consisting of thirty-nine pieces of oak so that the poles would slide more easily over top of them and then taken on eight poles, when I would have stopped, had I been observing the standard safety rules which stipulate that the cargo port must be shut as soon as it comes within eleven or twelve inches of the water; especially when one is riding at anchor in an open roadstead exposed to powerful currents and changing, unpredictable, gusting winds.[5]

Provisions were then placed in the storerooms and other goods stowed in the bottom of the hold; the spaces between the casks were filled with pieces of wood to prevent movement when the ship rolled.[6] Once the goods were on board, the captain became responsible for them, although he was not responsible for any damage that might occur during the loading.[7] If goods came on aboard in bundles too big to fit through the hatchways, the bundles were taken apart and the supplies thus exposed to damage and loss. The quality of the casks and packing left much to be desired. As Canadian colonial authorities pointed out in 1741 and again in 1749, poorly packed goods had little protection against the dampness aboard a sailing vessel.[8] Intendants in Canada urged that musket packing cases be wrapped in canvas to prevent rust and that swords be placed in cases rather than in bundles. They also wanted barrels to be identified clearly and different grades of nails not mixed up. These instructions speak volumes about the condition in which goods loaded in France sometimes reached their destinations in Canada.

With the exception of those used almost exclusively for troop transport, the majority of the king's vessels bound for New France sailed from Rochefort (figure 20). When the careening and ballasting had been completed, the crew climbed aloft and fastened the sails into position. The vessels were then towed, usually by 200 soldiers, down the Charente River a few miles. From there they proceeded to Île d'Aix for loading, and/or to La Rochelle to take on passengers.[9] The process of careening, ballasting,

Table 8 Cost of Fitting Out King's Vessels in 1743, for Six Months

Ship	Guns	Crew	Work days and work performed (livres)	Supplies and munitions (livres)	Salaries and wages for 6 months (livres)	Rations and fresh provisions and lay labourers for 1 month (livres)	Total (livres)
Le Dauphin Royal	74	620	20,235	55,231	96,580	81,952	254,088
Mars	64	430	16,210	45,255	56,815	55,922	174,202
Tigre	50	300	15,490	41,520	41,250	38,105	136,365
Zephyr	30	210	10,712	30,112	30,400	28,100	99,324
Flore	26	180	9,515	28,715	28,815	25,630	92,675
Sybille	14	120	6,329	17,412	16,923	14,795	55,459
Driade	10	80	4,212	14,312	13,988	11,210	43,722

and loading consumed from three weeks to one month. After returning from his voyage, the captain would spend about two weeks taking his vessel out of commission – unloading, unrigging, and paying off the crew. In New France, unloading took place over a period of about ten days, and reloading consumed about the same number. Often the only difficulty lay in finding sufficient cargo to fill the holds of ships sailing from Quebec City.[10]

All these operations were costly and required considerable manpower. For example, to equip a 26-gun frigate of 550 tons burden, such as the *Machault* in 1759, the services of persons skilled in some 50 different trades, from town criers to merchants and including 21 types of craftsmen, were employed (figures 8 and 9).[11] In fact, when a vessel was being fitted out, merchants were needed to supply equipment and provisions for the day labourers engaged in loading operations. While officials from the Admiralty attended to the legal formalities, boatmen and barge skippers took the cargo to the vessels. In the meantime, craftsmen such as carpenters, painters, and sailmakers made repairs and looked after last-minute preparations.

A few random examples serve to illustrate the cost of these operations. In the absence of precise statistics, these examples provide an indication of the size of the outlay for the French navy to equip its vessels. In 1743, to commission the *Rubis*, a 50-gun man-of-war, for a seven-month voyage and a 250-man crew cost 120,000 livres: 30,000 to obtain rigging and 90,000 to pay the crew, buy food, and defray other expenses. This total did not include the 25,000 livres spent during a stopover at Quebec City when most of the cost was because of the high rate of sickness on board.[12]

A detailed breakdown of the cost of equipping different types of sailing vessels for six months at sea in 1743 is provided in Table 8.[13] This is approximately the duration of an expedition to New France, and these vessels are the types that came to New France from 1755 to 1760. Between 1743 and 1755, however, costs rose probably by one third, as did seamen's wages, (a subject that I shall examine in Chapter Three). It is sufficient here to note that wages alone represented nearly 30 per cent of the total costs of fitting out a vessel. There is not enough information available on the commissioning of privately owned ships to permit a comparison.

Apart from the careening operation, the bulk of the work in fitting out a vessel was performed by crew members. Signed on by a petty officer, these sailors gathered in the port of embarkation. While the ship was being loaded, they remained on board, where they were lodged and fed. They went ashore only with the permission of a leading seaman or another officer.[14] While the work progressed, the captain complied with the legal formalities at the office of the port admiral. He obtained permission to leave port and paid the various port duties, such as anchorage, beaconage, and light dues. Upon entering or leaving port, he was required to provide a brief statement concerning his cargo. Of course, he would take particular care to read his instructions closely and would fasten a cannon ball to the sack of letters and papers he might have on board. In the event of danger, he would quickly dispatch the weighted sack to the bottom of the sea. In time of war, the captain would request a letter of marque. He could then attack other ships at sea in the name of the king, without being considered a pirate – by the conventions of the day, pirates were shown no mercy by victorious opponents.[15]

The dimensions, function, cargo, and origins of both the royal navy vessels and the merchantmen created limitations that affected the living conditions. The architecture of a vessel destined for New France was a particularly accurate indicator of its function. A private commission would use sailing vessels of limited size to transport manufactured goods and slightly larger vessels for foodstuffs. The royal navy which was responsible for their protection, often dispensed with guns in order to carry men and goods. There were certainly many ties linking France and New France and they were perhaps inadequately defended. The relatively short careers of most of the sailing vessels would suggest that they were poorly built. Architecture and cargoes definitely had an effect on how the vessels performed at sea.

As might be expected, the extent of the preparations for fitting out a vessel was determined by the size of the particular warship or merchantman. Similarly, a great deal more work was required to equip a flute for the colonies or a man-of-war fitted out for transport than for a man-of-war commissioned for battle.[16] These ships carried virtually no freight and therefore loading and packing cargo was much less complicated. Moreover, their voyages were quite often shorter. In most cases, commissioning a vessel was a long, delicate, and costly undertaking.

When all the preparations were complete, a commissioner representing the Admiralty inspected the ship's company – at least for the king's vessels. The passengers could then come on board and the crew was ready to hoist the sails. All that was needed was the wind to blow and in the right directions!

Chapter Two

The Atlantic Course

Of all possible characteristics, uncertainty is undoubtedly the one that best describes navigation in the North Atlantic under the French regime. From the time the vessels were loaded and the passengers taken on board, the waiting began. The captain had to wait for the right winds. He might cast off and then have to moor again because the winds were not as strong as he had thought or they had died down. Also because of the winds, he would not have even the vaguest idea of how long the trip might take. If favourable winds turned stormy, he might have to heave aback to change a topmast broken during the storm or to repair a serious leak. But sailors were not just at the mercy of the weather. They also had to rely on inaccurate charts, which could cause them to hit rocks in a fog, and on insufficient markers in the St. Lawrence River, which could cause them to run aground. To further complicate the voyage, the available navigational tools were often subject to human error. Meanwhile, enemy warships or pirates would sometimes suddenly interrupt a voyage.

Courses and markers

Having first hoisted a flag on the small topmast to announce that he was raising anchor, and having fired a shot to hasten any late arrivals, the captain would give the order to unfurl the small topsail for casting off. Upon leaving the Rochefort–La Rochelle region, ships would sail up to Isle Dieu or Belle-Isle and, from there, would head west.[1] In 1665, Jean Talon recommended a passage located between 46 and 46 $^2/_3$ degrees north latitude as the best course for crossing the Atlantic.[2] In practice, captains sailing to Canada tried to keep to a course between the 43rd and 47th parallels. Some pilots considered the route to Quebec to be between the 43rd and 44th parallels. Returning from North America, they would sometimes sail a few minutes beyond the 51st parallel, especially if they were

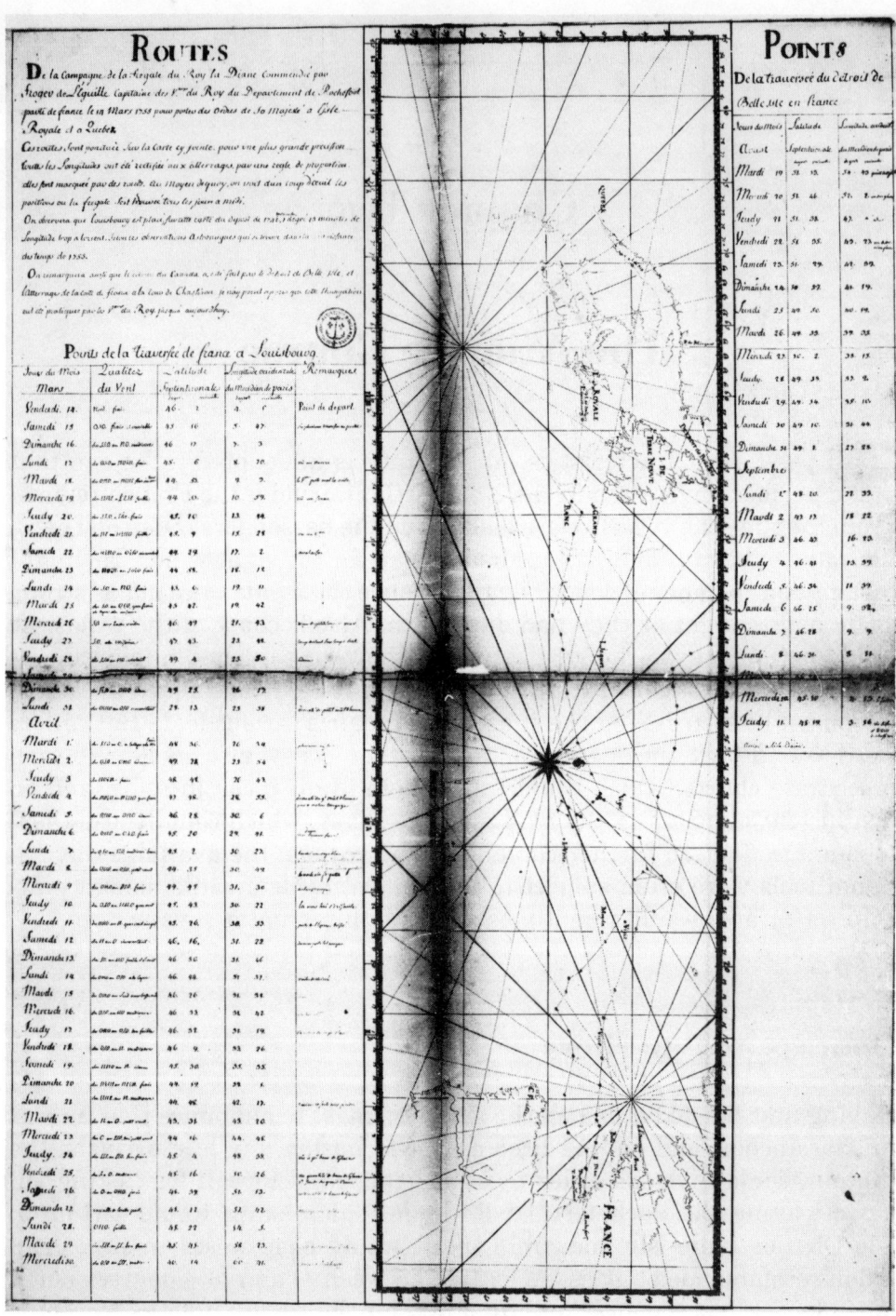

11. Courses followed by the king's frigate *Diane*, commanded by Froger de l'Eguille, captain of the king's vessels, department of Rochefort, which set sail from France on 14 March 1755 to carry His Majesty's orders to Isle Royale and Quebec City. (*France, AN, Marine, 4JJ, carton 13, bundle 47, logbook of the* Diane.)

taking the Strait of Belle Isle. Two criteria seem to have determined the choice of these routes: the winds, which shall be discussed later, and the currents. Currents in the South Atlantic pull westward, whereas currents in the North Atlantic pull eastward.[3]

Most likely because of these currents, the course sailed to America was located farther south; vessels would try to follow the more northerly route when returning to Europe. Adjustments in course were sometimes necessary and, as the captain of the *Chameau* indicated upon returning to France in November 1720, "pitching and rolling quite badly, [we] follow[ed] a course between 44 and 45 degrees latitude, to find gentler winds and calmer seas than one finds farther north".[4] The frigate *Diane*, which sailed to Louisbourg and Quebec City in 1755, probably followed a typical course (figure 11). Commanded by Froger de l'Eguille, the *Diane* left France on 14 March and dropped anchor at Louisbourg on 30 April. The records of latitude, determined every day at noon, indicate that the *Diane* sailed a course between 43 degrees, 31 minutes and 49 degrees, 50 minutes. Winds forced the frigate to tack and even to backtrack at times.

The most important event in these Atlantic crossings was probably the arrival at the Grand Banks of Newfoundland. This was important primarily for psychological reasons: having gone many days without knowing their exact whereabouts, the seamen finally had a point of reference to indicate that they were sailing in the right direction and were close to their destination. The presence of certain birds, "such as penguins, razorbills, and great auks", was a sign that the vessel was close to the banks, and the use of a sounding line made it possible to locate the bottom. For the sailors, arrival at the Grand Banks, which they called banking, was rather like arriving in port,[5] and they greeted the event with an enthusiastic cry of "Long live the King!"[6] Some pilots preferred to bank at 45 degrees, 30 minutes or even farther south if possible. In 1725, the man-of-war *Elisabeth* arrived at a latitude of 44 degrees. Its log-book read, "Lat 44°, long 327° 30', reached bank off Newfoundland; water – 130 fathoms: bottom – fine, gray sand".[7] In his discussion on navigation in Canada, Pellegrin, a former navy pilot who had become harbourmaster at Quebec City, recommended crossing the banks between the 44th and 45th parallels, and coming out along the 46th parallel, so as to locate the Green Banks.[8] Common use of this route is confirmed by the 1755 order to have fishing schooners "cross the western edge of the Grand Banks between 44 and 46 degrees when piloting vessels bound for Louisbourg".[9]

Vessels bound for Louisbourg would sight Scatarie Island and then sail around Cape Breton and into the Bay of Louisbourg (figure 16). Those sailing to Quebec City navigated close to the shallows off Île Saint-Pierre, entered the gulf between Cape Ray and St. Paul Island, and passed alongside Rocher aux Oiseaux. This was the course they followed upon entering and leaving the Gulf of St. Lawrence (figure 15). With the exception of fishing boats from St. Malo, which sailed through it annually, few vessels

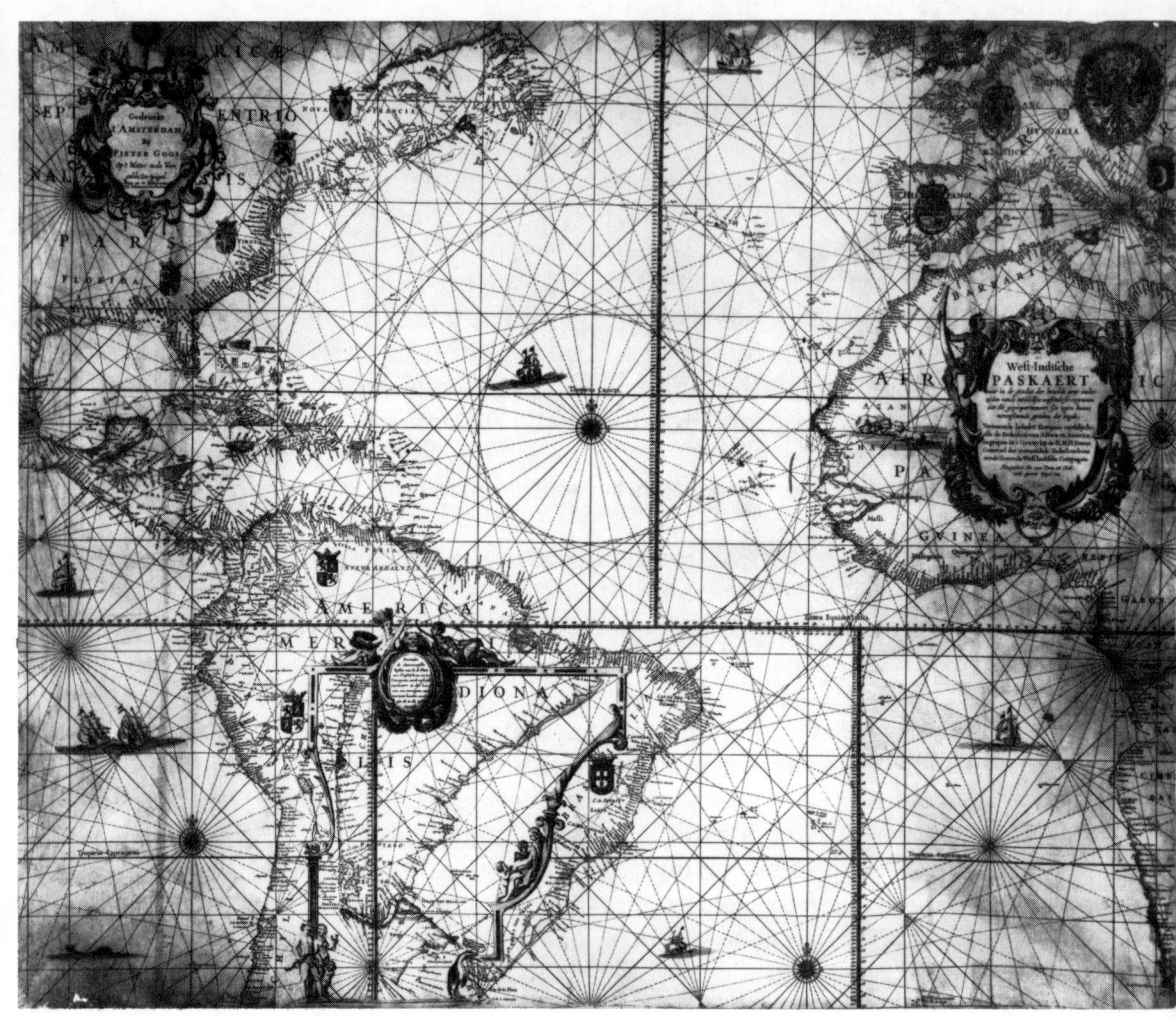

12. "West-Indische Paskaert" (1680), Pieter Goos. (*PAC, H1/10,000 [1680], NMC-11940.*)

took the Strait of Belle Isle to reach Canada.[10] The ice set in early in the autumn and thawed late in the spring, severely limiting access to the strait. Pilots used this route only during the Seven Years' War – but then almost exclusively. The frigate *Diane* was the first royal vessel to follow this course when it returned to France in 1755. Most of the vessels in the Dubois de la Mothe squadron took it a few weeks later. The route through the Strait of Belle Isle was actually the result of international politics: the English blockade of New France forced the French to slip through this passage. It was also consistent with the naval strategy of avoiding one's enemy whenever possible. In 1758, although not all captains agreed with their priorities, the authorities in France insisted that since the season was right, the *Outarde* and the *Aigle* should follow this course upon reaching Canada.[11] Unfortunately, it was here that the *Aigle* was wrecked.

Returning to France, all vessels, even those from the West Indies, would sail for the Grand Banks to take advantage of the prevailing westerly winds and currents. The use of this route by ships returning from the West Indies was actually one reason given to justify the establishment of Louisbourg in 1713.[12] As they approached the coast of New France, captains would usually make for the waters off Belle-Isle before turning south again toward the mouth of the Charente River.

The crews had various instruments to determine their headings and establish their positions as accurately as possible. A sounding line was commonly used, particularly for navigation along coastlines, to determine a ship's position and course. It consisted of a piece of lead coated with suet and attached to a rope. By letting it sink to the bottom of the ocean, the pilot could determine the water's depth; from the sound and from the pebbles that adhered to the suet, he could analyse the nature of the sea bottom. This instrument was essential for locating the Atlantic banks and the sand bars off the shores and islands of the St. Lawrence. Compasses were used in ocean navigation to determine direction, but they were accurate only as long as the iron axle of the steering wheel did not affect the magnetized needle. This problem confronted the captain of the *Rubis* in 1732; he resolved it by using another compass, which he placed some distance from the helm. The variation compass, which combined compass and sights, was also available to marine navigators. It made it possible to take bearings of the vessel's position by observing other objects or the stars.[13] In this way, pilots could determine the angle between the objects and the points of the compass, appraise the drift of the vessel, and correct its course accordingly. "All the way along I checked Sieur Lemere's compass and it has always been very accurate according to my observations since leaving Rochefort,"[14] commented La Jonquière in 1738, suggesting that French navigators had access to compasses and probably to other instruments manufactured by the Lemaire family, makers of celestial navigation tools.[15]

Using a *renard*, a disc representing the 32 points of the compass card, the pilot noted the direction being followed every half hour.[16] Each point was perforated by eight holes for the eight half hours of a watch, at the end of which the pilot would inscribe the directions in the ship's log. Pilots used the log and the hourglass to determine distances sailed and speeds attained. The procedure was explained by Champlain in his treatise on sailing and seamanship[17] and by La Galissonière in 1739. It consisted of throwing into the sea a small oak plank attached to a rope in which knots were tied at a distance of "47 feet, 6 inches, 7 $\frac{1}{5}$ lines apart, which gives 2853 fathoms for every 20 marine leagues or per degree of a great circle."[18] The number of knots played out in 30 seconds made it possible to measure leagues sailed in an hour. If, at the time of Maurepas and as a result of experimental surveys, the distance between the knots was set at $47\frac{1}{2}$ feet, then Champlain used a log-line with knots seven fathoms, or approximately 42 feet, apart. If the knots are spaced closer together, the apparent speed is obviously greater and the perception of the distances is also greatly affected. As a ship captain stressed in 1722, false measurements taken from a log-line by certain pilots "caused them to estimate a distance one eighth longer than it actually was".[19] The positions obtained using the log and compass were only estimates and thus quite imprecise. To compensate for this guesswork, pilots used astronomical observations.

Several instruments, such as the astrolabe (figure 23), the cross-staff, the English quadrant, and the graphometer, made astronomical surveys possible.[20] Using these instruments, navigators were able to calculate the lines of latitude. They determined either the sun's position in relation to the horizon at noon each day or the position of the pole star, and then made the necessary corrections according to marine almanacs such as the *Connaissance des Temps*.[21] In 1732 the captain of the *Rubis*, Desherbiers de l'Etenduère, claimed to have observed the pole star "with an instrument that I had designed for that express purpose".[22] That same year in France, Fouchy perfected a mirror instrument "intended primarily to measure the altitude of stars".

After 1731, Hadley's octant (figure 24) was used to measure altitude.[23] This reflection instrument, which made simultaneous sightings possible, was less sensitive to the vessel's movements and more accurate than the cross-staff or the English quandrant. La Galissonière was undoubtedly referring to an octant in his log-book entry in 1737 while sailing to Louisbourg on the *Héros*:

> By order of monsieur de Maurepas, I was given a new instrument for measuring altitudes, facing the sun. The first times I tried it I found it very hard on my eyes, and a few other officers found this too. However, Monsieur de Laiguille, who is a very good officer and a very careful observer, continued to use it and, once he got accustomed to it,

he found that it worked quite well. All the altitudes taken with this instrument that I have recorded under the others were done by him.

I feel that all the King's vessels should have such an instrument, because of the advantage it holds over all the ones we normally use, which is that it can measure altitudes even when the sky is overcast. I think it would be even better if the size of the arc were doubled (it would still be sufficiently portable), and if the coloured shade were enlarged or arranged so as to protect the eyes better than it does now.[24]

Precise determinations of longitude could not be made until the perfection of marine chronometers by John Harrison in the latter half of the eighteenth century.[25] Because the earth rotates 15 degrees every hour (or 360° every 24 hours), the difference between local time and the first meridian made it possible to calculate the longitude reached. Some French sailors, however, had used watches to try to establish longitudes as early as the beginning of the eighteenth century. Sieur de Radouays, second in command on the *Eclatant*, provided a good example of such an experiment, which was carried out while sailing over the Grand Banks in 1722.[26] It is the only record of such an attempt in all the documents consulted and, as such, it illustrates how difficult it must have been to popularize new techniques. The observation of lunar eclipses, predicted in tables for a precise time at the first meridian, also made it possible to determine the longitude reached by a vessel, if the local time was known.

Nautical observations were not restricted to determining the points of latitudes and longitude reached at noon each day, and sailors in the North Atlantic did not limit themselves to trying out new French inventions. They performed their own experiments. Voyages to New France were a source of inspiration for initiatives that brought technical progress and increased knowledge.

The points of latitude and longitude were shown on flat or reduced maps. French sailors had geographical maps of rectangular form with a network of equidistant parallels and meridians. Reduced maps were, in the words of Father Fournier, a seventeenth-century hydrographer, maps on which the meridians crossed in the same proportion as the parallels, so that each continent retained its actual shape.[27] The charts used in the seventeenth century were drawn by French hydrographers such as Le Cordier du Havre, who was mentioned by Damblimont, the captain of the *Arc en ciel* in 1687. In the eighteenth century, the Dutch maps of Pieter Goos and Gerard Van Keulen (Figures 12 and 13) were used almost exclusively until 1740. According to their users, these charts were not very accurate for locating the Grand Banks or the sand bars and islands of the Gulf of St. Lawrence. In 1733, La Jonquière wrote, "I found that in using my reduced Pieter Goos and Van Keulen map, I was ahead of the ship by forty-four leagues, which proves that the Grand Banks are illustrated too far to the east on all the Dutch maps."[28]

Navigation by reckoning was the cause of most errors. However, as La Jonquière wrote, pilots preferred to be ahead of their vessels. In that way, they were protected from the unpleasant surprises, such as a shore seen too late. For this reason, they tended to overestimate the distances travelled. The Dutch maps were not the only ones to contain errors and provoke the navigators' scepticism. In 1720, the captain of the *Chameau* noted "It is true that the French Neptune map shows the Spanish coast as being ten leagues farther away than the other maps, so one does not know which to rely on."[29]

Although the Goos and Van Keulen maps were still in common use at the end of the 1730s, charts from the Dépôt de la Marine (naval archives), including those of Nicolas Bellin, were appearing. The route taken by the *Diane* in 1755 (figure 11) is shown on a map from the Dépôt. Whereas the Dutch maps established their first meridian at Tenerife, French cartographers used the Paris Observatory. Although Bellin's maps were more reliable than the Dutch ones, they were not without their critics. Harbourmaster Pellegrin said they were fairly accurate concerning the route from the Grand Banks to the mouth of the St. Lawrence, but that the Green Banks and the shoals off Île St. Pierre were shown incorrectly, and Anticosti Island was shortened somewhat.[30] Generally, European maps were correct as far as the Gulf of St. Lawrence, but for the rest of the voyage, maps drawn by pilots such as Chaviteau or Pellegrin were probably more reliable. There were also pilot charts such as the *Flambeau de la Mer* which contained drawings of coastlines of explored territory in correct perspective. These drawings enabled the crew to recognize areas as the vessel landed, or places it was passing.

In summary, the underwater currents demarcating the course to New France forced vessels to limit themselves to a rather narrow corridor. Despite their limitations, navigational instruments both old and new allowed pilots to make their way there less blindly. This gateway was now open to new discoveries.

Speed and distances

Charts and navigational instruments notwithstanding, the time taken to sail across the ocean was determined ultimately by the speed of the wind. Sailing vessels could cover the 1,200 leagues (according to Lahontan)[1] from La Rochelle to Quebec City in nine weeks, or the 711 leagues (according to Denys de Bonaventure)[2] between France and Cape Breton in seven. The return voyage from Quebec City to France took five weeks, and from Louisbourg to France, four weeks. In practice, the vessels did not all travel at the same speed, as can be seen from Table 9. Royal vessels made the

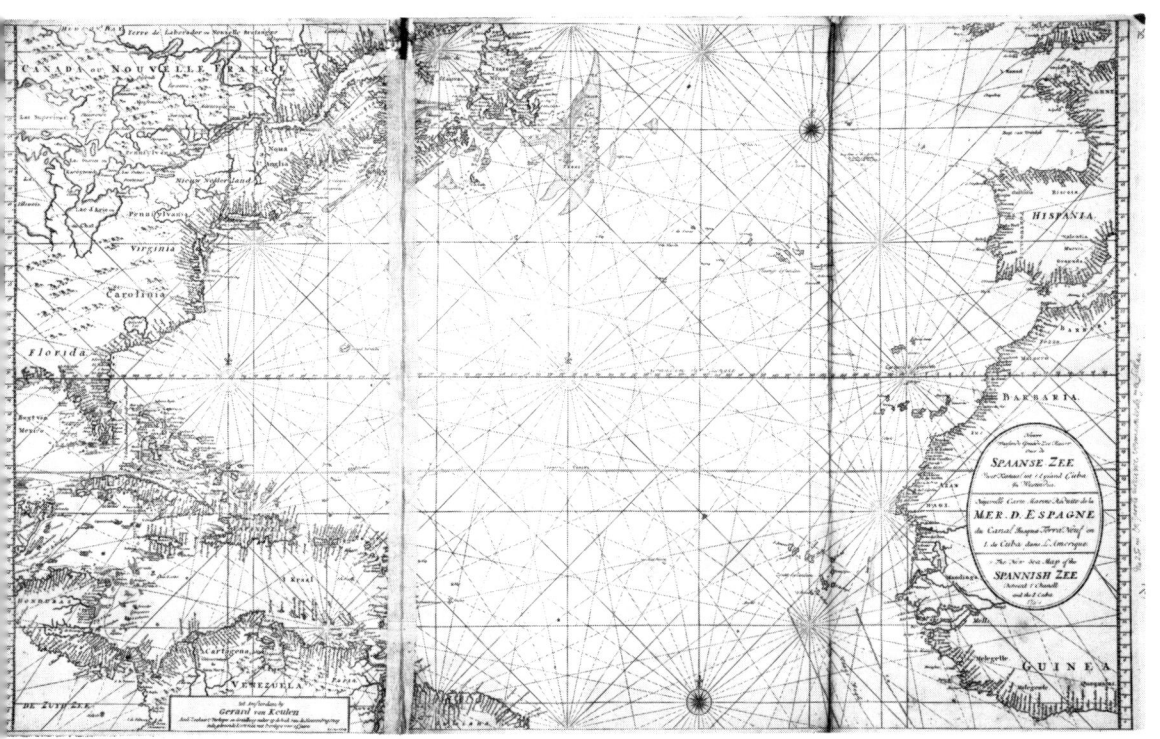

13. New scaled-down chart of the Spanish Seas from the channel to Newfoundland to the Island of Cuba in America, 1734, Gerard Van Keulen. (*PAC, A/1-3000, 1734,* Atlas Gerard Van Keulen, 169, p. 1, 15.)

14. Capture of the *Alcide* and the *Lys* in 1755. (*National Maritime Museum London, Public Visual Index, no. 1733.*) A year before war was declared, the English Royal Navy, having blockaded the coast of North America, succeeded in seizing two of France's 64-gun men-of-war. The fully armed *Alcide* tried to intervene between the English vessels and the *Lys* and the *Dauphin* – two French men-of-war fitted out for transport and *en route* to Canada, each with nine companies of soldiers on board. After 45 minutes of combat, the *Alcide*'s rigging and hull were riddled with hits and it was obliged to surrender. The *Lys* was taken a few hours later, its progress having been slowed by damage to its sails from enemy fire. The muskets of the soldiers on board were no match for the cannons of the enemy man-of-war, which closed in on either side. The *Dauphin* managed to escape in the fog. (*PAC, MG2B4, vol. 68, pp. 211-221, 394-404, 420-2.*)

Table 9 Crossing Times

Outward	France to Quebec City		France to Louisbourg	
	Number of ships	Days (avg.)	Number of ships	Days (avg.)
Royal vessels	57	58	64	49
Merchant vessels	30	71	7	58
Total	87	62	71	50

Homeward	Quebec City to France		Louisbourg to France	
	Number of ships	Days (avg.)	Number of ships	Days (avg.)
Royal vessels	32	37	47	31
Merchant vessels	5	33	none	none
Total	37	36	47	31

crossing in 10 to 12 days fewer than did merchant vessels.[3] The disparity seems to be much less pronounced for the homeward trip, but there is not sufficient data to establish valid statistics.

There are two reasons for the variations in crossing times. The king's vessels were generally much larger in size and capacity than those of the merchant fleet, so they rode better in the water and weathered storms more successfully. On rough seas, "a large man-of-war was more resilient than a frigate", according to Montcalm in 1756.[4] Also, merchantmen had fairly minimal crews, and that added to the difficulty of handling: there were fewer crewmen to hoist or bend the sails, or to make any necessary repairs.

The homeward voyage was three or four weeks shorter than the outward journey. "The reason for this difference is that, while the east wind may blow for 100 days out of the year, the west wind blows for 260."[5] In fact, the winds in the North Atlantic blow in an easterly direction much more strongly during autumn and winter,[6] and the vessels usually headed back to Europe in the autumn. Thus it was far easier to return to France than to reach Canada.

Among the vessels for which the travelling times between France and Quebec City are known, five took more than 100 days and eight crossed in fewer than 40 days. The longest crossing was surely that experienced by Jean Talon in 1665 aboard the *Saint-Sébastien*: it lasted 117 days.[7] In 1751 the flute *Chariot Royal* took 113 days.[8] Evidently, the intervening 86 years had not brought much improvement in courses or sailing vessels. There had perhaps been advances in navigational instruments but the winds had yet to be tamed. The 35-day crossing of the man-of-war *Arc en ciel* in 1687[9] appears to have been the swiftest. In 1756, the *Licorne*, the frigate that carried Montcalm to Canada, crossed in 37 days. Lévis, who

Table 10 Daily Distances of the *Actif*

Outward (East to West)		Homeward (West to East)	
Days	Leagues	Days	Leagues
1	54	6	53–64
3	42–44	2	42–49
4	31–38	4	31–33
15	20–27	6	21–26
8	10–19	7	12–19
14	2–9	1	3

left Brest at the same time aboard the frigate *Sauvage*, reached New France in 56 days.[10] The variation between the two frigates is an excellent example of the uncertainty surrounding the duration of Atlantic crossings.

Just as the length of the crossing varied from one vessel to another, so could the distance covered daily by any vessel. Many log-books contained notes regarding the distances covered each day. Days when a vessel was recorded as having sailed more than 50 leagues were extremely rare; with favourable winds, 20 to 30 leagues a day was a more usual figure. On the homeward trip, it was much easier to cover more than 30 leagues daily. The voyage of the *Actif*, which in 1755 transported nine companies of soldiers of the Languedoc regiment to Quebec City, was probably typical of its time.[11] It travelled from the coast of France to the entrance of the Gulf of St. Lawrence in 45 days, and made the return trip in 26 days. These crossing times are comparable to the average times noted for trans-Atlantic journeys. On the way to New France, the *Actif* exceeded 50 leagues a day only once; on the return trip there were at least six days when it covered 50 leagues, and once it even did 64 leagues.

Choosing the right season to hoist the sails and set off toward New France was as critical as timing the departure to pick up favourable winds. To all intents and purposes, the port of Quebec was inaccessible from 15 November to 1 May, because of the ice covering the river or drifting in the gulf. Even if the St. Lawrence did happen to be ice-free before the beginning of May, ice floes would break away from the Arctic landmass and float southward in spring, making navigation on the Newfoundland banks extremely dangerous. Mindful of the brevity of the shipping season, navigators considered it imperative to leave the shores of France before 1 May and to leave Quebec City before the end of September.[12]

Jean Talon recommended setting sail from France before 15 April and leaving Quebec City before the cold set in.[13] In practice, most vessels – at least those in the king's service – departed from France between 15 June and 15 July and set off homeward from Quebec City during the last two weeks of October. The expeditions between 1755 and 1759 took place somewhat earlier, with troops and merchant vessels arriving at Quebec City in May and June. "We have had something this year that I swear has never before been seen in Canada; a ship that left Bordeaux on January 30 was anchored at Île aux Coudres by April 23, and on the 11th and 12th of this month (November) three ships reached Quebec City."[14] Thus the navigation season between France and Canada was from the end of April to the middle of November. Even the last shipment of aid to New France, in 1760, at a time when the colony's needs were pressing, did not leave France until 10 April. Although financial, political, and climatic considerations had delayed this departure, it still fell within the normal limits of the shipping season. Departures from Quebec City were delayed as long as possible by the authorities to ensure that the maximum amount of cargo, and more particularly, the latest news, could be sent to France. In his diary in 1757, Bougainville wrote of the departure of the last ships for France on November 5 and 7, "It is high time, for on the 6th it was only 8 degrees outside."[15] The geographer C. Daney wrote, "It is not possible to horde the wind,"[16] and navigation in the North Atlantic illustrates this fact well, with its distances and its duration. The direction of the winds determined the navigation season and affected the lifestyle of New France, with its six months of intense activity and six months of waiting.

Climate and averages

Wind velocity could determine crossing times, and ice, the length of the navigation season; but those were not the only significant effects of these two climatic factors. Although head winds would force a vessel to bear, or zigzag, thereby lengthening the distance, exceptionally strong winds were just as detrimental, if not more. Galeforce winds and the storms usually accompanying them were probably the greatest fear of transAtlantic crews and passengers of the day. When gales struck, the crew had to reduce the sail area to withstand the buffeting. Winds and waves made handling difficult and sometimes carried equipment overboard. Such a situation was described by Captain Joseph Huault of the schooner *Aimable* in 1755:

> That on various occasions in the course of the crossing the deck took a severe beating from wind and waves; that during the storm she was obliged to go under bare poles for eight days without being able to hoist sail; that during this time her yards and sails were driven into the sea and lost, along with a twenty-one-foot oar, three forecastle timbers, a jury yard and a spar from that yard.[1]

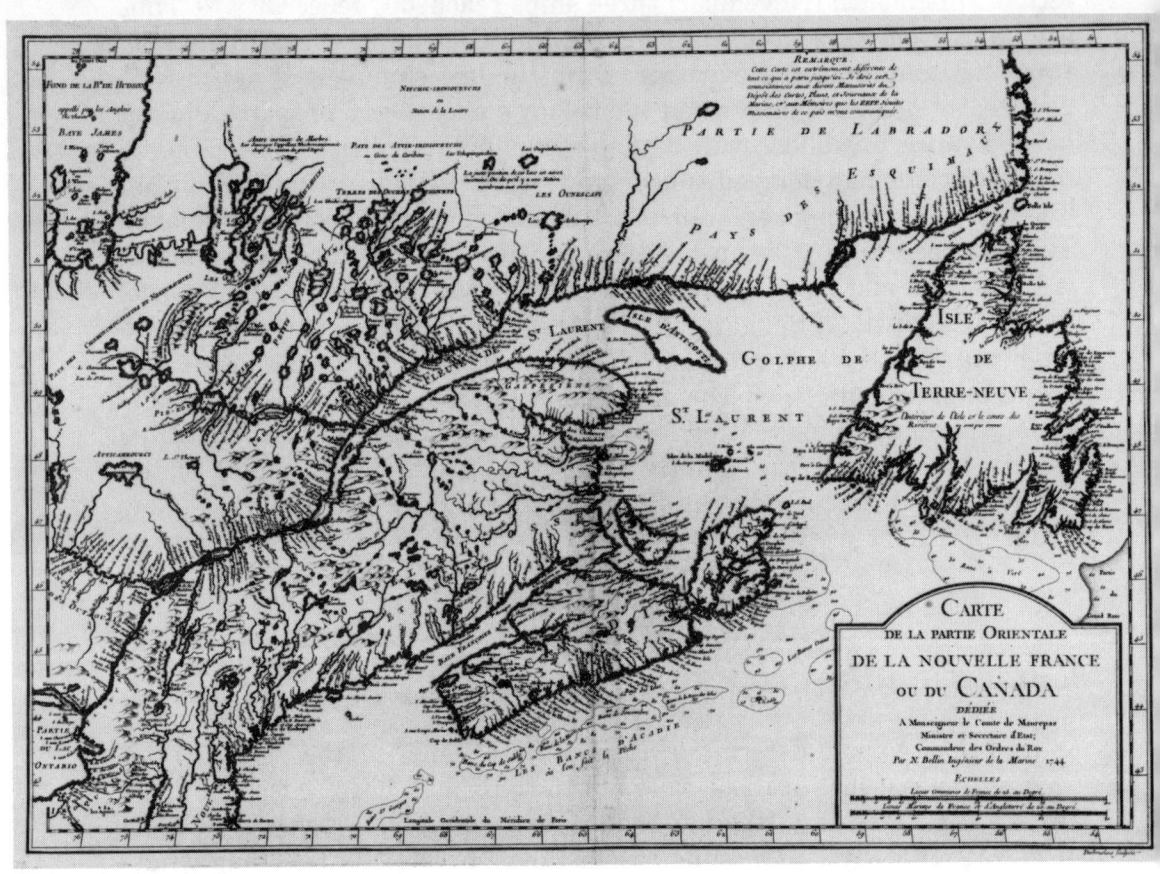

15. Map of the eastern portion of New France or Canada, 1744, Nicolas Bellin. (*PAC, H3/900.*)

"In stormy weather, it is impossible to stand, eat or sleep; everything must be secured, and, if we dared, we might be tempted to have ourselves tied down as well," wrote Montcalm in 1756, although his own crossing to New France was short.[2] Water leakage caused by a storm or from a crack in the hull could also spoil provisions and cargo. A violent storm raging about the *Chameau* in 1720 caused it to lose about 900 bushels of salt.[3] In addition to the already spoiled provisions, dry cargo could rot in the hold, because there was nowhere to spread out the wet bales to dry. The holds were crammed too full for anyone to make his way down to the bottom and thoroughly check the condition of the cargo.[4] Besides, it was thought that shifting the goods around might create disorder and hamper manoeuvrability in the event of an unexpected encounter.

Pumps, installed beside the masts, were the only means available for dealing with the influx of water. Pumping operations must have exhausted the crew members – especially if they were few in number, as was the case on a merchantman, or if the vessel was taking on 36 to 48 inches of water each watch, as the *Téméraire* did in 1692.[5] If pumping did not eliminate the water quickly enough, the captain might give orders to heave to; caulkers would then stuff oakum into the cracks and, if the damage was more serious, sailors might dive down and seal off the hole with a leaden plate.[6] Not only were pieces of equipment carried off by the waves and supplies ruined by moisture, but broken masts had to be replaced, and sailors sometimes had to work at night by lamplight stitching up sails torn by the wind. Returning from Canada in 1752, the flute *Seine* had its bowsprit broken and its foremast blown away during a storm.[7] To clear away and replace the broken masts, the crew was forced to cut the shrouds and backstays.

In addition to the exhaustion this extra duty would likely cause among crew members, storms also meant a marked disruption of the daily routine of sailors and passengers. Cooks could not risk building a fire on board, because of the danger of flames spreading. The man-of-war *Téméraire* barely escaped destruction by fire in 1692 when such an incident occurred near Newfoundland.[8] Everyone on board then had to go without soup and subsist on cold food and biscuits. This diet was certainly not ideal for restoring the strength of the crew. And how could people sleep in hammocks that were soaking wet? "By then, everyone wanted to get some sleep but all the beds were sopping, since the rain had seeped in through even the most imperceptible chinks, an unavoidable consequence of the vessel's violent tossing."[9]

To the list of dangers and discomforts connected with storms must be added those that accompanied fogs, which increased in frequency and density as the vessel approached the Grand Banks. The Récollet friar Sagard noticed the cold, damp fog that perpetually hung over the area, but he did not know what caused it;[10] the Jesuit Charlevoix reasoned however, that it arose as a result of underwater currents running against

16. View of the town of Louisbourg. (*France, Bibliothèque nationale, Maps and Plans, GeC 5019.*) This view of Louisbourg by Claude-Joseph, son of engineer Étienne Verrier, depicted the scene that greeted new arrivals to Isle Royale and those who stopped over there *en route* to Canada. The view of the city was to change little in later years, except for the addition of a commemorative gateway – the Frédéric – to the quay around 1742.

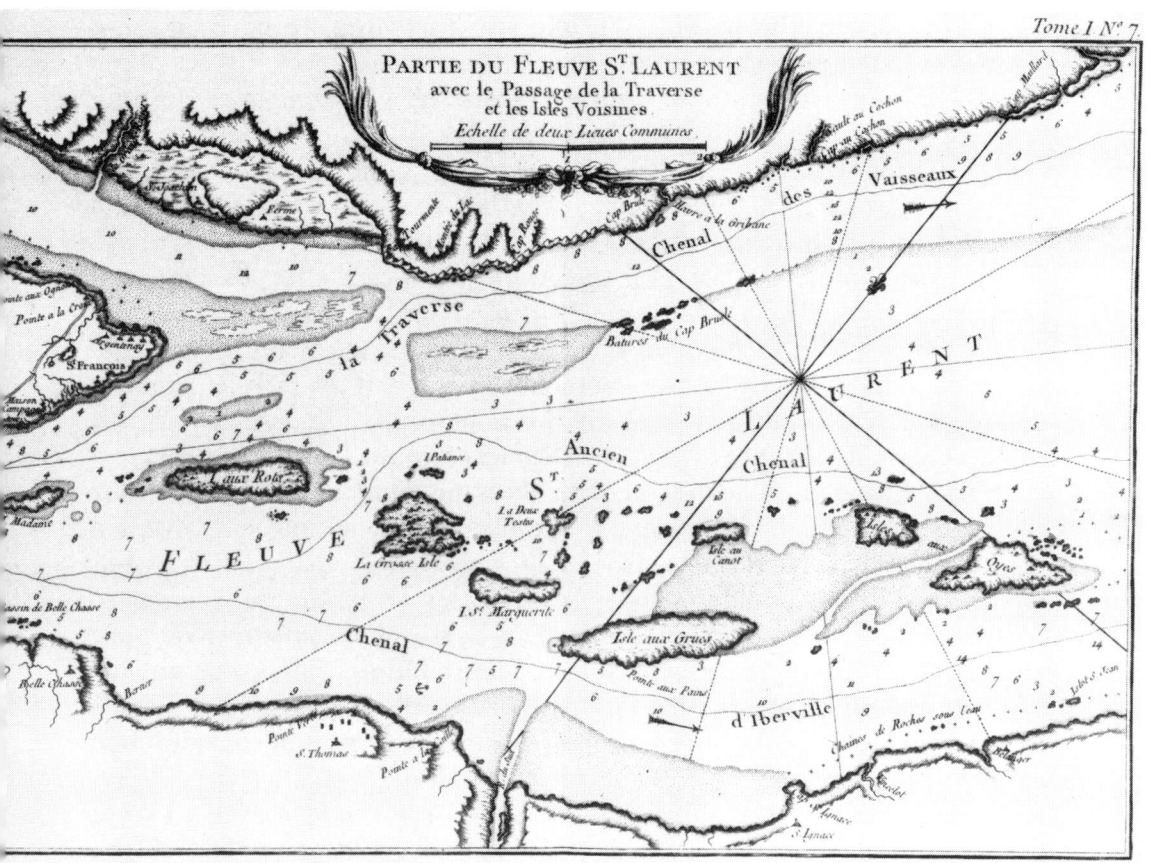

17. Part of the St. Lawrence River with the passage through the traverse and the nearby islands. (*Nicholas Bellin,* Petit Atlas Maritime: l'Amérique septentrionale, *1764, PAC.*) The new traverse and the old channel are well indicated.

the edge of the Grand Banks.[11] But it was far more important to foresee the consequences of the fog than to determine its causes. The most immediate effect was that it was impossible to take celestial observations to calculate latitude. "When, as is common in these waters, navigators are unable to take altitudes because of fog or bad weather, they are compelled to go under bare poles, and frequently even have to heave aback during the night; otherwise they would risk becoming stranded on these shores," wrote a passenger on the flute *Eléphant* in 1729.[12]

During such conditions, sailing vessels were in danger of running aground. The *Jason* narrowly escaped damage in 1737 on its journey carrying Intendant Gilles Hocquart to Canada.[13] Other vessels were less fortunate: it was in fog and stormy weather that the *Chameau* became stranded on the shoals of Isle Royale in 1725, the *Renommée* ran aground on Anticosti Island in 1736, and the *Aigle* was wrecked on Ile de Quincampoix in 1758. The list of accidents could continue indefinitely. The chances of running aground as a result of inaccurate calculations of distance were undoubtedly more remote, however, than the risks of running into pack ice or another vessel. In the hope of avoiding such hazards, captains posted lookouts to watch for ice when temperatures fell sharply; they also had drums beaten and muskets or cannons fired at regular intervals to signal their presence. These precautions did not prevent a fishing ship from La Rochelle from colliding with the *Rubis* in 1739, but fortunately it was not damaged.[14] In 1744, the *Trois Maries* was not so lucky when it was rammed by the French East India Company's *Brillant* and six of its crew members were lost. The remaining nine seamen survived by hurriedly scrambling onto the *Brillant*.[15]

As well as reducing the length of the shipping season considerably, ice created other very serious obstacles to trans-Atlantic travel. It restricted access to the Gulf of St. Lawrence to a single passage, except perhaps during July and August, when vessels could enter through the Strait of Belle Isle. During the rest of the year, they had to pass to the south of Newfoundland. Ice not only completely blocked the route at times, forcing ships to change direction, but also seriously hampered manoeuvrability. The flute *Rhinocéros*, nearing the shores of Isle Royale in March 1756, continued on its way under difficult ice conditions:

> despite a formidable barrier of ice stretching for the entire length of the coast, through which we could see no passage except, perhaps, at the very beginning where we were able to steer among the floes. However, these conditions did not prevail for long, and subsequently the floes became jammed together so tightly that in four and a half hours we were only two thirds of a league closer to our destination, making progress only by the use of a number of spars or poles, with which we pushed the ice aside to clear the way.[16]

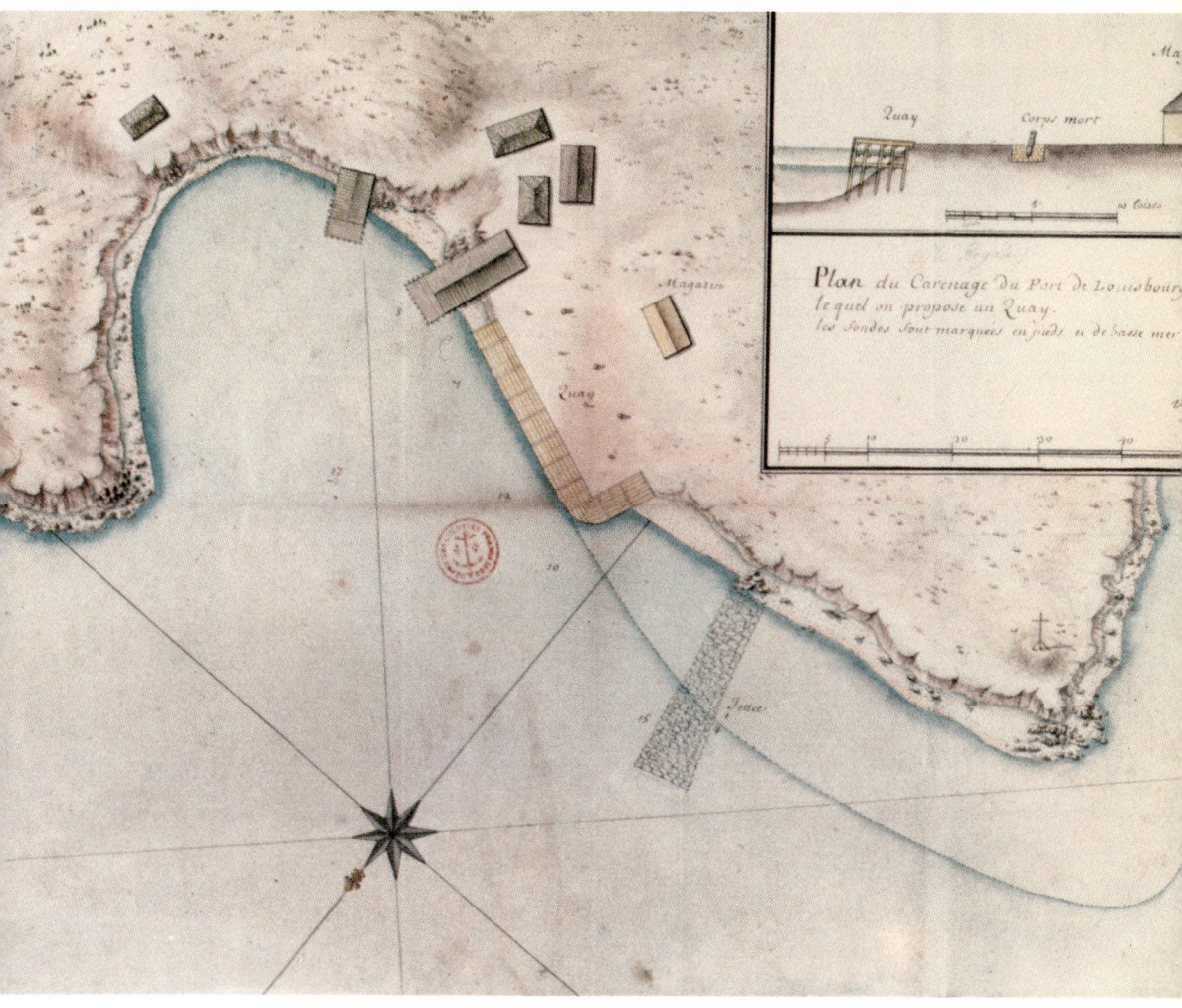

18. Plan of the drydock in the Port of Louisbourg. (*France, AN, Outremer, D.F.C., carton IV, no. 158*.) This plan, bearing the signature of the engineer Verrier, shows the cove used for careening, located in the southeast part of Louisbourg's port. It gives some idea of the facilities available for refitting sailing vessels. The frigate *Néréide* and the 80-gun man-of-war *Tonnant* were careened in this cove.

19. "A General View of Quebec from Point Levy", drawing by Richard Short, Print by P. Canot, 1761. (*PAC, C-118259.*) Although this drawing is from the time of the siege of Quebec, it undoubtedly shows the view seen by the sailors

and passengers on vessels that anchored in the port of Quebec during the first half of the eighteenth century.

20. View of the port of Rochefort. (*Cliché Musées Nationaux.*) This painting by Joseph Vernet, dated 1762, depicts the port of Rochefort in full operation. The scene includes a sailing vessel being careened, workmen unloading a boat, and passersby examining goods. The long building pictured is the Corderie, which manufactured ropes up to 20 inches in diameter and 200 metres long. Here at Rochefort, the king's men-of-war and flutes were fitted out for their annual voyage to New France and put out of commission when they returned.

21. View of the port of La Rochelle. (*Cliché Musées Nationaux.*) This painting by Joseph Vernet, dated 1762, depicts various port activities as well as several elements of the material civilization of eighteenth-century maritime France. Here government officials and immigrants board for their passage to New France. Soldiers waited to board at St. Martin on the Ile de Ré. The process of fitting out a man-of-war usually began at Rochefort.

22. View of the port of Bordeaux. (*Cliché Musées Nationaux.*) This painting by Joseph Vernet, dated 1759, looks at the port of Bordeaux from the Salinières side. Unlike Rochefort and La Rochelle, the port of Bordeaux fitted out mostly merchantmen. Most of the sailing vessels trading with New France left from here. During the Seven Years' War, for example, Gradis, Desclaux, and Jauge commissioned, with assistance from the state, approximately two thirds of the vessels sailing to New France.

What with the snow and blowing snow that frequently accompanied such ice, sailors sometimes had to travel for many hours "seeing neither sky nor earth". The snow stuck and froze on the cables, a complication that could have been avoided perhaps if the captain had left Quebec City sooner. Crews were sometimes faced with a cold so intense that sailors fainted on deck, and some had burns on their hands from pulling on frozen rigging.[17] The Jesuit father Aulneau, who left France on 31 May 1734 and disembarked at Quebec City on 16 August, described his passage to Île aux Coudres as follows: "It was there that we realized for the first time that it was summer, for since our departure from France we had been continually exposed to winter weather."[18] A journey across the Atlantic was thus not a relaxing experience, and all of these difficulties must have taken a heavy toll on the health of passengers and crew members. Climatic changes not only eliminated the possibility of establishing a routine, they also accentuated the hardships of the sailors' lives, and sometimes seriously hampered the shipowners.

Dangers and safety measures on the Atlantic

For the navigators of the eighteenth century, natural dangers were not the only threats to life: they also had to contend with the pirates and privateers who periodically disrupted normal traffic in the North Atlantic. Apart from the times of conflict in which the European powers opposed one another, trans-Atlantic shipping was sometimes obstructed by pirates who used the port of Salé in Morocco as their base of operations. These pirates seem to have been fairly active on the Grand Banks of Newfoundland in 1716, from 1723 to 1725, and in 1740.[1] Their main targets were fishermen. In 1725, the King of France sent vessels to patrol the banks to protect his nationals. Pirates wanted as much booty as they could get, and they showed no mercy. Undoubtedly, the nature of North Atlantic trade with its rather modest cargoes, limited piracy, for instead of the gold, sugar, and coffee carried by ships in southern waters these vessels held fish, furs, and manufactured goods.

In times of conflict among European powers, piracy was legitimized through two forms of state-sanctioned privateering: sailing vessels owned by private interests were specially equipped with men and arms to capture vessels of hostile nations on behalf of the king, and letters of marque were granted to captains of regular vessels, entitling them to seize any enemy vessels they might encounter. In contrast with pirates, privateers took prisoners, for whom they received a reward that could be used as a medium of exchange. The captured vessels would be sold to profit the outfitters of privateering vessels, with a share set aside for the king.[2] All the proceeds from captures made by captains in the French navy went to the royal treasury and to the crews.

To understand France's penchant for privateering, it is necessary to look back on the end of the seventeenth century and the naval battle of La Hougue in 1692. The defeat inflicted on the navy at that time, begun by Colbert 30 years earlier, was an indication that concentrations of naval forces and battles won do not always have the desired result. Colbert's successors, Louis de Pontchartrain and Jérome de Phélypeaux, were little interested in developing a royal navy; they were more concerned with the profitability of France's maritime operations. Their goal was to reduce the navy's costs and increase its revenues. Their administrations were in force at the time of the victories of Tourville, Jean Bart, and Duguay-Trouin over well-stocked merchant fleets as well as small divisions.[3] After the bitter defeat at La Hougue, these victories at sea had all the dynamism needed to steer France's maritime policy toward privateering.

When Maurepas came to power, the ministry started up the shipbuilding industry again. Most of the vessels built were less powerful than 74-gun men-of-war and were destined to be used for privateering. At the time of the Seven Years' War and Austria's War of Succession, France did not have enough vessels of sufficient might to seek out the English on every sea. During the Seven Years' War, both the state and private enterprise of England and France were active in privateering. Even before war was declared in 1756, Louis XV of France had promised privateers rewards of 100 to 300 livres for each cannon and 30 to 50 livres for each prisoner captured.[4] The French privateers paid a tax to the king when they sold their booty. England, by comparison, did not tax booty;[5] nor did it provide any financial incentives to privateers.

There are no statistics to measure the effects of piracy or privateering. A few figures will give some idea of the importance of this phenomenon, however, at least in the years 1756 to 1760, during which the French Royal Navy captured more than 170 English vessels.[6] The French merchant marine was also active, boarding 2,532 English vessels, compared with 944 for the English merchant marine.[7] Are these figures accurate or exaggerated? Guy Frégault, in quoting other sources, confirmed that in 1757 alone[8] the English fleet lost 571 vessels while capturing 364. The facts seem to indicate a French naval superiority.

French merchantmen captured more booty than their English counterparts in this competition, mainly because the English relied mostly on their royal navy to take the initiative in the privateering war. Of the 43 vessels captured by England between 1755 and 1760, and for which an inventory of the booty taken is on file at the Admiralty's court in London,[9] 18 vessels were halted by merchantmen and 25 by men-of-war of the state. By avoiding the enemy, as their orders recommended, the commanders of the French navy had little opportunity to take booty. The possibility of making a profit was a marvellous incentive to the English. In 1755, the

English Admiral Boscawen wrote to his wife that the seizures authorized during wartime would easily allow him to build a beautiful home in the English countryside.[10] At that time Boscawen was aboard the *Torbay*, one of the men-of-war involved in the first confrontation between the English and French royal navies during the Seven Years' War (figure 14).

In fact, the English Royal Navy halted more than 300 French merchantmen that year. This tactic of intimidation was apparently quite successful. In November 1756, a sergeant of the Bourgogne regiment wrote from Louisbourg:

> With our passing the activity of traders ceased, since they dare not chance navigation along these coasts, for fear of being raided by the English buccaneers and privateers so common in these waters, or being taken prisoner by the vessels of the English king that have been cruising ever since our departure from France for the islands.[11]

Combats between privateers were usually short-lived: by the time the adversaries had exchanged one or two cannon shots, one of the captains would usually recognize his weaker position and surrender. If he decided instead to resist, the fight soon became bloody. In one such instance in 1757, the *Robuste*, which had just left Bordeaux for Quebec, held off for four days against a 36-gun frigate. Ninety men were killed or wounded during the battle.[12] The *Robuste* returned dismasted to France. Whenever a vessel was captured, its crew members were taken prisoner and the victor took most of them on board. Members of the victor's crew then took charge of the captured vessel and sailed it back to port where it was sold, with the profits going to the shipowners. If intercepted by the enemy, a captain might also choose to ransom his vessel. He would promise to pay in return for unobstructed passage; to guarantee payment he would leave a few members of his crew as hostages.

Privateering wars were often the cause of unexpected and even cruel events. On 31 August 1756, the *Dauphin*, a snow of 120 tons burden *en route* to Louisbourg and Quebec City, was stopped 25 leagues west of Bordeaux by the *Cumberland*, a privateer from Guernsey. The *Cumberland*'s captain agreed to a ransom of 500 pounds sterling because he was unable to spare any members of his crew to sail the captured vessel back to England. He promised the *Dauphin*'s captain safe conduct in return for one hostage to guarantee payment of the ransom. Despite the promise of safe conduct, on 2 September the *Dauphin* was captured by another English sailing vessel, the *Boscawen d'Exeter*. With English sailors in charge, the *Dauphin* set sail for England, but on the morning of 16 September, she was re-captured by a privateer from St. Malo. At four o'clock the *Dauphin* was captured once more by an English vessel, this time the *Tartar*, a man-of-war of the royal navy, and was brought to Guernsey.[13] The *Dauphin* offered no resistance during this entire sequence of events.

23. Sea astrolabe (from a French model). The astrolabe was used to measure either the altitude of the sun at noon or that of the pole star at night. Using a graduated ring and a bearing plate and holding the instrument vertically, the user sighted the constellation in the upper sightvane and lined up its beam of light with the lower sightvane. The altitude was indicated by the angle inscribed on the ring.

24. Hadley's octant. (*Musée de la Marine, Paris.*) This instrument consisted of an eighth of a circle divided into 90 sections, a bearing plate, a sight, and two mirrors. One mirror was attached to the bearing plate; the other faced the sight and had a mirror finish only on its lower half. The instrument was held vertically, with the rim facing the observer, who aimed the sight at the horizon. The reflection of the constellation in the mirror affixed to the bearing plate was then lined up with the horizon. The position of the bearing plate on the rim indicated the altitude.

In an effort to mitigate these difficulties somewhat, the French fleet depended on a convoy system. In peacetime, king's vessels heading toward Canada and Isle Royale usually travelled together as far as the Grand Banks. The commanding officer on his way to Canada directed the convoy. When pirates were sighted, merchantmen gathered to place themselves under the protection of the king's vessels. However, these convoys attained any real size only during periods of armed conflict. In December 1744, for example, three vessels from the French navy escorted eight East Indiamen and 42 merchantmen back to France from Louisbourg.[14]

In wartime, convoys not only provided mutual protection, but also transported aid to the colonies. In fact, this was the special role of the convoy during the Seven Years' War. An aid convoy usually included armed men-of-war to serve as protection, partially armed men-of-war to provide transportation for troops and goods, and hospital vessels to care for the sick and wounded. Trading ships might also join the convoy, and frigates often sailed out in front.

Apart from the operation of the royal navy from 1755 to 1758, the most renowned convoys to New France were surely that of the Duc d'Anville in 1746, comprising 52 vessels, and that of La Jonquière in 1747, totalling 39 vessels. Storms and illness dispersed and immobilized the first. The men-of-war of the latter were defeated in a naval battle; only the merchantmen reached their destination.[15]

Although travel by convoy ensured mutual defence and the protection of weaker vessels by the stronger ones, it also imposed a series of constraints. The escort vessels had to limit their pace to that of ships whose progress was slow or faltering, and the time taken to cross the ocean increased accordingly. The risk of collision due to poor manoeuvring or fog increased with the number of units in the convoy; the chances of attracting attention were also much greater. Communication among vessels was another problem. To indicate various manoeuvres, the captains hoisted different coloured flags.[16] They used bullhorns to communicate with vessels outside their group and boats to visit from one vessel to another. In this way they could distribute supplies, exchange news, or prepare defence plans. If the wind rose or fog descended, however, they might well find themselves detained aboard the vessel they were visiting. In the final analysis, in peacetime or war, security at sea was the greatest difficulty along the trans-Atlantic route, and this factor placed heavy constraints on both the passengers and the crew.

Travelling up the St. Lawrence

Even when a crew had managed to leave the fog of the Grand Banks behind and entered the waters of the Gulf, it could not expect clear sailing.

In fact, the most perilous part of the journey was the trip up the St. Lawrence to Quebec City. "This is not a meagre watercourse like the Vienne, the Seine or the Loire; it is without dispute the finest river in the world, albeit not the widest in America."[1] This opinion, of Abbé Navières in 1734, certainly differed from that of Bougainville, who declared in 1756: "This river bristling with reefs and unparalleled for danger and difficulty of navigation; this is Quebec's most effective rampart."[2] Whereas Navières marvelled as a nature lover at the beauty of the river, Bougainville as a military man and a sailor, was impressed by its wild, untamed character and its defence capabilities.

After gaining entry to the river by navigating between Cap Desrosiers and Anticosti Island (figure 15), vessels sailed for Sept Îles, and then hugged the north shore as far as the Manicouagan sandbars.[3] To the Baron de Lahontan, who questioned the logic of this practice, the pilots responded that "the treacherous nature of the stormy northwest wind that prevails over the river for three quarters of the year was the reason that no one dared venture away from the north shores."[4]

In his dissertation on navigation in Canada, the Quebec harbourmaster Pellegrin supported this view and reserved the route along the south shore for when the winds were easterly or southeasterly.[5] From the Manicouagan sandbars, vessels crossed the river to reach their first anchorages, at Métis or Rimouski. The anchorages along the south shore were much better than those along the north shore and, from Rimouski on, vessels dropped anchor every evening. "We were constantly taking soundings because of the rocks on the bottom of the river, which make it terribly dangerous and forced us to cast anchor every night."[6]

As a result of these daily stops, the upriver trip took an average of 10 to 12 days; this explains the difference in time between crossings from France to Quebec City and those from France to Louisbourg. The voyage could last even longer if the captain had to wait for favourable winds or give the crew a rest. When illness scourged the *Rubis* in 1740, the captain was forced to make a particularly long stopover at Rimouski to give his vessel a thorough cleaning and airing.

From Rimouski, vessels followed the south shore as far as Île aux Lièvres, sailing between Île Verte and Île Rouge, north of the Kamouraska islands of Les Pèlerins and south of Île aux Lièvres. They then headed for Cap aux Oies, to pass north of Île aux Coudres and, after 1716, to set out along the new traverse between Île d'Orléans and Île aux Ruaux (figure 17).[7] After passing Point Levy, the vessels dropped anchor before Quebec City.

The anchorage along the river allowed the crew to go ashore and obtain fresh food. Seigneurs Lepage and Rioux of Rimouski and Île Verte frequently supplied animals and other provisions to passing vessels. Sailors and passengers could also take advantage of the opportunity to go hunting on the islands or on shore – although it was much more practical to rely on the Micmac Indians for a supply of wild game, since they were more familiar with the habits of Laurentian wildlife.[8] Some of the ship's company went ashore to gather wood, procure fresh water, cut trees to replace masts, or to bury passengers who had died on board. For the population along the river, the passage of ships from France presented an opportunity to hear news from home or to honour certain religious responsibilities. In 1741, for example, the seigneur of Rimouski and several local inhabitants had their children confirmed by the Bishop Pontbriand, who had arrived aboard the *Rubis*.[9]

Some passengers chose to disembark at these ports of call to complete their journey by land or on a swifter vessel. Others, like the passengers on the *Rubis* in 1740, left to escape the disease rampant on the ship.[10] Under the French regime, those arriving from overseas were not placed in quarantine. Even if there had been sickness on board the vessel, contamination could thus easily spread to the colony. An exception occurred in 1721, when French authorities ordered that vessels arriving from Marseilles or having called in at a Mediterranean port where there was an epidemic of the plague were to anchor near Île aux Coudres to await inspection by surgeons from Quebec City before continuing their journey.[11]

At the end of its trans-Atlantic voyage, a ship passing Sainte-Anne-de-Beaupré would salute the church with a few cannon shots, five or seven shots for one of the king's vessels.[12] This was the sailors' way of thanking Saint Anne, their patron saint, for having brought them safely to Quebec City at last.

The many difficulties faced by captains during their voyages up the St. Lawrence were to be alleviated somewhat by exploration of the river in the eighteenth century and by the use of pilots. In 1685, Governor Denonville, recognizing that the Dutch charts used by the navigators were hopelessly inadequate on the St. Lawrence, recommended that the services of the pilot Chaviteau be retained to chart the river accurately. Later, between 1725 and 1740, the first systematic exploration of the St. Lawrence River and the Gulf was begun as a result of the efforts of Testu de la Richardière, harbourmaster at Quebec City.[13] Accompanied by the king's pilots left in Quebec City for this purpose, La Richardière visited the north shore of the river with Dizé in 1731 and the south shore with Garnier in 1732. As Deshaies had in 1727, these pilots made surveys that geographers such as Nicolas Bellin at the navy map office would use later in drawing their charts. La Richardière explored the Strait of Belle Isle with the pilot Pellegrin in 1735, the Gulf of St. Lawrence with Joly in 1736, and the southern coast of Newfoundland in 1738.

These men were not alone in their attempts to expand the current knowledge of river navigation. Captains of the king's vessels also recorded a series of observations in their log-book. Tilly's description of the islands and anchorages of the St. Lawrence in 1727 and the views of the shoreline sketched at La Jonquière's request in 1733 and 1738 are good examples.

These views could well have appeared as illustrations on the charts the pilots took along with them.

"Although it is not the custom for pilots to take altitudes within sight of land as well-known as this, I did so as often as weather permitted, reasoning this to be of the utmost importance in perfecting the charts."[14] These words reveal La Galissonière's concern for scientific observation when he was in command of the *Rubis* in 1739. In 1743, Rossel, then captain of the *Rubis*, had calculations made of the distance separating Matane and Île aux Coudres, and, more important, the length of the islands and accompanying sand-bars lying between those two points.

Despite this exploration, and the dissertations on navigation written by Talon in 1665[15] and by Pellegrin in 1752 and 1757,[16] a trip up the St. Lawrence still posed problems. In 1755, the captain of the *Diane*, Froger de l'Eguille, noted that the charts were so bad that a captain should rely on the river pilots alone. The shortage of funds and, in the opinion of some, the faint-heartedness of French navigators hindered river navigation still further. The effects of these factors were felt most painfully during the siege of Quebec: the harbourmaster observed that, for lack of funds, no soundings had been taken in the traverse near Île d'Orléans for years,[17] and in October 1759 Vaudreuil and Bigot pointed out in reference to the new masters of Quebec: "the enemy brought sixty-gun men-of-war through passages where we hardly dared risk a hundred-ton ship". They continued on the subject of the traverse:

> Every year, before the arrival of the king's vessels, the towers that had been built expressly as landmarks on Île d'Orléans had to be whitewashed, and any trees that might have sprouted up in the swath cleared on Île aux Ruaux had to be chopped down to facilitate the passage. All these precautions were taken for any frigate. Whether it had thirty guns or sixty.[18]

Pilotage on the St. Lawrence River was handled initially by pilots from France, whose familiarity with the route increased with each voyage. Expert pilots, of whom there were very few, usually served aboard merchant vessels. For the king's vessels, "we do not have even one pilot who knows his way around the ports and roadsteads along the route",[19] wrote the captain of the *Chameau* in 1720. This improved to some degree after La Richardière was named port captain at Quebec City. Each spring, around the beginning of June, the port captain or his representative would go downriver to await the king's vessel at Kamouraska or Île Verte. The ship's captain announced his arrival by firing several cannon shots, and the port captain went on board to pilot the vessel to Quebec City. He would conduct the vessel back when it departed in October.

If they needed pilots, at least for the passage from Île aux Coudres to Quebec City, merchant vessels could count on the services of men such as Tremblay or Savard, who would board at Île aux Coudres. There were certainly not enough Canadian pilots, a fact reflected in Montcalm's recommendation in 1756 that a school for pilots be established at Quebec City.[20] This need had become glaringly evident in 1755, when the Dubois de la Mothe fleet arrived in Canada. The authorities had had to engage the captains of merchant ships, including Abel, Vitré, Chabosseau, Raby and Roy, to pilot the fleet's vessels. Trained pilots and reliable charts, "constitute our sacred law and prophets, obedience to which can transform a hard and dangerous voyage into a joyful outing" – yet with all the advances in pilotage and cartography, a trip up the St. Lawrence could never be described as an easy outing. Too many vessels were to be stranded or wrecked in these waters.[22]

After either a safe or a difficult crossing, arrival at Quebec City (figure 19) brought a great feeling of relief. The crew and passengers could at last set foot on terra firma. They were no longer at the mercy of such fickle elements as the sea and the wind. The captain of the *Rubis* in 1732, in recounting his arrival at Quebec City, describes a scene that must have been repeated thousands of times. Entering the Basin of Quebec on 24 August at eight o'clock in the evening, Captain l'Etenduère dropped anchor in 18 fathoms of water.

> We got under way the next morning, the 25th, the feast of St. Louis, at ebb tide, with the small topsail trimmed. Stemming the current, I slipped into place in the roadstead of Quebec, where I cast anchor in eighteen fathoms corner of Île d'Orléans slightly apart from Pointe des Pères and the bell tower of the Recollet friars from the southwest end of the General's house, which is the best anchorage for men-of-war. I moored across with the flood, then backed both anchors and saluted with nine cannon shots, to which the merchantmen responded in like fashion.[23]

The St. Lawrence River, with its currents and the surveys it spawned, was like an extension of the ocean for a ship's crew. Nature seemed to increase the number of obstacles just as the voyage was coming to an end, reminding the crew of the many constraints experienced during the transAtlantic crossing. Safe passage required men who were able to overcome these obstacles.

Chapter Three

The People and Their Occupation

Various forces and many interests might have prompted individuals to undertake a voyage that would place them at the mercy of the ocean for at least two months. The conditions that prevailed on such oceanic crossings were examined in the preceding chapter. In this chapter, we shall look at the men and women who embarked on such an adventure. How many crewmen were required to sail these vessels toward New France? How many passengers were crowded between-decks, imagining this new country, dreaming of material or spiritual conquests? How did they pass the time on these long voyages?

The crew

Upon meeting the merchant vessel *Marie-Elisabeth*, the Chevalier de La Clue, captain of the 64-gun man-of-war *Triton, en route* from Toulon to Louisbourg in 1751 (figure 26), wrote in his log: "I sent my boat to fetch the captain, not wishing to make him lower his, as this is quite troublesome for merchantmen, which have only a small crew."[1] As Table 11 indicates, the crews of merchant vessels were indeed quite limited.[2] On the average, there were not more than 60 crewmen, unless the capacity of the vessel was more than 500 tons. The crossing of the Atlantic, under the usual conditions, must have been most exhausting work for these small crews.

The size of the crew on a merchantman varied according to the ship's tonnage. To have a crew of 15 or more, a vessel had to have a capacity of more than 100 tons; at least 45 men were needed for vessels upwards of 250 tons. The two ships listed in Table 11 as more than 500 tons – 550 to be exact – were privately owned frigates that were outfitted first as privateers and later as escort ships.[3] They were not true merchant vessels, but rather warships, each carrying 26 guns. Vessels under 50 tons were

Table 11 Complements in the French Navy and Merchant Marine

Navy

Type, size	Number of vessels	Average Number of Men
man-of-war, 80 guns	3	877
man-of-war, 74–70 guns	7	700
man-of-war, 64 guns	12	514
man-of-war, 60–62 guns	4–2	415
man-of-war, 54–56 guns	2	273
man-of-war, 50 guns	6	330
man-of-war, 48 guns	2	250
man-of-war, 46 guns	3	173
man-of-war, 42 guns	1	260
frigate, 30 guns	7	230
frigate, 28 guns	1	286
frigate, 26 guns	6	190
frigate, 24 guns	3	218
frigate, 22 guns	1	150
frigate, 20 guns	1	120
corvette, 10 guns	5	80
corvette, 16 guns	2	123
corvette, 14 guns	2	80

Merchant marine

Size	Number of vessels	Average Number of Men
500 tons and over	2	166
400–499 tons	2	40
350–399 tons	1	57
300–349 tons	8	45
250–299 tons	4	45
200–249 tons	8	37
150–199 tons	5	25
100–149 tons	28	17
50–99 tons	25	14
0–49 tons	6	11

used usually for coastal trade and rarely embarked on trans-Atlantic crossings, so the smaller crews were not nearly so much of a drawback.

Men-of-war were manned usually by more than 250 crewmen, frigates by 120 to 230, and corvettes by 80 to 120. Men-of-war and frigates were considerably larger than merchant vessels, but the size of the crews on royal vessels related more to the number and calibre of the vessel's guns. According to a naval department document, the larger calibre cannons had to be manned by more men.[4] A four-pound cannon required only two men to operate it, but a 36-pound cannon required a minimum of 15 men;

24- and 18-pound cannons required nine men; 12-pounders, seven men; eight-pound cannons four men; and six-pounders, three men.

Flutes – royal vessels with a capacity of between 600 and 800 tons – had crews of 80 to 100 members. Unlike the men-of-war, these vessels had no offensive or defensive military function: they were transport vessels slightly larger than merchant ships. A vessel fitted out for transport use would have only 20 or so cannons and its crew would also be much smaller. For example, in 1755, there were only 300, instead of the usual 500 to 700, crewmen on the vessels transporting four infantry battalions to New France.[5] These 300 sailors must have been sufficient to sail a 64- or 74-gun man-of-war because the soldiers had no duties on board. Overall, the function as well as the size of the vessel determined the strength of the crew.

Judging from about 50 crew lists,[6] the captains recruited most of their sailors from the towns and villages near the seaports where their vessels were fitted out. In fact, from the Colbert era on, the recruitment of sailors was based on the class system. All males between the ages of 17 and 50, in the coastal provinces of France, were registered and assigned to one of three or four groups, or classes, according to their province and its population. Every three or four years each class had to serve on the king's vessels for one year.[7] In other years, the seamen were free to sign on with the merchant captains of their choice. If a sailor was unable to honour his contract with the king, he had to find a replacement. This class system is undoubtedly the reason for the difficulty in recruiting crews for the larger number of king's ships in commission during periods of conflict, such as the Seven Years' War. In 1758, for example, the commanding officers of the *Aigle* and the *Outarde*, which the king was equipping to send to Canada, barely completed their crews.[8] The officers could count on foreign sailors, particularly the Spanish, however, to fill any available positions on the French sailing vessels.

The recruiting problems on the king's vessels also affected the merchant marine. Naval ordinances gave commanding officers of the royal fleet the authority to fill any vacancies in their crews with sailors taken from merchant ships. This procedure was common in the colonies, particularly because there was no class system in Canada and French vessels were not allowed to recruit sailors from the colonies unless they guaranteed their return passage.[9] The only practical way to find recruits, therefore, was to raid the crews of merchant ships. It was not difficult for royal vessels to justify this practice. Indeed, their role was to protect trade, and how could they fulfill that mandate if they were unable to sail because of insufficient crew? Although naval captains could commandeer sailors from the merchant marine, merchant captains were forbidden to sign on men from other ships, a law that increased their dependency on the king.[10]

Just as the size of the crew varied according to the size and function of the vessels, so too did the number of positions to be filled. The larger the crew, the more varied were the services required. The crew consisted of four major categories: chief officers, petty officers, other officers, and crewmen. Table 12 lists the various positions for officers and crewmen by category.[11] This table applies to both the French navy and the merchant marine, although the merchant marine required many fewer positions.

The number of positions for chief officers depended on the class of the vessel. A first-class vessel would have two captains, two lieutenants, and two midshipmen, whereas a fourth-class vessel would have only half that number. Second-lieutenants and midshipmen were very scarce on merchant vessels. As well, merchantmen did not have chaplains and only half of them carried surgeons. Ship's boys and officers in trades not directly associated with ship handling were the most dispensable, especially if the crew numbered only 15 or 20 men. On the king's vessels, officers accounted for 32 per cent of the complement and able seamen for 43 per cent. In the merchant marine, able seamen represented 41 per cent, and officers 38 per cent.

France's 1681 naval ordinance stipulated that, for physical reasons, seagoing men were to be between the ages of 17 and 50.[12] According to Table 12, the average age of able seamen was 26; of ordinary seamen, 21 years; and of ship's boys, 15 years. The average age of petty officers, who were mostly specialized workers and career men, was 29 years. They were about the same age as the chief officers, except for the captains, who had an average age of 36. Although the average ages indicated in Table 12 are for crews in the merchant marine, seamen on the king's vessels were the same age, as a result of the rotation set up by the class system. Generally we could conclude that a Frenchman could be a ship's boy at 15, an ordinary seaman at 20, an able seaman at 25, and an officer at 30 years of age. In short, and as was the intent of the ordinance, the men who went to sea were in their prime.

The king did not pay nearly so well as private enterprise. On the king's vessels, only senior officers were paid more than their colleagues on merchant vessels. Moreover, officers in the merchant marine could take on private cargo to supplement their wages (figure 28). They would load a few tons of merchandise, without paying any shipping charges, and sell them at a profit in the colonies. Louis Houin, captain of the *Duc d'Anjou*, a 105-ton ship fitted out at Les Sables d'Olonne for a voyage to Isle Royale in 1756, was taking private cargo of 30 barrels of liquor, six barrels of plums, 12 small barrels of vinegar, four small barrels of almonds, 30 hams, 100 cheeses, and 15 hundredweight of rope.[13] His brother Jacques, who was surgeon on the same ship, the second captain, and the lieutenant were taking about the same. Merchant officers thus had a good means of augmenting their incomes.

Other crew members in the merchant marine were paid two or three times what their counterparts in the royal navy earned. Table 12 lists the wages for crewmen on the king's vessels during the Seven Years' War. In the merchant marine, wages increased by 50 to 100 per cent within ten years. Because of the lower wages paid in the navy, the class system was clearly useful, not only for finding the seamen required, but also for keeping them. When entering into service, a sailor usually received one or two months' wages in advance.[14] One third of his wages for the expected duration of the voyage went to his family, and the captain would pay the balance when the journey was over. Thus the seaman could not gamble away his entire salary *en route* or spend it during stopovers.

The wages of seamen serving on the king's vessels were comparable to those of soldiers on duty in Canada at that time. The wages of seamen on merchant ships were more in keeping with those of a journeyman.[15] In addition to their wages, however, seamen on merchant ships received rations for every day they were at sea, an advantage that was no doubt negligible considering the short term of employment each year. A comparison of these wages with the costs of some standard consumer goods provides an idea of the value of this remuneration. In 1757, a 180-pound barrel of flour cost 27 livres; a barrel of suet, 50 livres; a bottle of Burgundy, one livre, ten sous; two pounds of Gruyère cheese, 46 sous; and two pounds of butter, 40 sous. A shaving mug sold for eight sous; a pound of candles, 12 sous; a hammer, two livres; a pair of tongs, three livres; a saw, five livres; and a plane, two livres.[16] (All workers had to supply their own tools.) The cost of these few food and household products clearly indicates that the seamen's wages were quite meagre.

In fact, the wages paid to seamen seem to reflect the low esteem in which they were held by society. The authorities realized the worth of seamen's work, of course, and praised their bravery, especially in wartime,[17] but although satisfied with the work, they despised the men themselves. According to Lahontan and Diéréville, sailors were just as superstitious as the Ancients, refusing to sail on a Friday and believing that Saint Elmo's fire was a storm warning.[18] Chabert de Cogolin felt that sailors knew much more about the effects of phenomena than the causes.[19] Jean-François Duchêny, a Quebec merchant, declared scornfully that he had "never met any of the sailors in that crew, or in any other", since he "never associated with such people".[20] And when the authorities proposed the construction of a shed in Quebec City to store the rigging of the king's vessels, they specifically mentioned the repairs that would be required continually because of the sailors.[21]

The sailor was not a simpleton, however. Referring to the sailors serving on privateers in 1757–1758, the directors of the Bayonne chamber of commerce declared, "ignorant as they are, they know how to count". A seaman who received an advance of 200 livres was not much use in combat: "This seaman knows his best interests; he sees and determines that considerable seizures will have to be made if there is to be any prize money left after the advance has been deducted."[22] Seamen preferred to return to port and sign on again rather than to fight a battle of uncertain outcome. In appreciating the work and despising the man, public opinion tended

Table 12 Ages and Wages of Sailors in the French Navy Between 1745 and 1755

Positions	Ages — Crew lists from 1745 and 1755		Monthly Wages — Merchant vessels				Monthly Wages — King's Vessels
			Wages 1745		Wages 1755		Regulation Wages circa 1755 (livres)
	Number of men	Average age	Number of men	Average wage (livres)	Number of men	Average wage (livres)	
Captain	0	0	0	0	0	0	0
Chief officers	43	36	15	100	32	155	300
Second captain	42	28	11	72	33	124	200–300
Lieutenant	25	29	6	50	17	89	100
Second lieutenant	12	27	8	57	4	108	0
Midshipman	13	23	5	32	9	50	50
Surgeon	26	30	8	32	17	65	50–75
Writer	0	0	0	0	0	0	45–50
Chaplain	0	0	0	0	0	0	30
Petty officers	0	0	0	0	0	0	0
First boatswain	25	34	0	0	26	77	40–50
Second boatswain	0	0	0	0	0	0	36–45
Boatswain's mate	22	34	9	40	14	66	30
First pilot	16	30	6	51	9	65	40–50
Second pilot	13	19	12	32	0	0	30–40
Master carpenter	35	33	9	44	26	76	36–40
Carpenter's mate	13	28	1	27	13	56	18–30
Master gunner	16	31	2	37	10	60	40–50
Gunner's mate	0	0	0	0	0	0	24–36
Gunner's assistant	0	0	0	0	0	0	30
Master caulker	6	33	0	0	6	7	24–36
Caulker's mate	0	0	0	0	0	0	16–24
Anchor master	9	33	0	0	9	75	24
Leading seaman	14	28	0	0	13	50	21
Coxswain	12	29	0	0	12	65	21–24
Boatman	0	0	0	0	0	0	18–21
Master sailmaker	5	23	0	0	5	57	21–30
Sailmaker's mate	0	0	0	0	0	0	0
Other officers							
Gunsmith	0	0	0	0	0	0	18–24
Gunsmith's assistant	4	23	1	30	3	42	12–15
Second surgeon	0	0	0	0	0	0	24–30
Surgeon's assistant	7	22	0	0	7	45	15–18
Apothecary	0	0	0	0	0	0	18–24
Cook	26	27	4	22	23	41	0
Baker	8	24	1	16	7	32	0
Able seaman	554	26	165	30	267	42	10–15
Ordinary seaman	224	21	27	16	132	24	0
Ship's boy	111	15	28	9	65	13	3–6

Table 12 (cont.—) Ages and Wages of Sailors in the French Navy Between 1745 and 1755

Positions	Ages Crew lists from 1745 and 1755		Monthly Wages Merchant vessels				Monthly Wages King's Vessels
			Wages 1745		Wages 1755		Regulation
	Number of men	Average age	Number of men	Average wage (livres)	Number of men	Average wage (livres)	Wages circa 1755 (livres)
Chief officers	161	30	53	N/A	112	N/A	N/A
Petty officers	206	29	40	N/A	164	N/A	N/A
Other officers	45	24	6	N/A	40	N/A	N/A
Complement	1,301	25	319	N/A	780	N/A	N/A
Without ship's boy	1,190	26	291	N/A	715	N/A	N/A

to lump all seamen together. Chief officers, however, were judged individually. They were not anonymous persons like seamen or petty officers. The authorities praised their exploits or criticized their mistakes.[23] Some chief officers even had their praises sung: "Grand Courval, Sans Egal & sans crainte, Ta valeur nous est connue, nous suivons tes vertues..." [Captain Courval, we bid you cheer! Without equal and without fear, greatness have you ever shown, your virtues all to us are known].[24] These verses are from a song written in honour of François Louis Poulin de Courval, a captain in the French navy, born in Quebec City in 1728.

In summary, considering the space available on board, the manoeuvring of a sailing vessel required the services of a large and youthful crew. Sailors were paid poorly, and because the profession had little to offer, recruitment was difficult. Moreover, sailors were in no position to demand better treatment.

The passengers

The crew members were not usually the only persons on board. They rubbed elbows with passengers, who frequently were not at all used to ocean voyages. Who were these passengers and why were they travelling to New France? Were they treated differently, according to their social rank or who they were?

Many were going because of their work. For the government officials, a position in the colony was an important or a necessary step in their careers. The missionaries or nuns were going to convert the North American Indians, and the soldiers were being sent to conquer and defend half a continent. The fishermen on board were going to work on the coasts of

LE PORT DE BREST
Vu du Chenal devant le nouveau quai aux canons

25. View of the port of Brest. (*Musée de la Marine, Paris, ph 15544.*) This etching was made in 1776 from a painting by Nicolas Ozanne. Although it was made a quarter of a century after the period in question, the port scenes depicted are no doubt quite similar to those at the time when soldiers were commissioned to patrol the North Atlantic, and that troops on their way to help New France embarked between 1755 and 1757.

Newfoundland, the Gaspé Peninsula, or Cape Breton Island, for shipowners who in most cases remained in France. Others made the trip for business reasons: merchants or clerks sought to establish contacts and to sell cargo. Many of these passengers would sail back across the ocean: the fishermen usually returned at the end of the fishing season and the government officials went back eventually to pursue their careers. Some returned to France for personal reasons, to collect inheritances or further their education, whereas others went because of their health, to be treated and take the waters.[1] Only the soldiers and the members of religious orders often stayed on in the colony.

From 1720 to 1740, another type of passenger was forced to make the crossing to New France. During these years, the colony received a number of prisoners. Most were petty thieves, poor men who had been sentenced for poaching on the property of a nobleman or for attempting to cheat the tax collector. There were also libertines, who had been sent away by their families to protect the family honour.

The last category of traveller was composed of immigrants in search of a new life. They were often craftsmen, such as the 24 carpenters who left France for Quebec City in 1749 to work in the shipyards.[2] Merchant vessels also had to transport a certain number of apprentices, who had been hired by the first colonists for a three-year period. Their number depended on the tonnage of the vessel. There seem to have been very few stowaways: only seven were recorded for the century preceding the conquest of New France – a young boy who hid to follow his father, a captain; three fishermen wanting to return home; a criminal fleeing justice in New France; and two adventure-seekers from Marseilles.[3] The attractions of a clandestine voyage must have been very limited.

Officials, soldiers, prisoners, and missionaries usually travelled on the king's vessels without charge. During periods of conflict, such as the Seven Years' War, when the royal vessels could not be spared they would use merchant vessels chartered by the king. Others who wished to travel on the king's vessels had to pay 150 livres for their passage if they were at the captain's table, or 30 livres for the same rations as the crew.[4] All other passengers travelled on merchant vessels. The fishermen's passage was paid by their employer. Each captain had to take from three to six apprentices, depending on the vessel's tonnage. Skilled workers counted as two men, a policy that explained the contention that many of these workers were not so skilled as the captain claimed.[5] Both the shipowner and the captain used this policy to their advantage. Other passengers generally had to pay 150 livres for a crossing in peace time. In 1758, Abraham Gradis profited from the war by demanding 250 livres per soldier to take troops to New France.[6]

In times of peace, particularly between 1730 and 1744,[7] the king's vessels generally carried 150 to 200 passengers to New France. This number usually included about 75 to 100 recruits and 40 to 60 prisoners on seaman's rations; 20 to 30 officers and missionaries who dined at the captain's table, and their servants, who ate in the pantry. These passengers might have included a few wives of officers or of government officials. The *Jason*, a 50-gun man-of-war with a usual crew of 230, had 437 people on board when it was preparing to set sail from La Rochelle (figure 21) for New France in 1737.[8] On their return to France, the king's vessels could transport 50 to 75 passengers, including 15 to 30 discharged or retired soldiers. They also took on criminals, who were condemned to the galleys.[9] During the Seven Years' War, soldiers were often the only passengers aboard royal vessels. Sixty-four-gun and 74-gun men-of-war sent to New France from 1755 to 1758 carried eight or nine companies of soldiers, or 330 to 360 men. This meant that 6,000 soldiers were transported to Louisbourg and Canada during those four years.[10] These vessels were obviously fitted out as transport vessels, usually at the port of Brest (figure 25).

It is much more difficult to determine the number of passengers who travelled on merchantmen, because of the lack of documentation. Quite often, there were only the three or six apprentices prescribed by law, unless the captain had found some way to avoid this requirement. If there were soldiers on board, the party rarely numbered more than 20 men; at most, a ship would carry a company of 50. The explanation for these small numbers was the size of the vessels and the hope of reducing losses by dividing the men among several ships.[11] Passenger lists for the merchant vessels fitted out at Bordeaux (figure 22) and travelling to Louisbourg and Quebec City between 1755 and 1759 show very few civilians.[12] Clearly, this was a very difficult period. If an estimated 10,000 persons, including 3,500 military personnel, emigrated to New France between 1630 and 1760,[13] however, then the number of civilians aboard merchantmen must have been limited in peacetime as well. During the Seven Years' War, civilians travelled on the 24 vessels carrying passengers from Bordeaux. Most of the ships had one or two passengers; one carried four; and the 400-ton *Nouvelle Victoire*, 16. Among the *Nouvelle Victoire* passengers were some women:

> I certify that Madame Lilie Demeloize, thirty-two years of age, wife of Monsieur de Pean, assistant major of the troops at Quebec City; Madame Marie de Lery, twenty-nine years of age, wife of Monsieur Darpantigny, infantry lieutenant; Marie Latache of Quebec City, lady's maid to Madame de Pean; François Ollivie of Coué in Poitou, twenty-four years of age, are all Catholics of long standing who wish to embark on the ship *Nouvelle Victoire* of Bordeaux, with Captain Joseph Fossecave, to voyage to Quebec City where they are going on business, signed at Bordeaux, this twelfth day of April, 1755.[14]

Péan, Bigot, Imbert, and LeMercier were state employees who had boarded the royal frigate *Fidèle* in March of the same year.[15]

26. Men-of-war sailing from the Toulon roadstead. (*France, Bibliothèque Nationale, Estampes (Prints), Cliché Giraudon L6976.*) In the eighteenth century, the port of Toulon also commissioned a few of the vessels sailing to New France, although not nearly so many as the ports of France's west coast.

Generally, the passengers did not enjoy their trans-Atlantic crossings, especially when the seas were a little rough. Bougainville probably summarized their feelings best:

> No words can describe the suffering that we endure in this miserable vessel. The lurching is horrible and continuous. We don't know where to place ourselves or how to hold on. We could break our necks at any moment. The almost continuous beating of the waves inundates us with vile salt water. It is not a mere matter of buckets of water; our animals and fowl are dying by the numbers. I won't even speak of the damp and cold that must be endured without a fire and out in the open every day. The despotic lurching rules more than our lives, our movements, our attitudes, our rest; we must fight it at every morsel we bring to our lips and every time we must satisfy a need.[16]

Despite quite a rapid crossing, Montcalm wished never again to take to sea once he had returned to France after the war. Marie de l'Incarnation seems to have been the only person who was not critical of her voyage. Although she spent three months at sea, she was delighted with the comforts provided her and her companions in a large, well-ventilated cabin.[17]

The passengers' inactivity must have made them more sensitive to inclement weather and to the continuous pitching of the vessel. Whereas the naval soldiers on the king's vessels had musket and cannon practice three or four times a week, the soldiers on board had no assigned duties. When infantry battalions were being transported to Canada by the Dubois de la Mothe squadron in 1755, the authorities strictly forbade ships' captains to make the soldiers work. At the very most, soldiers sailing on merchant vessels were permitted to defend the ships during an attack.[18] Other passengers had almost nothing to do. "As one gets little exercise, one soon becomes heavy and fat," wrote Diéréville in his travel diary,[19] and in notes on his travels, Father Charlevoix concluded: "As you can see they are mere trifles which at best would amuse those with nothing to do on board ship."[20] In exceptional situations, such as when illness struck the crew or when the sailors alone could not handle the ship in a storm, the captain might ask the passengers to help in the sailing.[21] This unplanned participation was undoubtedly sufficient to confront them with the difficulties of a seaman's life.

The cramped quarters and the boredom and frustration from inactivity occasionally led to fits of bad humour among the passengers. Some unpleasant character traits became more evident. The Sulpician Joseph Dargent commented on the rude conduct of Jean-Baptiste Duquesnel, captain of the *Jason* in 1737:

> He received me as he did all the others and he treated me as he does the officers and passengers all the rest of the time, that is, quite rudely,

as he has never had a good word for anyone on the vessel. Thus he was known to all as a boor.[22]

Sailors were not the only persons on board who were disliked by officers and some passengers: royal envoys were nothing but "scoundrels" and even those in holy garb were sometimes embroiled in disagreements. Following his voyage in 1734, the Jesuit father Nau wrote to his superiors:

> My lord Bishop arrived at La Rochelle when we no longer expected him and he sailed with us. He brought with him a dozen or so priests he had collected from the streets of Paris and at the doors of churches, men who for the most part were ignorant and uneducated, and who believed that they had the right to insult everyone, who quarrelled continually amongst themselves and who even dared attack the ship's officers; they would have found themselves clapped in irons if not for the esteem in which the prelate was held. We avoided them as much as possible and attempted to keep to ourselves along with three Sulpician fathers, men of intelligence and rare piety.[23]

Living in close quarters did not mean that passengers would associate with just anyone, however. Intendant Gilles Hocquart wrote about a surgeon's wife to whom he had given passage on the *Héros* in 1731: "although I assigned her to the captain's table, at the State's expense, Monsieur le Comte Desgouttes made her eat alone. It would not have been proper for her to eat at his table or in the pantry." Hocquart went on to describe her as "not suitable in terms of birth and fortune".[24] Mingling among the social classes would have to wait for the Revolution.

The sailing vessel, or "floating city", as it was called by Abbé Navières in 1734,[25] was a veritable social microcosm. Although limited space aboard ship forced the passengers to be in close contact, everyone remained somewhat aloof. The Jesuit Nau's attitude in this regard is typical and most enlightening. Passengers travelling to New France bear witness to the state's role in this matter. Travellers preferred to sail on the king's vessels, no doubt because of their spaciousness and the cheaper passage. In fact, the state was unable to meet the demand and found it necessary to charter merchantmen to transport soldiers, for example, despite the fact that only a small minority of the population travelled. In all, a voyage across the North Atlantic was not particularly easy.

Crew members' duties

Whereas inactivity was the daily routine for passengers, crew members did not have as much free time. The 1681 *Code de la marine*, for the

27. Planes from the *Machault*. (*Parks Canada*.) These three different types of planes were used for making grooves and working on wood that was very rough surfaced or concave in shape. They were probably from the tool box of the *Machault*'s carpenter.

merchant marine, and the 1689 *Code des Armées Navales*, for the king's vessels, set out the sailors' duties and their training. In the group of chief officers, the captain had ultimate responsibility for the vessel he commanded, the cargo, and all passengers. Pierre Hévé, a Quebec navigator, who was hired as a captain, refused to set sail and demanded compensation when the vessel's owners tried to impose a revised contract on him. It would have placed him under the supervision of one of the owners, who was to go on board as the cargo manager.[1]

The captain's responsibilities ranged from preparation of the vessel, and sometimes the very choice of the ship, to the laying up. To become a captain, at least for a merchant vessel, a sailor was required to have a minimum of five years' navigation experience. Before receiving his captainship he also had to take an examination. The candidate was questioned by a professor of hydrography and two other captains before officials of a court of admiralty. The examination was not compulsory for a candidate with two years' experience as a pilot, who would have been on several naval campaigns, and passed an examination conducted by the same panel with two additional pilots. Although most of the chief officer positions were reserved for nobility,[2] the rank of captain could be obtained only after several years of service at sea, for an officer must have held the positions of naval cadet, midshipman, and lieutenant before being given command of a man-of-war. Because the captain of a royal vessel had a much larger crew, he could entrust routine navigation duties to his subordinates. The captain of a merchant vessel, who was often also pilot of his ship, however, was at the helm more often.

Inventories of the belongings of a few ship's captains indicate that some officers were concerned with basing the practical aspects of sailing a ship on theoretical knowledge.[3] These documents list books on navigation, law of the sea, history, and geography, which would seem to reveal the practical concerns of their owners. The choice of titles was very limited, however, for books were difficult to obtain in the colonies. Nevertheless, the libraries of these captains were relatively well stocked and compared favourably with those of professionals and colonial merchants. This is all the more surprising in light of the risk of damage to books aboard ship. But unlike some professionals, a naval officer had to apply his technical knowledge to practical situations, and needed to refresh his memory continually.

The lieutenant was in command of the vessel after the captain or second captain, and reported to the captain. He was usually responsible for port watch, whereas the captain was responsible for starboard watch. The crew was divided into two equal groups. One was responsible for handling the port side, the other for the starboard. When it was time to cast or weigh anchor, and during storms, all crew members had to be at their posts: it was a full watch. While at sea, each group was replaced every four hours, hence the expressions "starboard watch" and "port watch."

28. Chinese porcelain bowl from the *Machault*. (*Parks Canada*.) Measuring 11 cm high with a rim 25.5 cm in diameter, this bowl is a fine example of the approximately 1,500 porcelain pieces found in the cargo of the *Machault*. They were part of the goods taken on board by officers for private sale.

In the French navy, a lieutenant could command frigates and corvettes. The duties of midshipmen were similar but subordinate to those of lieutenants.

The writer, posted mainly on the king's vessels, was a type of notary or clerk. He kept a record of the rigging and merchandise stowed and distributed on board and of the food consumed; he also maintained the crew list, and recorded any deaths or desertions.

The positions and duties of the petty officers comprised four major categories: ship handling, piloting, gunnery, and maintenance. The boatswain had prime responsibility for the physical operation of the vessel. Officially, he gave orders to the entire crew and looked after all ship handling; in fact, he was concerned mainly with the stern of the vessel to the mainmast during the main watches. He saw that the vessel was properly loaded and rigged for smooth sailing, and that the rigging was always in good order. He was assisted by the boatswain's mate, who, although his subordinate, carried out similar duties at the bow of the vessel and would replace the boatswain in his absence. In addition, there was an anchormaster (bosseman), who was responsible for lowering, raising, and maintaining the anchors, and leading seamen (in French, literally, quartermasters), who, according to the ordinance, commanded one quarter of the crew for one quarter of the day. The leading seamen were responsible for the cleanliness of the ship and for operating the pumps when necessary. As was the case with chief officers in the navy, the position of boatswain was not reached until the positions of leading seaman, anchor master, and boatswain's mate had been held. The coxswain and boatman were also petty officers. They were responsible for the manoeuvring of their boats when launched and for their maintenance on board.

The master pilot alone set the ship's course. He had to have extensive experience at sea, often acquired by serving as an assistant pilot. The pilot was also responsible for purchasing the charts, octants, and astrolabes required for guiding the vessel through the voyage. Some pilots had long, busy careers travelling the same routes. For examples, Jacques Chaviteau made 25 voyages between 1701 and 1725, 22 of which took him to New France.[4]

On the king's vessels, the master gunner was a petty officer responsible for all artillery on board. He inspected the cannons and the magazine regularly. He was responsible for the gun room, where the hatchway leading to the powder room was located, and for the arms that were stored and the passengers who slept there. He also arranged the cannonballs by calibre and prepared the charges for firing the cannons.

The petty officers responsible for the maintenance and preservation of the vessel were specialized workers who came on board with their own tools. The number of these workers and their assistants depended on the size of the vessel. The master carpenter inspected the planking, masts, and yards to check their strength and make the necessary repairs (figure

29. Rafts used during the siege of Quebec City. (*National Maritime Museum, London, Public Visual Index, no. 1466.*) These rafts were intended to destroy the English fleet. In the summer of 1759, however, they were ignited too soon and had burned completely before they reached the English ships anchored near Quebec City.

27). The master caulker ensured that all seams were caulked with oakum and covered in pitch and tar and that the cargo ports were watertight. When necessary, he installed leaden plates over the most seriously damaged areas. Since he occasionally had to go underwater without special equipment to check the ship's condition, his was undoubtedly the most dangerous trade.[5] The master sailmaker checked the suit of sails and mended torn sails. The cooper, responsible for the maintenance of all containers and the repair of water barrels, was not on board as frequently as the other craftsmen. He would sometimes make barrels to be used in the colonies for reloading the ship.[6] On merchant vessels, the master carpenter often had to do the work of caulker, sailmaker and cooper as well because of the limited number of crewmen.

While the petty officers attended to the sailing and pilotage and gave the appropriate orders, other officers were also carrying out important duties. The cooks and bakers fed the crew; the gunsmiths looked after the guns. The remaining 60 per cent of the crew simply took orders. While the ship's boys, who were on their first voyages, ran errands, the ordinary seamen learned about the able seamen's duties, for which they did not yet have the ability or the strength. The able seamen handled the sails and the anchors. Depending on their abilities, they hoisted, trimmed, and took in sails; raised or cast anchor; took turns at the pumps; fired the cannons; and rowed the long boat.

Briefly, these were the main duties of sailors at sea. It was often extremely demanding work: lifting an anchor weighing as much as 8,000 pounds, moving a 92-foot-long yard, or untangling a rope rendered stiff by the damp and cold.[7] In port the sailors became dockers, loading and unloading their vessels or those of others. In Quebec City, the sailors were sometimes also required to work on the fortifications or help defend the city's batteries in times of conflict. Such was the case in 1709 and 1759 (figure 29).[8]

Because of the many different skills and tasks practised on board a sailing vessel, the job of a sailor was a highly specialized one. This specialization also involved a rather developed feel for the laws and biases of the hierarchy. But a maritime career was particularly notable for the priority it gave to the aptitudes and skills of the individual crew members. In the eighteenth century, navigation was already too unpredictable an undertaking to entrust the vessels to incompetents or persons too inflexible to adapt to difficult circumstances.

Chapter Four

Life Aboard Ship

Whether a sailor was part of the enormous crew crowded onto a 50-gun man-of-war, or one of the dozen or so confined in a small brigantine, the voyage to New France required him to adapt to the special conditions inherent in life at sea. The billows need only be a little too high, for example, and water would seep in from all quarters, drenching the sailor's hammock or berth. The outfitter laid in a store of provisions sufficient to last the trip to Quebec City – but how concerned was he with the quality of these foodstuffs? They could be sufficient in quantity, yet fail to provide the nutritive elements essential for a healthful diet. And if too few sanitary precautions were taken, disease could claim any number of lives. Before the chaplain led vespers, sailors danced on the forecastle while passengers took air on deck. These distractions were often enough to prevent passengers from getting on one another's nerves unbearably, or to stop a cranky remark from sparking a free-for-all. If tempers did flare, the captain would likely have to punish the unruly sailor or quarrelsome passenger.

Routine and sleeping quarters

We can only guess at what the sailors' daily routine must have been like. The documentation on the daily course of activities aboard the king's vessels is scant; of course, there is even less for merchantmen. In the French navy, bells and drums were used to signal the hours of rising, meals, watches, and sleep for one and all, thereby setting the pulse of life aboard ship. The sailors also punctuated their work with shouts. "There were sometimes more than 100 men pulling the same rope and it fell to those with the loudest voices to call out in a certain way to help the men pull together at the same time."[1] The day began about seven with prayers, then breakfast.[2] To ensure the manning of the ship 24 hours a day, captains adopted the system of watches and the division of the crew into two groups, as described earlier. While one group worked, the other rested.³ To avoid having the same sailors always working the same hours, there was a change in shift halfway through one watch, between four and eight in the evening.⁴ This enabled everyone to eat about 6:00 p.m.

> Although I've cracked most double-entenders in the jargon of navigation, my probings of "amas" long yielded naught but exasperation: I'd said this swinging grave had a moniker preposterous, but gads, was I mistaken: on close examination I find it a most suitable appellation whose meaning comes across to us. "Amas" is surely valid when your travels 'cross the seas Are in such close confines' – en masse – or when, so oft, alas! your berth's infested with a mass of vermin and of fleas.⁵

These satiric lines about his hammock were penned by an officer on the *Argonaute*, a 600-ton East Indiaman with a crew of 154 men. The *Argonaute* called in at Louisbourg on the homeward leg of a voyage to the Indies that was to take from 1742 to 1744. These witty few lines clearly convey two rather disagreeable aspects of life aboard ship: the lack of hygiene and the wretched sleeping facilities.

A sailor's hammock consisted of a piece of canvas six feet long by three feet wide, which he suspended from the beams, either by all four corners or by means of a rope attached to the two ends.⁶ These hammocks were also known to the French as "branles" or "swings", because their rocking motion matched that of the vessel – hence the "swinging grave" mentioned by the officer of the *Argonaute*. Hammocks were used in turn by different sailors each watch, because there was only one hammock for every two seamen. The sailors slept fully clothed, so as to be ready in case of emergency. They were also supplied with a blanket. Crews on fishing vessels used straw pallets, which afforded better protection from the dampness and cold.⁷

Since the hammocks were suspended from the beams, all hands slept in the between-decks. They often had to stoop when making their way to bed, for there was little headroom. On an 80-ton brigantine, such as the *Madeleine*, the between-decks was only three and one-half feet high, and on 50-gun men-of-war the height was only five feet.⁸ Sailors were not the only passengers to sleep in the between-decks: soldiers and prisoners bound for the colonies also had to hang their hammocks there. The other passengers slept in the Sainte Barbe, or gun room, in the stern of the ship, on bunks set up in two or three tiers. These cots were corded with spun yarn, and each had a mattress. If there were too many passengers to be accommodated in this area, some would have to sleep in the between-decks with the crew. A makeshift partition of wood or canvas would be rigged up if necessary to provide a measure of privacy.⁹

Although the passengers might have been isolated somewhat from the crew, they certainly were not protected from the noise: the rudder tiller passed through the gun room. Comfort was not often available, as this account by a traveller of 1734 makes clear:

> At the mere sight of the Saint Barbe, which was to be our sleeping quarters for the voyage, our hearts sank, mine first of all. It is a room about the size of the Rhétorique of Bordeaux, in which hang a double tier of cots meant to serve as beds for passengers of both sexes, junior officers and gunners. We were crammed into this dark, foul place like so many sardines; it was impossible to get into bed without banging our heads and knees twenty times. A sense of propriety prohibited us from undressing, and after a while our clothes caused us appalling discomfort. The motion of the vessel would dismantle the apparatus, slinging people into each other's cots. Once I was dropped, still in my bed, upon a poor Canadian officer, descending upon him like the Angel of Death. I lay there for five or ten minutes, unable to extricate myself from my cot, with the officer half suffocated and barely able to summon the strength to swear.[10]

In the infirmary, which was forward in the between-decks, the sick were provided with bunks like those of the passengers in the gun room. The chief officers and important passengers, such as governors, bishops, and intendants, slept in rooms or cabins located under the quarterdeck. These rooms had locks and some were panelled to quieten noises from outside. Some were also decorated with paintings. Even privileged passengers did not always find the accommodations to their liking, however. Governor Denonville, for example, transferred to a different vessel in 1685:

> Seeing that Madame de Denonville could not but find herself in jeopardy in the storeroom; even though she was given as much space as possible, it was necessary to put in five beds so that a room twelve or thirteen feet long by eight feet wide had to lodge nine children and adults. These circumstances, compounded by the heat and the distress caused by seasickness, could place my wife in grave danger, especially in her pregnant condition.[11]

The wardroom, a large chamber used for chief officer meetings and as a dining room, was also under the quarterdeck.

The kitchens for the captain and crew were in the forecastle. Live animals, which were usually transported only on the king's men-of-war, shared this area. Sometimes a few cages of fowl and pens of livestock were put between-decks, in the area in front of the sail-makers. Men-of-war usually transported pigs, sheep, chickens, and a few head of cattle to be eaten during the voyage. It was also necessary to transport some animals to New France to establish herds of livestock there. Despite the limited space available, horses also had to be taken on board. One can easily imagine the difficulties with having live animals on board, especially if the crossing was rough. After passing through a violent storm *en route* back to France in the autumn of 1720, the commander of the *Chameau*, Voutron, wrote:

> It [the storm] cost us three head of cattle, along with many sheep and fowl that we had on board. Mr. Raudot's two mares, which I neglected to mention earlier, were also battered to death, despite the fact that they were between-decks with all the necessary precautions. It was neither the season or the climate to be transporting animals.[12]

Most of the provisions were stowed in the hold or in the storerooms; powder, vegetables, and sea biscuit, in particular, were kept in the storerooms, which were lined with plaster and hung with matting to protect against moisture. On merchant vessels (and sometimes others), regulations notwithstanding, captains occasionally had to stow goods on deck or below the upper decks.[13] Protesting the claims of his ship's outfitter, one captain declared in 1747: "he does wrong to forget that in order to find a place for his goods I gave up my own cabin for the whole journey. My room was full and so was the wardroom, so that whatever the weather, sunshine or rain, we had to eat out on deck."[14] Under such circumstances, the crew and passengers had little space to stretch their legs (figure 30).

Religious services, such as catechismal instruction, took place on deck. A greater number of passengers and sailors could thus participate – the soldiers without leaving their stations (if they were busy with the sails, for example). The decks were also the setting for the crew's recreational activities. It was there that sailors organized dances and that, upon reaching the Grand Banks, a baptismal ceremony described in the section on recreation was held in honour of those crossing for the first time. Weather permitting, crews took their meals on deck, but the cold and rain so common in the Atlantic forced them to eat in the between-decks more often than not.

As we have seen, seamen were provided only the bare minimum of space and sleeping arrangements. This paucity extended to their clothing as well. There was no uniform, not even for sailors on the king's fleet. Only the chief officers and the soldiers aboard these vessels wore a uniform of sorts, made up of breeches, jacket, and jerkin.[15] A few rare, brief inventories of sailors' belongings mention, in exceedingly small quantities, woven shirts and breeches, jerseys, cloth caps, woollen stockings, cloth handkerchiefs, French sabots and shoes, and a canvas or leather bag for carrying a few spare articles of clothing.[16] The clothing of the seamen was sorely inadequate as protection against the cold of the North Atlantic. In 1692, D'Iberville described the alarming state of the sailors aboard the *Poli*, then sailing to France, as follows: "[we sailed] with many of my men sick from the cold, having none but cloth garments, most lacking both shoes and stockings, obliged to wear their clothes still wet, not having any extra to change into, and becoming chilled through to the marrow".[17]

The scarcity of spare clothing frequently meant having to work in wet clothes, an invitation to fevers and colds. In 1762, an ordinance decreed for the first time that sailors were to change into dry clothes when those worn were wet.[18] It also required sailors to change their shirts at least once a week. The lack of proper apparel raises the matter of the sailors' personal hygiene, a problem inevitably connected with the cleanliness of sailing ships themselves. Seamen could not change their clothes regularly. Moreover, water aboard ship was too precious to be used for washing laundry frequently. Under these conditions, the ship's environment was ideal for parasites. Why should the sailors worry about personal hygiene when the vessel on which they lived was far from immaculate? Under the *Code des Armée Navales*, the vessel was to be swept once a day, animal droppings were to be thrown into the sea twice daily, the between-decks was to be aired during good weather, and vinegar was to be used as a disinfectant whenever necessary.[19]

The inclement weather of the North Atlantic often rendered these tasks impossible. It takes little imagination to understand the effect that rain or a strong wave could have had on animal droppings left on a deck that was scarcely waterproof. The humidity generated by large numbers of persons and animals living between-decks also caused problems, because condensation developed on the vessel's walls and beams. Coils of wet ropes accumulated on the fore-decks and the pumps were not equal to the task of removing all the stagnant water that had seeped into the hold (figures 34 and 35). These problems all contributed to the unsanitary conditions. The day after a storm had to be used "to air out the ship, which reeked of the myriad foul odours concentrated aboard".[20]

In addition to all the other drawbacks, the sailor was never well rested. He had to sleep fully clothed and never for more than four hours at a time. The passengers did not have to worry about the night watch, but their quarters, like those of the sailors, did not provide much privacy. In fact, they provided none at all. Passengers and sailors alike had to negotiate the continual darkness of the between-decks with their heads stooped. The port-holes were always closed, unless the vessel was engaged in a naval battle. Lanterns and candles were not permitted because of the danger of fire. The upper decks were the only areas of the vessel where passengers and crew alike could meet outside of working hours. On the North Atlantic, this was not often possible. This was the environment in which a sailing vessel's occupants were obliged to exist.

30. View of cross-section of a three-decker man-of-war. (*Atlas de Colbert, France, Service hydrographique de la Marine, man. 140, Cliché Giraudon, LA154958.*) Except during periods of conflict, such as the Seven Years' War, men-of-war with more than 56 guns did not frequent North American waters. The vessels that sailed there were usually one- or two-deckers and were smaller in size. It is therefore probable that the vessels that usually sailed the route between France and New France were less spacious, causing even more congestion on board.

Diet

According to studies conducted for the United Nations,[1] a male of 25 years weighing 65 kilograms and living in a temperate zone with an average temperature of ten degrees Celsius uses 3,200 calories a day if he works at an eight-hour job requiring no heavy physical labour. If the temperature falls five degrees, he burns an extra 48 calories, because his heavier clothing dulls his movements. If he weighs 80 kilograms, his caloric expenditure is 3,733 units; with strenuous physical labour, he burns 4,000 to 4,500 calories. Age, weight, physical activity, and climate are thus four factors influencing an individual's energy requirements. In the eighteenth century, the average age of sailors was 25, but the temperatures to which they were exposed while crossing the Atlantic must often have been below ten degrees Celsius. There is no mention in the documentation of the average weight of crew members, but we know their physical activity was usually gruelling.

A seaman's caloric intake was determined by his daily rations (table 13), which provided him with a maximum of 3,693 and a minimum of 2,692 calories. This is far from the 4,500 calories he needed. The caloric value of a petty officer's rations was markedly superior, ranging as high as 5,009, no doubt enough to facilitate a small but lucrative trade in extra rations. Table 13 indicates the daily rations on royal vessels setting out on a six-month voyage; specifically, it describes the rations to be provided aboard a frigate that made the journey from France to Louisbourg in 1757 and was captured on the way back.[2] More than half the calories contained in the rations of seamen or petty officers were derived from the biscuit and wine they received at each of their three daily meals. Ship's biscuit, made of "pure wheat, unmixed with bran", was baked four to six weeks before the vessel sailed and had to be stored carefully in a closed place.[3] The quality of the flour used was certainly not always the best, as reflected in the following extract from a statement of examination of 50 small barrels of flour at Quebec City in 1713. The inspector declared that the flour had been "originally in good condition, but it is now old and has suffered some deterioration; it would therefore be advisable not to carry it elsewhere, but rather to sell it in town since it is not fit to be made into anything but biscuit".[4]

For the journey, outfitters packed the biscuit, or "hard-tack", in sacks large enough to hold 55 to 60 pounds. According to a 1739 document on the preparation of these biscuits, they were shaped like pancakes, "composed of fourteen ounces of dough and cooked long enough to reduce the weight to eight or nine ounces of dough at most".[5] Each man received roughly the equivalent of two biscuits daily to make up his ration of 18 ounces. In port, the entire company enjoyed fresh bread, but at sea only petty officers and the sick were entitled to it, and even then not regularly. Because the nutritive value of bread was less than that of hardtack, a ration of fresh bread was 24 ounces.

Each crew member was allowed three quarters of a pint of red wine, which was mixed with enough water to produce three half-litre mugs of drink.[6] Most of the wine was from the Bordeaux region, although the captain brought about a 30-day supply from Saintonge on board as well. This wine was consumed first, because it did not keep well, as the captain of the *Eléphant* discovered on a journey to Quebec City in 1728.[7] He had laid in two casks of Saintonge: one to be tapped at Quebec City and the other when the vessel returned to France. Once the casks had been opened, the wine quickly turned to vinegar. In addition to the wine, each man consumed approximately two casks of fresh water during a voyage from France to Quebec.[8] The outfitters also provided about a ten-day supply of aqua vitae: the use of cider and beer was reserved generally for coastal traffic rather than trans-Atlantic voyages, except in the case of merchant vessels departing from New France.[9]

A sailor's breakfast consisted of only wine and ship's biscuit. If, to his misfortune, a squall should arise, hardtack would form the bulk of his other meals as well, for the cook could not then use the cauldron because of the great risk of setting the vessel on fire. "During those days we lived on biscuit and a few morsels of bread which each procured as best he could," wrote Father Aulneau in 1734, following several days of stormy weather.[10]

A petty officer was entitled to a sardine and a little meat or cheese every morning. For the noon meal on "fish-days" – Wednesdays, Fridays, and Saturdays – a seaman received either rice, cod, cheese, or vegetables. On other days – "flesh-days" – he was entitled to salt beef or pork. Vegetables and rice were cooked in the broth from the boiled meat or fish. The crew could eat fresh meat only in port – when the vessel was being fitted out or during stopovers.[11] The live animals brought on board were kept for the table of the captain and his guests; the sick, however, were allowed chicken and mutton. At supper, in addition to his biscuit and wine, each seaman consumed four ounces of vegetables – peas, broad beans, or kidney beans.

As well as bread and wine, a sick man's rations included eggs, fresh meat, rice, butter, plums, and sugar (Table 14). If he were to have a meal of butter, rice, and chicken, he would receive 3,409 calories, or the maximum possible from his ration. If, instead, he ate an egg, mutton, plums, and sugar, his ration would provide no more than 2,938 calories. For those who were sick, and whose physical activity was therefore limited, the energy supplied by this ration was certainly sufficient. No doubt sailors adjusted to the caloric insufficiency of their diet, but it must have cost them a great deal of energy. This want of calories perhaps explains some seamen's aversion to physical exertion; in 1736, for example, the company of the *Renommée* refused to work even though their refusal placed their ship in greater jeopardy.[12] An inadequate supply of calories induces fa-

Table 13 Daily Rations For a Petty Officer and a Seaman, For a Six-Month Journey

Petty officer

	Food	Old measure	Metric equivalent	Calories	Number of Days
Daily:	Biscuits	18 oz	550.08 g	1907	136/182
	Bread	24 oz	733.44 g	1907	46
	Saintonge wine	1¹/₈ pt	1250 ml	963	30
	Bordeaux wine	1¹/₈ pt	1250 ml	963	142
	Aqua vitae	⁹/₃₂ pt	250 ml	613	10
Breakfast:	Heads and trotters	4 oz	122.24 g	460	91
	Cheese	1¹/₂ oz	45.84 g	177	91
	Sardines	1	(50 g)	90	182
Dinner:	Salt pork	9 oz	227.04 g	1089	78
	Salt beef	12 oz	366.72 g	1254	46
	Cod	6 oz	183.36 g	818	23
	Cheese	4¹/₂ oz	137.52 g	532	20
	Vegetables	6 oz	183.36 g	629	9
	Rice	3 oz	91.68 g	329	6
Supper:	Vegetables	4 oz	122.24 g	419	182

Seaman

	Food	Old measure	Metric equivalent	Calories	Number of Days
Daily:	Biscuits	18 oz	550.08 g	1907	136/182
	Bread	0	0	0	46
	Saintonge wine	³/₄ pt	690 ml	531	30
	Bordeaux wine	³/₄ pt	690 ml	531	142
	Aqua vitae	¹/₁₆ pt	60 ml	147	10
Breakfast:	Heads and trotters	0	0	0	91
	Cheese	0	0	0	91
	Sardines	0	0	0	182
Dinner:	Salt pork	6 oz	183.36 g	726	78
	Salt beef	8 oz	244.48 g	836	46
	Cod	4 oz	122.34 g	545	23
	Cheese	3 oz	91.58 g	355	20
	Vegetables	4 oz	122.24 g	419	9
	Rice	2 oz	61.12 g	219	6
Supper:	Vegetables	4 oz	122.24 g	419	182

Table 14	Daily Rations For the Sick			
	Food	Old measure	Metric equivalent	Calories
Daily:	Fresh bread	24 oz	733.44 g	1907
	Wine	3/4 qt	690 ml	531
Breakfast:	Egg/or	1	(50 g)	82
	Butter	1½ oz	45.84 g	328
Dinner:	Mutton/or	8 oz	244.48 g	291
	Chicken	8 oz	244.48 g	315
Supper:	Plums/or	4 oz	122.24 g	73
	Sugar	½ oz	15.28 g	54
	Rice	2 oz	61.12 g	219
	Butter	½ oz	15.28 g	109

tigue. This was probably the cause of the deep sleep that some sailors experienced. They "go off to bed, and without the aid of a candle they find their hammocks as easily as a rabbit finds its warren. No sooner do they lie down, that they are fast asleep. You could fire every cannon on board and still not wake them," recounted Diéréville.[13]

The dearth of vitamins in the rations is even more surprising.[14] A lack of vitamin A, which is derived from milk products, cod-liver oil, and eggs, causes dryness of the skin and poor vision. Nevertheless it was almost totally absent from the sailors' diet. Only cheese, eaten on some 20 occasions during a six-month voyage, provided a few units of it. This lack of vitamin A must also have slowed the growth of the young ship's boys serving aboard the vessels. The relatively small physical stature of the population in general, however, suggests that this deficiency was not confined to sailors' rations.

Vitamin B, contained in cereals and vegetables, was present in reasonable quantity in the seaman's diet; thus he must not have suffered excessively from nervous or digestive problems. Vitamin C, found in green vegetables and fresh fruit, was totally lacking; its absence allowed scurvy to wreak havoc aboard ships sailing the Atlantic. (This will be explained at greater length in the section on illness.) A lack of vitamin D, found in oily fish, cod-liver oil, and milk products, can cause rickets. Sunlight probably compensated to some extent for this deficiency in the diet, although the fog and rain of the Grand Banks were perhaps too prevalent for this to have been the case.

The ration described above was that of seamen serving on the king's vessels. The passengers on these vessels – such as soldiers, prisoners, and apprentices – received fare known as the supply officer's ration.

The food provided for the seamen aboard merchant vessels was never documented this precisely. Sources do, however, contain lists of provisions laid in for certain voyages, so that some conclusions may be drawn about the food on board.[15] These items were essentially the same as the basic ration for crewmen in the king's fleet. When Abraham Gradis advised the captain of his ship, the *Mercure*, bound for Louisbourg in 1758, "You must be sure to feed your crew in accordance with standard practice," he was no doubt referring to a ration similar to that provided on the king's vessels.[16]

Although the nutritive quality of provisions left something to be desired, the quantity seems to have been more than sufficient for the trip to New France. When leaving the shores of France, the king's vessels laid in enough provisions to last from six to seven-and-one-half months, the time needed to sail to the colonies and back. Captains occasionally reduced these quantities by amounts equivalent to a one- or two-month supply to allow for the purchase of fresh food when calling in at the port of Quebec.[17] This custom ended, however, when the Seven Years' War broke out and the intendant issued an ordinance forbidding the merchants of Quebec City to sell foodstuffs to the crews.[18] The authorities also recommended that troop transport vessels leave in the colonies any excess provisions they might have.[19]

Few complaints on the quality of food have been recorded. The documentation provided only one such example: on the last aid convoy to New France in 1760, the contents of the horse and beef barrels were rotten.[20] The rarity of these complaints is perhaps more comprehensible when we consider that the persons most likely to be unsatisfied did not have the means to make themselves heard. Most of the passengers who left firsthand accounts of life on the high seas were guests at the captain's table and these administrators, chief officers, and missionaries enjoyed a more interesting menu than did the ship's company. The dishes served at the captain's table could be quite varied: fruit and vegetables accompanied fresh meats, which could be seasoned with a variety of condiments. Nevertheless, some passenger complained that the food was not salty or spicy enough.[21] Coffee and spirits might round off the meal.[22] Father Labat, a missionary who travelled from France to the West Indies on one of the king's ships, described a bill of fare probably typical of a captain's table:

> As soon as Mass was over, we sat down to breakfast. Usually we were served a ham, or pâté with a stew or fricassée, butter and cheese, a remarkably good wine, and fresh bread morning and evening. We had dinner after the pilots had taken altitude, that is, after they had observed the position of the sun at noon to determine the elevation of the pole from the ship's current location. Dinner consisted of a large tureen of soup served with the boiled meat, which was always fowl, Irish beef brisket, pickled pork and fresh mutton or veal; these were accompanied by chicken fricassée or something else. These three dishes were then withdrawn, and replaced with a plate of roast meat, two

bowls of stew and two salads. For dessert we had cheese, some stewed fruit, fresh fruit, chestnuts and preserves.

Supper was similar to the noon meal: we were offered a large tureen of soup, then a chicken, two plates of roast meat, two stews, two salads and dessert; and, since there was ample stock of spirits, we were served unstintingly.[23]

The contrast between this fare and that of the crew explains why these products were kept under lock and key. Just as the food itself differed, so did the manner of preparation and consumption. For the sailors, only a large cauldron was needed to cook their soup, beef, or pork (which the cook would have soaked beforehand to extract the salt). The seamen gathered in messes of seven, each of which was given a common grog-tub, mess bowl, cup and plate. Each man did, however, receive a spoon to himself.[24] No one was permitted to eat alone, or at other than the appointed meal times. Since they had no table, they ate seated on the decks, sometimes on a pile of planks or a chest. Diéréville, the king's scribe, left eloquent testimony to the hygienic qualities of such a setting: "I felt particular revulsion at the sight of the mess bowl. What a disgusting collection of towels and eating utensils! The dishes were never scoured clean, and they were wrapped round with a greasy rag to prevent them from toppling over."[25]

Many more utensils were used to prepare the dishes served at the captain's table. Indeed, the cauldrons, plates, and other tableware (figure 33) found on sailing ships compared favourably with those of a typical middle-class household.[26] There were pots and pans of various types, as well as items such as pasty moulds. Servants could set the table with hors d'oeuvre plates and silver flatware. Each diner had his place at the table designated from the beginning of the voyage, so that the servers could give each guest the same serviette every meal.[27] This practice must certainly have improved hygiene and decreased the risk of contagion to some degree.

Except for a privileged few, the passengers and crew alike did not eat well aboard ship, although they did not go hungry. Social distinctions applied here as elsewhere. The sea voyage aggravated the inadequacies of the normal diet on land, usually resulting in a vitamin deficiency.

Illness and medical treatment

Inadequate clothing, lack of attention to hygiene, and improper diet, combined with strenuous physical labour and often deplorable climatic conditions, provide some insight as to why disease could take such a toll on the crews of Atlantic-going vessels; in fact, it would be more surprising if the opposite had been true. The most frequently encountered, and seemingly inconquerable, disease was scurvy. It was as devastating in 1756, Montcalm noted in his letters,[1] as it had been in 1692 – yet from the end of the seventeenth century, and no doubt even before that, there were known remedies for the disease. The *Arc en ciel*, a royal vessel that crossed from France to Quebec City in 1688 and from there to Africa, set some one hundred scorbutic sailors ashore on the African coast. Lacking the "lemons and herbs which are infallible cures for scurvy", the captain sent men to look for lemons and oranges on the Senegalese coast.[2]

The major cause of scurvy was, of course, the absence of vitamin C in the diet. The wisdom of the day, however, attributed this disease to a steady diet of salted foods.[3] To regain his health, the sufferer was advised to eat fresh meat and vegetables – two limited commodities aboard a sailing ship. The effects of scurvy usually began to appear "after four or five months" at sea.[4] Although voyages to New France did not take that long, scurvy was still a major problem. When on 23 August 1692 the captain of the *Aimable* wrote in his log, "Have visited all our sick and found among them a large number of cases of scurvy as well as fever," the vessel had left Brest only 22 days earlier.[5] It was heading toward Cape Breton and Newfoundland in the company of the *Bon* and the *Téméraire*, and after two months at sea, each vessel had 79 to 80 men down with scurvy. Either the men had been on land for too short a time before signing on again, or they had come from environments where the diet was simply inadequate. Hunger must have been as strong a motive for joining the service as was the call of the sea.

The other truly devastating form of illness was fever – "common", "hot", "malignant", or "purple". In 1697, the intendant and the bishop of Quebec called for a medical award to the surgeon Michel Sarrasin in recognition of the services he had rendered aboard the *Gironde*, where there had been a serious outbreak of purple fever.[6] Fevers sometimes took on epidemic proportions, resulting in many fatalities among the crew and passengers. Such was the case, for example, aboard the *Rubis* in 1732, 1740, and 1743, and the *Léopard* in 1756.[7] Of a crew of 270 serving on the *Rubis* in 1740, 42 died during the course of the journey and 147 were sent to hospital when the ship arrived at Quebec City, leaving a skeleton of 81 to man the vessel. Some historians maintain that the fever found aboard ship was actually exanthematic typhoid.[8]

Although chief officers and distinguished passengers enjoyed a special diet, they were not immune from sickness. Governor Vaudreuil had to spend two weeks in bed to recuperate from his trip to New France in 1724.[9] Others were less fortunate: Brother Charron died aboard the *Chameau* in 1719, and the new bishop of Quebec, Laubérivière, died a few days after his arrival in 1740.[10] In the enclosed environment of a sailing vessel, illness did not respect social barriers.

There were also the more deadly diseases, such as smallpox, which swept the *Jason* in 1737: "Smallpox continues to plague the ship; Mr. Hocquart's cook was stricken today and by midnight he was dead."[11] As if these illnesses were not enough, there was the occasional outbreak of food poisoning, although with less deadly consequences. "The night of the twenty-first to twenty-second, thirty people fell sick with developing colic and high fever – and all people who had eaten at the captain's table or in the pantry. None of the crew was affected. Today, Friday the twenty-third, they are almost all in good health again."[12] These symptoms of food poisoning appeared on the *Rubis* in 1741, and comment aptly on the quality of stored and preserved foods on sailing ships of the eighteenth century. Were such maladies even more common among the seamen than among those dining at the captain's table? Considering the existing sanitary conditions, that would be a fairly safe assumption.

Although the dietary deficiency in vitamins and calories seems to have been the source of many health problems, it was not the only one. The absence of proper precautions regarding clothing and food handling was undoubtedly the second most significant cause of infections. The quotation earlier from an officer of the East India Company regarding the infestation of lice on his man-of-war is underscored by this affirmation by the Jesuit Nau on board the *Rubis* in 1734: "Each time we left the between-decks we found ourselves covered in lice. I even found them in my slippers. The source of the infection: 80 dealers in contraband salt who had languished in prison for a year and who were veritable ant-hills of lice."[13]

The sailors were often obliged to work in dirty or wet clothes on vessels that, because of the climate, could not be cleaned properly. Such working conditions led to chills, fevers, and the spread of disease. Dental hygiene was not sophisticated either, as indicated by this passage from the diary of Robert Challes, a writer aboard an East Indiaman: "My teeth are beginning to itch; I'll scrape them tomorrow and not before."[14] These causes of illness, which the crew was usually powerless to combat, were sometimes compounded by human negligence. When the *Léopard* arrived in Quebec City in 1756 with an epidemic on board, the blame was on its chief officers, who had "not once had the between-decks, where all the odours were concentrated, scrubbed and swabbed."[15]

The most immediate result of all these illnesses was to weaken the crew by decimating the ranks. The sailors who were not sick had to replace their bed-ridden co-workers, and thus overtaxed their own health. The crew on the *Mars*, a man-of-war belonging to the squadron of the Duc d'Anville in 1746 "worked as hard as could be expected of men worn out by scurvy and other diseases".[16] At times it was necessary to press the passengers to help crew the vessel, as was the case on the *Chameau* in 1720 and the *Rubis* in 1734.[17] And when the crew and passengers reached the limit of their endurance, the captain sometimes changed course: if

Table 15 Seamen Hospitalized at the Hôtel-Dieu in Quebec City, 1755–1759

	Number of ships	May	June	July	August	September	October	November	December	Total
1755	5	0	0	16(3)	0	0	1	0	0	17(3)
1756	14	9	64	16	20	8	1	0	0	118
1757	19	0	1	12	42(12)	135(21)	26(16)	(7)	(3)	216(59)
1758	26	11	24(14)	102(1)	64(6)	50(12)	7(5)	8(2)	0	266(30)
1759	14	8	25	9	0	0	0	0	0	42
Total	78	28	114(4)	155(4)	126(18)	193(33)	35(21)	8(9)	(3)	659(92)

bound for Quebec City, he would call in at Louisbourg to give everyone a rest. The captains of king's vessels could then commandeer sailors from trading vessels to replace crew members. To the merchants who complained about this practice, the captains' retort was that the king's vessels were there to protect trade and if lack of a crew prevented them from sailing, no such protection was possible.[18]

The arrival at Quebec City of vessels full of sick men precipitated a significant rise in the occupancy rate for hospital beds during the summer months. In the last five years of French rule alone, at least 659 seamen were hospitalized at the Hôtel-Dieu in Quebec City (Table 15).[19] The figures in Table 15 do not include seamen admitted to the Hôpital Général or cared for in private homes. For example, in 1755, after part of the Hôtel-Dieu was destroyed by fire, some 40 sailors from the *Actif* were hospitalized in a private home. Moreover, these statistics cover only seamen and officers, but during those years disease and illness were just as rampant, if not more so, among the passengers. As Doreil reported, more than 300 soldiers were hospitalized in 1756 and 250 in 1757.[20] Most were from the La Sarre, Royal-Roussillon, and Berri battalions. The seamen hospitalized between 1755 and 1759 were from 60 merchant vessels and eight navy vessels. Thus, merchantmen were not spared from illness, but because they had smaller crews, disease would have been confined to less epidemic proportions.

The hospitalization of scores of sailors undoubtedly meant extra work for the surgeons and nuns in Quebec City, but the worst consequence of the arrival of disease-ridden ships was the spread of infections among the colonial population. The Louisbourg parish records show, for example, that following a stopover there in 1732 by the *Rubis* there was a noticeable increase in the community's mortality rate. This occurred again in 1757 with the arrival of the Dubois de la Mothe squadron and, as the minister noted, "It is unfortunate that the disease should have been transmitted to the inhabitants."[21] The squadron's return to Brest in the autumn had the same tragic consequences for that city.

Conditions were not any better in Canada, where in the absence of a quarantine system, illnesses spread among the population. Governor

Denonville bemoaned the situation at the end of the seventeenth century, and in 1756 several nuns and the Quebec City military surgeon caring for seamen from king's vessels fell ill and died. What way would there have been to stop the spread of disease when, as Abbé Paris wrote, "Several passengers sought to avoid contagion by leaving the ship for a number of coastal boats, but they were not spared, as they already carried within themselves the poisons they had picked up during the crossing"?[22] It would have been difficult for the local inhabitants to avoid contamination. When the man-of-war *Aigle* was shipwrecked in the Strait of Belle Isle in 1758, the survivors reached Rimouski in November, only to discover that its population had been decimated by a pestilence three months earlier.[23] It is quite possible that the illness had been introduced by a vessel during a stopover there that summer.

A modicum of hygiene and ventilation would have been enough to combat a number of these illnesses. One experiment conducted by De la Saussaye, captain of the *Rubis* in 1735, testifies to this. To eradicate the disease rife on board,

> and not knowing the reason for it, I decided to rig up an air scoop in the aft hatches using a stuns'l to direct air into the hold, from which there came the most awful smell. The scoop was turned to catch the wind and raised about ten feet above the quarterdeck, so that the air circulated throughout the hold; the smell completely disappeared and the air was so fresh that those who went down into the hold were more cold than hot.[24]

De la Saussaye was also very careful to have his vessel cleaned and disinfected once or twice a week, and, as a result, far fewer cases of illness occurred. In 1740 as noted earlier, still aboard the *Rubis*, De la Saussaye was to be much less fortunate.

To look after those who fell ill, all the king's vessels had a surgeon and several assistants on board. Despite ordinances calling for their presence aboard vessels on the high seas, surgeons were not as common on merchant vessels. Crew lists for some 50 vessels fitted out for voyages to New France in 1745 and 1755 indicate that only half the vessels had surgeons. "Surgeons are asses. A sick man has to be watched carefully if he is to be cured of medicine, the cruelest disease of all."[25] This view at the end of the seventeenth century on the abilities of surgeons in general was echoed in 1757 by lieutenant Rossel: "Blood-letting was a very common practice and it was my experience that the ones subjected to this the fewest times were the ones who recovered most quickly."[26] With such a reputation, surgeons were perhaps not essential.

Most surgeons, at least those practising in the merchant marine, were about 30 years of age, and they received wages on par with those of petty officers. They had usually spent some time working in a hospital,

31. Model of a 50-gun man-of-war. (*Eglise Saint-Sauveur de la Rochelle, Cliché Giraudon, LA 17559.*) This model is typical of the men-of-war that travelled regularly between France and New France in the eighteenth century, particularly between 1730 and 1745. The *Rubis*, the *Héros*, and the *Jason* were all 50-gun men-of-war. This was no doubt a votive offering of a crew following a difficult crossing.

where, under the watchful eye of a physician, they learned how to administer purgatives, let blood, and dress wounds.[27] They then hired on to serve at sea. In addition to this practical training, some had theoretical knowledge. Jean Lacoste, a surgeon from Bayonne who signed on to the *Heureux Moine* in 1740, owned a book entitled *Recueil de remedes faciles et domestiques* ("A Treasury of Easy Home Remedies") and two manuscripts – a treatise on the anatomy of nerves and arteries and a collection of miscellaneous articles on surgery.[28] He was probably more educated than most of his colleagues.

Although many surgeons' knowledge perhaps left something to be desired, their medicine chests were well stocked: stimulants and narcotics nestled beside liniments, purgatives, and gargles.[29] The Quebec City Hôtel-Dieu sometimes had to supply medicines for vessels returning to France – typically Canadian remedies such as pine gum and maple sugar.[30] Ultimately, however, when one does not have a great deal of confidence in the surgeon, there is nothing better than a personal remedy to fight off a fever:

> There is an awful rumour about anthrax going around, so De la Chassée and I are forced every morning to drink a little brandy with some crushed garlic in it and to toss back or swallow all the garlic at once. It stinks so much we can't stand one another. He calls it "chasing out the devil for Belzébuth."[31]

Fortunately, despite the spectacular nature of some epidemics, some sailing vessels were unscathed. The situation differed from one vessel to the next, and from one year to the next. The vessels of the royal navy seemed to be the most vulnerable, particularly in wartime. Hasty preparations for departure were no doubt often responsible for these diseases. Although numerous medications were available, medicine seems to have been generally ineffectual aboard sailing vessels. Illness made no distinction among the social classes, because those in privileged positions could not escape from the sick. On land they could flee an epidemic; at sea it came to them. At sea, illness was the victor over privilege.

Religious practice

The naval ordinance of 1681 stipulated that all vessels making sea voyages were to carry a chaplain approved by the captain.[1] In fact, only the king's vessels carried chaplains. Any members of religious orders aboard merchantmen travelling between France and New France were merely passengers. The church was unable to supply the captains of all the vessels with chaplains, and many crew lists ended with a note that it had been impossible to procure the services of a chaplain. The absence of chaplains on board did not mean, however, that religious practices were ignored during sea voyages. Most instructions from owners to the captains of their vessels began with a recommendation that the members of the crew be required to say prayers morning and evening and to refrain from swearing. "He will take care to have prayers said morning and evening and do his utmost to see that God is not offended by those aboard his vessel," recommended the owner to Captain Leblanc of the *Marie-Anne* in 1716.[2]

It is impossible to know whether all the captains obeyed these instructions or how much attention the sailors paid to them. Religious beliefs certainly emerged, however, when some danger threatened. "At that same time we said our prayers and made a vow to be fulfilled in Quebec City if the Lord was good enough to take us there,"[3] said Captain Rozier of the *Renommée* in 1753, when huge waves were sweeping the ship. And when the Canadian officer Beaujeu heard sailors devoutly singing the Lord's praises during a storm, their invocations seemed to him to be "not at all normal for that sort when they are not in danger".[4] When their vessel was in distress, seamen usually made a vow: for example, they would take up a collection to have a mass said. As well, the chaplain on board could give general absolution. In Canada, crews went to Sainte-Anne-de-Beaupré to fulfill their vows, making a pilgrimage to hear mass and make votive offerings (figures 31 and 32).[5]

The seamen and passengers prayed to God when they were in danger and they also thanked him for safe journeys. One captain concluded his log with a grateful "God be praised", and the passengers of a vessel that arrived in Quebec City in September 1753 attended a thanksgiving mass the next day for their safe voyage.[6] The seamen's special devotion to Saint Anne probably explains their custom of saluting the church at Sainte-Anne-de-Beaupré with several cannon shots as they sailed by.[7]

On the king's vessels, in addition to leading daily prayers, the chaplain said mass and recited the Angelus before meals. On Sundays and feast days, attendance at mass and vespers was mandatory for the entire crew:

> The routine aboard ship is most edifying; prayers are said three times a day – in the morning, in the evening before the crew sups and at nightfall, when the litany of the Blessed Virgin is recited. Each time, God's blessing is asked for the King and the crew, and the prayers always end with cries of "Long live the King!" On Sundays and feast days vespers are said on deck so the whole crew can take part, without even leaving the rigging,

explained Montcalm in his journal in 1756.[8]

Despite the many deaths at sea, the documents make no mention of any funerals on board sailing vessels in the North Atlantic. A comment

32. Ex-voto: Painting attributed to Michel Dessaillants de Richeterre and donated to Sainte-Anne-de-Beaupré around 1717 by a Mr. Roger. (*Musée de Sainte-Anne-de-Beaupré.*) Further information is provided in the article entitled "L'ex-voto de monsieur Roger" by J.P. Asselin, in *Revue de Sainte-Anne-de-Beaupré*, 86:10. October 1958. The coast in the background somewhat resembles the entrance to the port of Louisbourg. At certain times, boats had to make a path through the ice to enter the port as the passengers of the boat in this picture are doing.

33. Pewter tableservice from the *Machault*. (*Parks Canada*.) A plate, soup bowl, teaspoon, and goblet from the *Machault*. These pieces were probably used at the captain's table.

by Bougainville in 1758 would indicate that these ceremonies were often rather hasty:

> One of our sailors died and this morning his body was thrown into the sea. Such funerals are carried out at no cost and without ceremony. On board ship, we die as we lived.[9]

The death of an officer entailed a more elaborate ceremony, as described by Robert Challes in the account of his voyage to India:

> The chaplain said the mass for the dead and the crew gave a military salute with drum rolls and cannon shots. The service ended with the singing of the prayer for the dead and sprinkling of the holy water before the body was sent to its grave at the bottom of the ocean.[10]

Liturgical celebrations sometimes had to be cancelled because of bad weather. Stormy seas caused Montcalm to miss all the ceremonies of Holy Week in 1756. On stormy days, chaplains had difficulty just reading their breviaries, according to Abbé de la Maraudière.[11] In these circumstances, all chaplains were not equally co-operative, however:

> The abbé wanted to say mass, despite all our protestations that the sea was too rough and the vessel was rolling too wildly. He wanted to say mass, and despite everything we said to try to stop him, he said it, saying it was his business. He spilled the blood of Our Lord all over Mr. de Verville's sleeve and the corporal and the cloth. It would be better not to have any chaplain at all than to have one like him who nips wine and picks fights with the officers and the entire crew.[12]

This incident took place aboard the frigate *Paön, en route* from France to Louisbourg in 1722. The previous year, the chaplain of the *Portefaix*, who had been denied permission by the authorities to take a private cargo of several hundredweight of cod, had been physically dragged back onto the vessel after its stopover at Louisbourg.[13]

The naval regulations determined that chaplains were to repeat in French what they recited in Latin, provide religious instruction for the crew, deliver a sermon every two weeks if they had any talent for preaching, and visit the sick every day.[14] The king's vessels regularly carried missionaries, who would often provide chaplaincy services during the crossings to Canada. If by some stroke of luck for the captain, a bishop was travelling to Canada, he would assume responsibility for the spiritual life aboard ship. Men such as Saint-Vallier, Dosquet, Laubérivière, and Pontbriand were thus called upon to provide religious instruction or to organize discussions on morals.[15]

Missionaries often had to catechize ship's boys and sailors who were most recalcitrant, considering themselves too old or too smart to be sub-

34. Pump from the *Machault*. (*Parks Canada*.) There was usually a pump located near the mainmast of each sailing vessel. It was used to pump out water that had seeped into the vessel. Pumping was often a strenuous task for the crew, especially if the vessel had been damaged.

jected to the missionaries' questioning. Seamen, who were not so proud or so concerned about what others might think as were members of the middle class and the aristocracy, were more willing to confess their sins.[16] The missionaries also tried to convert Protestant sailors, who occasionally signed on to the king's vessels, despite their strong religious beliefs. "Those who belong to the so-called Reformed church are well-instructed, it must be admitted," wrote Father Crespel after spending several days trying to convert a Calvinist seaman.[17] Religious practice was a concern of the state, which used it to establish authority. Religious observance on the king's vessels was governed by law; those who did not attend services were sentenced to six lashes, and blasphemers lost a month's wages. Under such restrictive conditions, it is difficult to distinguish between personal religious beliefs and the required practices. Objectors must have found it very difficult to have their convictions respected. Religion was not always just a refuge from fear, however. It was sometimes an expression of thanks – the humble thanks of those who knew how to give it.

Insubordination and discipline

Failure to attend religious services was not the only dereliction to incur the rigour of authority. As in armed forces generally, desertion was undoubtedly the greatest problem affecting crews of navy and merchant vessels in the eighteenth century. On merchantmen, even those with small crews, the desertion of one or two sailors during fitting out, usually after they had collected one or two months' advance pay, was not an unusual occurrence. Joseph Froment, a Canadian signed on the *Hasard*, a 60-ton vessel fitting out at La Rochelle in 1757, jumped ship with two months' pay.[1] Mass desertions were much less frequent, but they did occur. In 1744, 33 men deserted the *Atalante*, a fishing ship fitting out for a voyage to Isle Royale.[2] The entire crews of the *Samson* and the *Bayonnais*, which were to have escorted a flotilla of merchantmen to Canada, jumped ship in 1758.[3]

Seamen not only jumped ship during fitting out, to take advantage of easily earned advances, but also deserted at ports of call. They would cite a too-exacting or too-brutal captain as their provocation. The following remarks by the Chevalier de la Clue, captain of the *Triton* in 1751, show clearly, however, that the reasons given by deserters could not always be accepted at face value:

> Sieur Jean Arismeinge, captain of the *Renommée* from Bordeaux, lodged complaints with me against his sailors, who were deserting him, and brought me two of them whom he had arrested. I had them clapped in irons aboard my vessel and sent an officer aboard the captain's to question the crew in order to find out if it was harsh treatment by the

captain or his officers that was causing the desertions. The men said they could not complain about the treatment they were given, nor about the food, but that they were made to work without respite. The real reason was that the *Renommée* was about to return to France. They thought the voyage had been too short, that they were going to be part of the class that would be called up for service, and to escape this fate they wanted to go to America. I recommended to the captain not to overwork his crew. I threatened the sailors with severe punishment if they left the vessel without leave, and after keeping in irons a few days those who had been arrested, I returned them to their captain and heard nothing more of the matter.[4]

Under the naval ordinance of 1681, sailors who were apprehended after jumping ship during fitting out were to be condemned to make the voyage without pay. Those who deserted *en route* were flogged.[5] Before 1689, deserters from the king's vessels were punished by death.[6] Under the code of 1689 they were condemned to the galleys for life. Some captains preferred having deserters given a ducking. Using a hoist attached to the end of a yard, the executor would suddenly let the condemned sailor fall into the water a few times. A dry ducking was when the fall was broken just at the surface of the water. The authorities could also order a keel hauling. The executor would then drag the condemned sailor from one side of the vessel to the other, under the keel through the water.[7] The risk of drowning the sailor, who had been knocked out against the hull, was very great indeed.

Theft on board does not seem to have presented a very serious problem. Sailors' belongings were probably too meagre to arouse the envy of their fellows. Provisions, on the other hand, were kept under lock and key, and even the kitchen boiler was sometimes padlocked. If the whipping given a ship's boy who had borrowed a few things from a sailor is an indication, the punishments meted out most certainly discouraged offenders. "His tar-covered pants were pulled down, and he was tied to the pump handle, which served as a wooden horse; the pilot lashed his bare bottom with a cat-o'-nine-tails refurbished with several brand-new thongs full of knots."[8] Attempted revolt and mutiny were perhaps less frequent, but they caused a great deal more commotion because they prompted legal proceedings.

Sailors' revolts usually took the form of a refusal to work: to take the helm, for example.[9] The mutinies could lead to assault against officers if the sailors persisted in their disobedience. A crew could also refuse to continue a voyage if the vessel ran aground, until its condition was checked. In 1731, when the *Vierge de Grace* collided with another ship in the roadstead at Quebec City, the sailors refused to set sail until shipwrights had inspected the hull. The captain had the two noisiest crew members locked up, since "as has happened a few times before, they might be tempted to drill a few holes in the bilge in order to force Sieur Lilleronde to put into port again, which could have meant total loss of the cargo".[10] Mistrust was common. Sometimes officers provoked the revolts of their subordinates. The crew members of the *Saint-Antoine* from Cherbourg refused to obey Captain Pierre Robin, who tried to force them to sail along the north side of Île aux Coudres without a pilot, and took their orders from the executive officer instead.[11]

Despite their bad reputation, particularly in the eyes of the authorities, sailors were no rougher a group than any other. In ports of call, after a prolonged visit to the local taverns, they occasionally got into a few brawls. But the eighteenth-century judicial archives in Quebec City made mention of only three fights that led to the death of seamen.[12] One of these sailors was killed by his ship's first mate. The sailor had attacked the officer, who had wanted to send him back to the ship after the sailor had complained about the food. Although the officer was cleared of any responsibility in the affair, perhaps the blame for such incidents did not always rest solely with the rowdy sailors.

"It is useless to preach to sailors the obedience observed in convents; it is no more strict than that observed at sea,"[13] wrote Robert Challes in his travel diary. And sailors had every reason to be obedient, life aboard ship being so strictly ordered, with rigid series of do's and don'ts. Do respect the officers, do smoke only near the foremast and with a bucket of water nearby, do inform on deserters within 24 hours, do return the balance of your pay if a captain must lay up in the colonies. Don't go ashore without leave, don't stay ashore all night, don't sleep undressed, don't smoke at night or during religious services, don't have drinking parties on board.

Sailors had many constraints placed upon them, and few excuses were accepted. Breaches of discipline were usually punished by a reduction in rations, cut in pay, and a stint in irons. When the offence was more serious, or it had happened more than once, the captain could punish the sailor by a ducking or make him run the gauntlet, that is, force him to run between two rows of men who whipped him as he passed.[14] Since running a tavern was strictly forbidden aboard ship, alcoholism must not have been a very serious problem. Nor did captains complain very often about insubordination. The crime rate was probably no higher among sailors than in any other group. Do's and don'ts may seem theoretical, but in the reality of the isolated world aboard ship, how could the sailors ignore these regulations? Desertion was perhaps the only means of protest available to them.

Recreation

Although drinking might not have posed much of a problem at sea, sailors did make up for it somewhat while in port. Describing Canadian *coureurs de bois* when they returned from a trip, the Baron de Lahontan wrote:

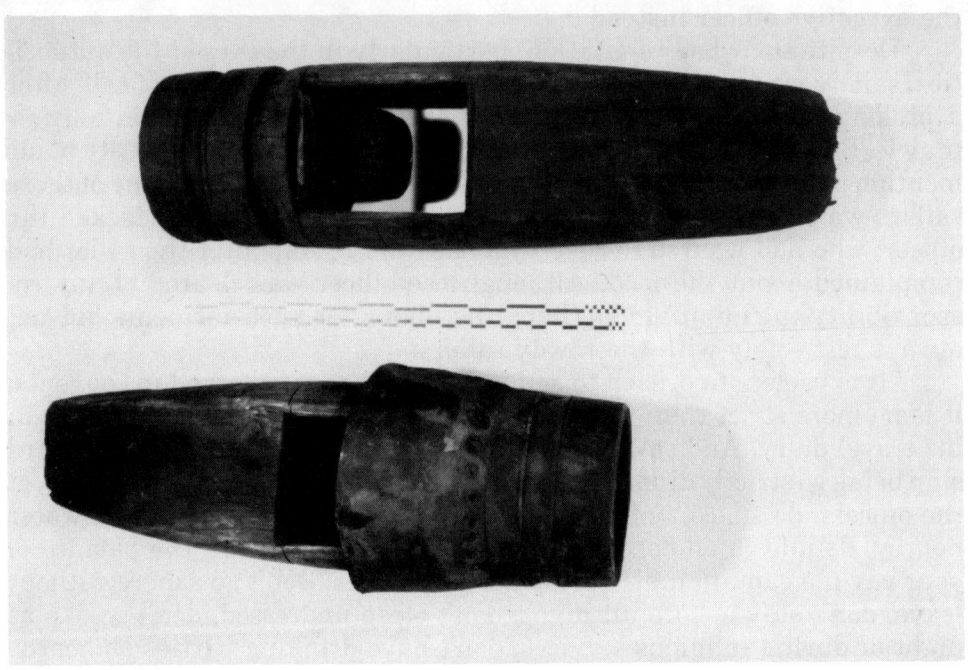

35. Pump's piston from the *Machault*. (*Parks Canada*.) This pump's piston from the *Machault* is made of elm; its movement inside the pump sprayed the water into the deck.

They plunge themselves into sensual pleasure up to their necks. Wine, women and song, everything! They set off again when they have spent all their money, thus dividing their youth between misery and debauchery. In a word, these trappers live like most European sailors.[1]

Such is the stuff of reputations. Considering the large number of taverns in a small town like Louisbourg in the eighteenth century, tavern keepers must have relied heavily on the patronage of sailors to make ends meet.[2] The situation was doubtless much the same in Quebec City, where between 1660 and 1760 there were nearly 200 innkeepers and tavern owners. The wife of François Boucher, an innkeeper in Cul-de-Sac, gave the following account in October 1739: "Friday night, five sailors from the ship commanded by Sieur Ricoeur, which had run aground at Cul-de-Sac, went to her place, where they stayed about an hour and a half, during which time they drank a bottle of wine each."[3] The sailors were waiting until high tide to return to their vessel.

There were a few events to break the monotony during the trans-Atlantic crossings. The biggest, and certainly the most interesting for the sailors, was the mandatory baptismal ceremony for all vessels and individuals crossing over the Grand Banks for the first time. This ceremony also took place at five other points: the Strait of Gibraltar, the Dardanelles, the Arctic Circle, the Equator, and the Tropics.[4] Seamen and passengers who underwent the baptism at the Equator were exempt from all the others. Each novice on his first crossing had to report to a crew member, who was disguised to look as boorish as possible. He then had to sit on a pole over a barrel full of water and make an offering of money to the crew. If he refused to make this small contribution, the sailors would let him fall into the barrel. On the Grand Banks, where the weather was harsh, rather than give the recalcitrant traveller a bath, the sailors would soot him. The money collected would go toward buying the crew-members a little brandy to quench their thirst. Unlike the crew, who profited from it, the passengers did not seem to appreciate this experience. Missionaries, among others, saw it as mockery of the sacrament of baptism and thought it rather vulgar.[5]

Arrival over the Grand Banks permitted sailors and passengers to catch a few cod and other fish. After weeks of highly salted food, fresh fish was greatly appreciated. As another distraction during the crossing, the crew might fire a salvo from their muskets at an ice floe, and the captain might have a couple of cannon shots fired in the direction of Rochers aux Oiseaux as the ship entered the Gulf. "We fired a cannon shot, which raised the alarm throughout the feathered republic, and a thick cloud of birds a good two or three leagues round formed over the two islands," wrote Charlevoix in the account of his travels.[6] Those aboard sailing vessels on 25 August could celebrate Saint Louis' Day in honour of the king. At sea, this celebration meant a few cannon shots and a lavish meal at the captain's table. In port, the ceremony was more elaborate: the crew dressed ship and the highest-ranking commander of a king's vessel usually gave a banquet, to which he invited the local government and port authorities.[7]

The officers sometimes listened to music in their leisure time, and a few even played an instrument:

> Monsieur de Fontenu who loves music and sings well, brought a musician with him: He had a harpsichord, a bass, and other instruments, which were joined by the three oboes belonging to the crew of Monsieur le Chevalier de Chavagnac. When the weather was fair we held concerts and the pleasure this provided made us forget we were at sea."[8]

This is an excerpt from the travel diary of the scribe Diéréville, written during his return voyage from Port Royal to France in 1701 aboard the *Avenant*. Chavagnac was the captain and Fontenu the purser.

Besides these distractions, the sailors could always smoke a pipe, dance on the quarterdeck, or belt out a few songs. Appendix L presents a rather saucy version of the song "M'en revenant de la Jolie Rochelle". If the sailors played cards, chess, or dice, they were not permitted to play for money. Passengers often had only reading and writing to occupy themselves. "I write only to amuse myself and pass the time," said midshipman Parscau Duplessis.[9] But as Diéréville wrote, "You can't always be reading,"[10] or as Montcalm concluded, "Anyone who thinks going to sea provides an opportunity for serious, methodical study has never been aboard ship."[11]

When they tired of such pastimes, passengers had nothing to do but talk and watch other vessels that might happen along. For the author of a memoir written in 1762 who said, "One might put forward the postulate that recreation is as necessary to man as is food," these few distractions at sea must not have satisfied all needs.[12] Recreational pursuits seemed to have been reserved largely for the crew, as was the work aboard ship. Along with any soldiers who might be on board, the sailors took part in any leisure activities, sometimes to their advantage, but usually simply for relaxation. They had to wait for stopovers to forget their troubles by drinking. The missionaries, members of the bourgeoisie, and government officials on board were usually unwilling to do more than watch, no doubt refusing to take part in anything connected with a sailor's life. The need for escapism and the silent protests of the sailors were undoubtedly the results of the physical restrictions placed on them by the life style aboard a sailing vessel.

Conclusion

The theme of trans-Atlantic communications between France and New France during the eighteenth century can perhaps be summarized in four words: presence, uncertainty, effort, and privation. Sailing vessels of between 35 and 1,500 tons criss-crossed the Atlantic. These vessels, which might have as many as 80 guns, defended themselves or escorted other ships. They made commercial trade possible and supplied European countries with fish. The ships were indispensable to the network of political and economic ties they created between France and its colony.

The presence of the state and of private enterprise was ensured on the North Atlantic through two categories of outfit, each with five types of vessels. In peacetime, one or two vessels sufficed to ensure the royal presence, either to supply the colony or to defend the interests of the merchant fleet. In wartime, the state played a larger role, and in 1757, for example, one-quarter of the French fleet was sailing in North American waters. The French presence later diminished, more as a result of an improvident shipbuilding policy than by choice. France's strategy, however, was to bring assistance to its colony, rather than to assure control of the route. This assistance required expenditures of millions of livres to fit out all these vessels, particularly because men-of-war equipped to sail to Canada were fitted out as transport vessels, which required longer loading times, greater quantities of supplies, and larger crews. These men-of-war would escort merchant ships whose tonnage was sufficient to meet the requirements for trade, and whose activity would depend completely on the protection they received in the convoy.

Wind and storms, fog and ice, inaccurate maps and instruments, and pirates and privateers combined to make North Atlantic crossings precarious. The course had to be adjusted continually and thus the duration of the voyage was equally uncertain. Extra distances and delays, losses of equipment, or wrecks loomed as hazardous barriers between France and New France. Many persons probably considered the crossing too risky, and such fears must have substantially limited the population of New France. The general perception of the Atlantic was no doubt as inhibiting as the geographic reality itself. Fear of the unknown was probably as great an obstacle as the 1,200 leagues of inadequately charted ocean.

But the Atlantic route, like the route up the St. Lawrence, also provided an opportunity for initiative. Here, sailors developed and experimented with new navigational instruments. They conducted systematic explorations and improved their maps. The North Atlantic navigators responsible for these initiatives, such as La Galissonière, La Jonquière, and Cogolin, thus made their contributions to the Age of Enlightenment and to the advancement of scientific knowledge. Where could one find a more stable link between two civilizations? The Atlantic Ocean was the catalyst.

> I have been to Canada seven times, and while I have always made it safely, I must say that even the best of these voyages gave me more gray hairs than I got from all the other trips I have made to other places. Anywhere else we normally sail, we do not suffer or take the risks we take sailing to Canada. It is a continual torment to body and soul.[1]

These remarks of a captain in the French navy suggest that the route to New France was exceptionally difficult, but sailors and passengers continued to make the trip, sometimes many times. They were prepared to make the effort required to get to New France, either for their occupations or for business purposes. They accepted the unpleasant conditions even if this meant sharing accommodation with passengers from different social backgrounds. The sailors manning the vessels lived alongside passengers, who often treated them with contempt. They made few complaints about being poorly paid or overworked or about working conditions, which were often very difficult. These sailors are somewhat of a mystery to us, just as the ocean must have been to them. But also like the ocean, they were rich in resources – the resources of vigour and youth.

An eighteenth-century sailing ship was a restricted environment, where two societies had to co-exist, avoiding contact as much as possible. The sea failed to break down social barriers. The two lived quite differently: one group was almost totally inactive, whereas the other was overworked. For both groups, however, comfort was limited. Although the influential passengers had more space, they too suffered when the elements were unleashed. For the sailors, bedding was scant, there were few changes of clothes, hygiene was impossible, and the diet so deficient that sickness could sweep easily through the ship. The seamen moved about in a world of do's and don'ts where it was difficult to distinguish between personal convictions and the requirements imposed by others. Their reputations reflected the contempt in which they were held by their contemporaries, but although they might have had good reason to be less disciplined or more quarrelsome than other social group, they were not permitted to be.

The title of this study, *Between France and New France*, may have appeared too general, as vast as the ocean separating the two countries, but it seems a just tribute to the great ambition and courage of those who dared to brave the North Atlantic. *Between France and New France* describes a means of transport, a communications link, a human experience, and a living environment. An Atlantic crossing was not only a military, commercial, and scientific adventure, but also a social adventure. Even with all its physical limitations, the voyage could not erase prejudices. It demonstrated political and economic strategies for development. It challenged men to test the limits of their endurance. It was a victory over fear. In view of the enormous challenges of the time, it was, without doubt, a great accomplishment.

Appendices

Appendix A King's Vessels at Quebec City From 1713 to 1754[1]

Year	Name	Type	Captain	Place and date of construction		Remarks
1713	—	—	—	—		no vessels
1714	*Afriquain*	man-of-war	X	Bayonne,	1692	—
1715	*Afriquain*	man-of-war	Voutron	Bayonne,	1692	—
1716	*François*	man-of-war	Voutron	Le Havre,	1688	—
1717	*Astrée*	frigate	X	Brest,	1707	—
1717	*Victoire*	frigate	X	Dunkerque,	1704	—
1718	*Eléphant*	flute	X	Brest,	1718	forced to turn back
1719	*Chameau*	flute	Querquelin	Holland,	1716	—
1720	*Chameau*	flute	Voutron	Holland,	1716	Father Charlevoix aboard
1721	*Chameau*	flute	Lamirande	Holland,	1716	—
1722	*Chameau*	flute	Beaumont	Holland,	1716	—
1723	*Chameau*	flute	Beauville	Holland,	1716	—
1724	*Chameau*	flute	Méchin	Holland,	1716	Vaudreuil aboard
1725	*Chameau*	flute	Saint James	Holland,	1716	wrecked off Isle Royale
1726	*Eléphant*	flute	Desgouttes	Brest,	1718	—
1727	*Eléphant*	flute	Tilly	Brest,	1718	—
1728	*Eléphant*	flute	Desgouttes	Brest,	1718	—
1729	*Eléphant*	flute	Vaudreuil	Brest,	1718	wrecked off île aux Coudres
1730	*Héros*	man-of-war	L'Etenduère	Rochefort,	1721	—
1731	*Héros*	man-of-war	Desgouttes	Rochefort,	1721	—
1732	*Rubis*	man-of-war	L'Etenduère	Le Havre,	1728	epidemic
1733	*Rubis*	man-of-war	La Jonquière	Le Havre,	1728	—
1734	*Rubis*	man-of-war	De Chaon	Le Havre,	1728	—
1735	*Héros*	man-of-war	De Forant	Rochefort,	1721	—
1736	*Héros*	man-of-war	St. Clair	Rochefort,	1722	—
1737	*Jason*	man-of-war	Duquesnel	X	1723	Hocquart aboard
1738	*Rubis*	man-of-war	La Jonquière	Le Havre,	1728	—
1739	*Rubis*	man-of-war	La Galissonière	Le Havre,	1728	—
1740	*Rubis*	man-of-war	La Saussaye	Le Havre,	1728	Mgr. Lauberivière aboard
1741	*Rubis*	man-of-war	Méchin	Le Havre,	1728	Mgr. de Pontbriand aboard
1742	*Rubis*	man-of-war	Conteneuil	Le Havre,	1728	—
1743	*Rubis*	man-of-war	Rossel	Le Havre,	1728	—
1744	*Gironde*	flute	L'Etenduère	X	1737	—
1745	*Gironde*	flute	Tilly	X	1737	—

Year	Name	Type	Captain	Place and date of construction		Remarks
1746	Duc d'Anville	squadron comprising 7 warships, 1 hospital ship, 4 flutes, 3 corvettes, 2 frigates, 2 fire ships, and 33 transport ships				
1747	La Jonquière	squadron comprising 5 warships, 1 frigate, 1 flute, 6 East Indiamen, and 26 merchant ships				
1747	Emeraude	frigate	La Jonquière	X	1741	part of the La Jonquière squadron
1747	Alcyon	man-of-war	X	Toulon,	1724	
1747	Gironde	flute	Sr Cosse	X	1737	—
1747	Northumber-land	man-of-war	Périer de Salvert	Great Britain,	1705	La Galissonière aboard
1748	Friponne	frigate	Le Gardeur de Tilly	X	1747	Bigot aboard
1748	Zephyr	frigate	Nepveu	X	1728	—
1749	Diane	frigate	La Jonquière	Toulon,	1741	—
1749	Léopard	man-of-war	Daubigny	Toulon,	1726	La Jonquière aboard
1750	Diane	frigate	Du Vigneau	Toulon,	1741	—
1750	Anglesea	frigate	Gomain	Plymouth,	1694	—
1751	Chariot Royal	flute	La Filière	Le Havre,	1749	—
1752	Seine	flute	Vautron	Toulon,	1718	Duquesne aboard
1753	Seine	flute	Beauchêne	Toulon,	1718	—
1753	Tigre	man-of-war	La Villéon	Toulon,	1724	demolished at Quebec City
1754	Caméléon	flute	Foucault	X	1751	—

Legend: X = not specified
        — = nothing remarkable

Appendix B King's Vessels in New France From 1755 to 1760[1]

Name	Guns	Type	Voyages: Year–destination	Place and date of construction		Remarks
Abénaquise	36	f	1757–L	Quebec City,	1756	captured in 1757
Achille	64	m	1757–L	Toulon,	1745	—
Actif	64	m	1755–Q	Brest,	1750–52	fitted out for transport
Aigle	50	m	1758–Q	X	X	wrecked in the St. Lawrence
Aimable	X	b	1756–L	X	X	—
Alcide	64	m	1755–Q	Brest,	1741	captured *en route* in 1755
Algonquin	72	m	1755–Q	Quebec City,	1750–52	fitted out for transport
Amphion	64	m	1758–L	Brest,	1748–52	—
Apollon	50	m	1755–Q, 1757–L, 1758–L	Rochefort,	1738	captured in 1758
Aquilon	46	m	1755–L	Toulon,	1731–33	hospital ship
Arc en ciel	50	m	1756–L	X	1745	captured in 1756
Aréthuse	36	f	1758–L	X	1757	—
Atalante	X	f	1759–Q	Toulon,	1740–41	sank in 1760
Belliqueux	64	m	1757–L, 1758–Q	Brest,	1755–56	captured in 1758
Biche	X	c	1758–L	X	X	scuttled in 1758
Bienfaisant	64	m	1758–L	Brest,	1751–54	captured in 1758
Bizarre	64	m	1755–L; 1757–LQ	Brest,	1749–51	—
Brune	30	f	1757–L	Le Havre,	1753–55	—
Célèbre	64	m	1757–LQ; 1758–L	Brest,	1755–56	lost in 1758
Chariot Royal	36	fl	1756–L	Le Havre,	1749	captured
Chèvre	X	fl	1758–L	X	1751	scuttled in 1758
Capricieux	64	m	1758–L	Rochefort,	1752–54	burned in 1758
Comète	30	f	1755–57–58–L	Brest,	1751–52	—
Concorde	X	f	1756–L	Brest,	1754–55	—
Dauphin Royal	70	m	1755–L; 1757–L	Brest,	1735–38	fitted out for transport
Défenseur	74	m	1755–L; 1757–L	Brest,	1752–54	fitted out for transport
Diadème	74	m	1757–L	Brest,	1755–56	—
Diane	30	f	1755–Q; 1758–L	Toulon,	1741–44	captured in 1758
Dragon	64	m	1758–Q	Brest,	1745	—
Duc de Bourgogne	80	m	1757–L	Rochefort,	1747–51	—

Name	Guns	Type	Voyages: Year–destination	Place and date of construction		Remarks
Echo	X	f	1758–L	X	1757	captured in 1758
Entreprenant	74	m	1755–Q; 1758–L	Brest,	1749–51	—
Espérance	74	m	1755–L	Toulon,	1722	fitted out for transport
Eveillé	64	m	1757–L	Rochefort, 1751–52		—
Fauvette	X	b	1755–Q	X	X	—
Fidèle	26	f	1755–Q; 1758–L	X	1747	scuttled in 1758
Fleur de Lys	30	f	1757–L	Brest,	1753–54	—
Formidable	80	m	1757–L	Brest,	1749–51	—
Fortune	46	fl	1757–L	Rochefort, 1755–57		—
Glorieux	74	m	1757–L	Rochefort, 1753–56		—
Hardy	64	m	1758–L	Rochefort, 1748–50		—
Hector	74	m	1757–L	Toulon,	1752–55	—
Hermione	26	f	1757–L	Rochefort, 1748–49		captured in 1757
Héros	74	m	1756–Q; 1757–L	Brest,	1750–52	fitted out for transport
Illustre	64	m	1755–Q; 1756–Q	Brest,	1749–50	fitted out for transport
Inflexible	64	m	1757–L	Rochefort, 1752–55		—
Légère	X	b	1756–L	X	X	—
Léopard	64	m	1755–Q; 1756–Q	Toulon,	1726–27	demolished at Quebec City
Licorne	X	f	1756–Q	Brest,	1754–55	—
Lys	64	m	1755–Q	Brest,	1745–46	captured *en route* in 1755
Magnifique	64	m	1758–L	Brest,	1747–48	diverted
Messager	X	fl	1758–L	Rochefort, 1752–53		lost in a collision
Macreuse	X	b	1755–Q	X	X	—
Opiniâtre	64	m	1755–Q	Brest,	1748–50	fitted out for transport
Outarde	X	fl	1755–L; 1756–58–Q	Rochefort, 1753		—
Pomone	X	f	1759–Q	Toulon,	1748–49	lost near Quebec City
Prudent	74	m	1758–L	Rochefort, 1751–53		—
Raisonable	64	m	1758–L	Rochefort, 1754–55		captured in 1758
Rhinocéros	X	fl	1755–L; 1756–L	X	1751	—
Sage	64	m	1757–L	Toulon,	1749–51	—
Sauvage	X	f	1756–Q	Brest,	1754–56	—
Sirène	30	f	1755–Q; 1756–Q	X	1744	—
Sphinx	64	m	1758–L	Brest,	1752–55	—
Superbe	70	m	1757–L	X	1735–38	—
Tigre	X	f	1758–L	X	1758	ex-HMS *Tiger*
Tonnant	80	m	1757–L	Toulon,	1753–55	—
Vaillant	64	m	1757–L	Toulon,	1753–55	—
Valeur	20	f	1755–L; 1756–Q, 1758–Q	Rochefort, 1753		—
Zephyr	X	f	1758–L	X	1728	—

Legend: L = Louisbourg, Q = Quebec City, m = man-of-war, f = frigate, fl = flute, b = barge, c = corvette, — = nothing remarkable, X = not specified

Appendix C
Survey of the *Chezine*[1]

> Copy of a letter from the Master Shipwright and his assistants at Plymouth to the Navy Board dated 14th of March 1760.

In obedience to your directions of the 4th past we have been on board the La Chezine, lately taken by His Majesty's Ship Rippon; and find her almost a new Frigate; she is said to be not more than 16 Months Old, and to have been built at Nantes in France. She has ports on her upper deck for twenty-four guns, but think 'twill be difficult to fight the two foremost; as she is not only very narrow on her upper deck, but also has a thin lank Bow; the metal she has on board are of different Bores, yet most of them are for a six pound shot; her ports on this deck are very small, both Fore and Aft, and up & down, as will appear by the Dimensions annexed, and as her Topside Tumbles home very much, being no more than 22 ft. 6$^1/_2$ in. broad from outside to outside of the Plank at the height of the waste rail on midships, and there being no more than 8 ft. 4$^1/_2$ in. between the upper edge of the spirkiting of this Deck, and the outsides of the Comings of the Main Hatch, we think it little enough for working her guns in time of action; Her Cables come in upon the upper deck where she has only one pair of Riding Bitts. She has Ports for six guns on her lower deck of very small dimensions likewise; and what is yet a further Inconvenience, neither can they be worked we think for want of height, being no more than 4 ft. 4 in. between the plank of this and the upper deck; she has no Cabbins, nor guns on her Quarter Deck or Forecastle; neither are there any Ports on either. The Captains cabbin is on the upper deck. Forward and Abaft are Cabbins for other Officers, and Storerooms on the lower deck. She has no Platforms below this Deck: but being deep in Hold, there is room for making one Afore and another Abaft, whereon a Fireplace and Storerooms etc. may be erected, her present fireplaces being under the Forecastle on the upper deck on each side. Under the after Platform, we think there will be sufficient room for a magazine, brandy, fish and Breadroom. The Scantlings of her Frame are slight, but her Decks are kneed with one substantial wood hanging, or lodging knee at each end of each beam. The Plank and thickstuff on her sides both within and without board is chiefly Oak, but the fastnings are with Nails. We can say little of her shape more than what appears above water: except that the waterline she is now paid up to, promises a body formed for sailing well.

Upon our duly considering her construction so far as can be seen of her by us, more particularly above water; we are apprehensive she never can fight any guns upon her lower deck; and that it is incommodious fighting them on the upper deck, for want of more breadth thereon; that her Scantlings are small, not sufficient for a heavier metall than a six pound shot; and her ports extreme small also; nor will they bear widening sufficiently, we fear, without wounding overmuch her Port Timbers. We can't therefore presume to recommend her as a Frigate very fitting to be purchased for His Majesty's service. We have hereunto annex'd her principal Dimensions and Tonnage with some few scantlings; all that we could conveniently take as also the dimensions of her masts and yards.

Dimensions of Masts and Yards

	Masts		Yards	
	Length yds. ins.	Diam. ins.	Length yds. ins.	Diam. ins.
Main	24.24	20	22.16	15
Top	14.38	$12^{1}/_{2}$	15.9	$10^{1}/_{2}$
Gallant	7.30	$6^{5}/_{8}$	9.21	5
Fore	22.33	$19^{1}/_{8}$	21.1	$13^{3}/_{4}$
Top	14.9	12	14.8	10
Gallant	7.9	$6^{5}/_{8}$	8.27	$4^{1}/_{4}$
Mizon	17.26	$13^{3}/_{4}$	19.6	$9^{5}/_{8}$
Top	9.34	9	10	$7^{1}/_{2}$
Gallant	3.3	$4^{1}/_{4}$	None	
Bowspritt	14.30	$19^{3}/_{4}$	14.8	1.0
Crossjack	. . . .	. . . .	13.0	$8^{5}/_{8}$
Jibb	10.20	$7^{7}/_{8}$	. . . .	. . . .

Principal Dimensions & Scantlings of the Rippon's Prize, La Chezine

				feet	ins.
Length by the Keel for Tunnage				99	9
On the Lower Deck from the Rabbit of the Stem to the Rabbit of the Post				119	6
Breadth Extream				30	2½
at the Top Timber Line from out to outside of the Plank			Afore	20	0
			Midships	22	6½
			Abaft	13	7
Depth in Hold				12	8½
Burthen in Tuns			404 16/94		
Draught of Water			Afore	12	3½
			Abaft	14	4
Lower Deck	Beams round			0	6¾
	Plank thick			0	2½
	Height from the Plank	To the upper Edge of the Upper Deck Beam at the middle of the Beam	Afore	4	4
			Midships	4	4
			Abaft	4	4
		To the Port cells		1	4¼
	Ports	Deep		1	11¾
		Fore and Aft		1	11½
		No. on each side 3			
	Beams	Sided		0	11
		Moulded		0	9
		One Dagger Knee to each Beam, sided		0	8
Upper Deck	Beams			0	6¼
	Plank thick			0	2½
	Height from the plank	To the upper edge of the Quarterdeck Beams at the middle of the Beam	Afore	5	3
			Abaft	6	4¾
		To the waste		4	3
		To the Port cells		1	4
		To the upper edge of the Fore Castle Beams at the middle of the Beam	Afore	4	7½
			Abaft	4	10
Upper Deck	Ports	Deep		1	9¼
		Fore and aft		1	11
		No. on each side 12			
	Beams	Sided		0	10¼
		Moulded		0	6½
	Knees	One hanging knee to each beam, and the lodging knees to the Beams of the Main Hatch Sided		0	6½
Fore-castle	Beams Round			0	5¼
	Plank thick			0	2
	Long taken at the aft side of the Bollard Timber			25	0
	Beams	Sided		0	7
		Moulded		0	4½
Quarter Deck	Beams round			0	6¼
	Plank thick			0	2
	Long taken in midships at the aft part of the Stern Timber			51	6
	Beams	Sided		0	7½
		Moulded		0	4½
	Quarter Deck and Fore Castle Beams no Knees, but a piece of thickstuff brought on the clamps, and scor'd up into the Beams and bolted through the sides and through the Beams.				
Scantlings of the Frame	Second Futtocks, At the Upper Deck, Top of the Side,	Sided		0	9
		Moulded		0	7
		Sided		0	8
		Moulded		0	5
		Moulded		0	3½
	Space between the Timbers			0	9
	Fore	Thwartships		4	3
		Fore and Aft		5	0
	Main	Thwartships		5	0
		Fore and Aft		7	5½
	After	Thwartships		4	3½
		Fore and Aft		4	10
Height of the Lower Deck Port Cells from the water				3	9½

Appendix D
Scientific Observations Made During Atlantic Crossings[1]

Longitudinal observations which one can make whenever latitude has been calculated at sunrise or sunset.

Yesterday, July 15, when our pilots saw the sunset, at 44 degrees, 20 minutes, I made a type of longitudinal observation using a good watch belonging to Mr. de Montlouet, a sub-lieutenant. He had not touched the watch since Brest. This watch read 10:04 when the sun was setting, which at this latitude is 7:34, giving a difference of 2 hours, 30 minutes or 37 degrees, 30 minutes difference in longitude. This places us at 333 degrees, 30 minutes from the Tenerif meridian, because Brest is situated 11 degrees east of the meridian, and adding 37 degrees, 30 minutes

      37 D. 30 m.   we get
    333 D. 30 m.   11 degrees
    371 D. 00 m.

east of Tenerif. However, the equation for clocks given in *Connoissance des tems* indicates that we should subtract approximately 1/92 from the time shown on a good watch when it has been set by the sun on May 20. I should therefore subtract approximately 2 degrees, 30 minutes from my longitudinal calculation and, on that basis, I am only 336 degrees east of the Tenerif meridian and, consequently, still 6 degrees from the Grand Bank, of which our pilots hope to have a sounding this evening. From the outcome we will know which of us was wrong. Nevertheless, I feel I should point out here how I came to my conclusion. The most recent large-scale charts of Canada show Cape Race as being only 250 leagues from Quebec City, in a straight line, which, in latitude, equals 18 degrees difference. There are also 18 degrees from Paris to the Tenerif point. These two totals come to 36 degrees. There are still 36 degrees, then, from Cape Race to Tenerif because, according to the gentlemen at the Academy, there are 72 degrees from Paris to Quebec City and, consequently, Cape Race is situated only 324 degrees from Tenerif, and as the watch puts me only as far as 336 degrees, according to it, I am still 12 degrees from Cape Race. That is why I said I was still 6 degrees from the Grand Banks, because from Cape Race to the eastern edge of the Grand Banks, that is about the difference. [p. 249–250.]

... July 22. Yesterday we sounded the Banks, which proves that our pilots calculated our position as about 180 leagues ahead of where we actually were. It shows that their charts are inaccurate and that their log-line measurement is incorrect, leading them to believe they have gone one eighth of the way further than they have. In addition, yesterday, when we sailed north all day, I checked our watch glass and found that it gained 8 minutes a day over a good watch. Without doubt, these three factors were enough to put us ahead in our estimates by 180 leagues without our having to attribute the error to currents, as pilots always do. What I have just described gets to the crux of the matter, that it is important to adjust the log-line measurement, to correct variation compass faults and, especially, to procure new charts with the longitude markings adjusted at several locations, because I have just witnessed a situation clearly illustrating this problem. Mr. de Kersalaun, sub-lieutenant of this vessel, marked and followed his course on two different charts. On July 15, he calculated his position by the new chart as 19 leagues east of the Banks, and the same point on the other map placed us 18 leagues west of the Banks, for a difference of 80 leagues. The new chart proved to be the better one; it shows the Cape where we place it here, that is, at 324 degrees longitude. [pp. 250–251.]

... I also observed and allowed others to observe latitude with an instrument which has a much larger arc than the cross-staff and the English quadrant, and which offers a decided advantage because of its great precision and convenience.

On several occasions, I also observed the variation, at different times of the day, our pilots having gone up to three weeks without having an opportunity to take observation at sunrise or sunset. They all agree that this means of observation, with the astronomical circle, has its advantages and that the variation compass I brought is much superior to the ones the King supplies. [p. 252.]

... Although I have not had an opportunity to observe an eclipse, I still feel I cannot use the 9-foot 3-inch telescope that I brought, at sea. It can only possibly be of use in a sheltered roadstead and then only to observe the moon, not Jupiter, which is impossible to keep within the field; the harder one tries, the sooner one loses it, you lose it as soon owing to the reversal of the image. A 7-foot telescope would be quite useful to us; the moon is wide and one can keep the object in view. This way, I think one could observe a star in the proximity of immersion and emersion, when the sea is calm and condition[s] are not very turbulent.

If I may make an observation which reveals my feelings regarding long telescopes, it is clear we would have a decided advantage in bringing a good 4-foot telescope with us, which we could use often for observation purposes. It would be useful on occasions when the moon was more than three days either side of full, which would give us 22 days per month on which we could observe the immersion or emersion of the dark side. I admit there are still 30 degrees near the zenith where observation is impossible. [pp. 253–254.]

... August 27: A strong wind from the east reduced us to using only the lower sails on the 25th and 26th. I was still hoping to use this past night to calculate longitude by a star of the third magnitude which was eclipsed by the moon. I thought I could do this, because even if I had not been able to witness the exact moment of immersion on the bright side with my 7-foot telescope (because the moon had only been on the wane for 3 days) I would have had about an hour after the emersion on the dark side, as our 3-foot navigational telescope is adequate for that purpose and I could still have used my own, the way I set it up, unless the sea was extremely rough. As it was, the night was so black we didn't even see the moon clearly. [pp. 258–259.]

Appendix E
Altercation between a French Man-of-War and Three English Vessels, 1743[1]

This morning at four, at the break of day, I sighted a small ship ahead of me going east. I headed north to try to gain some information from her about the Banks. A half hour later I sighted three ships windward of me in the fog following the same course as the first. I then resumed my NNW course, on a port tack closer to the wind, which was from the west. These three ships sailed toward me. I should mention that, at the time, I had full reefed my topsails. I prepared myself for combat. Then the English captain hoisted his flag and pennant and enforced his colours by a shot. The other vessels also hoisted their English flags. Within a half hour, they were upon me. I hoisted my flag and pennant and enforced my colours by a shot leewards.

    The English captain hove to a short distance ahead and to windward of me, and the other two ships kept coming straight for me. One came under my lee and the other stayed windward of me. I continued on my course without touching the tiller, sailing well within gun range almost across the English captain's bow, being unable to pass to windward of him. He called out to me to heave to, so I brailed my lower sails. As I did this, he fired and damaged the brail of my mainsail and the other hit a chicken coop and injured a young chicken and a soldier. I continued to brail my lower sails and hoisted my large topsail on the masts. Then the English captain called out to me to lower my boat. When I refused, he lowered his and sent an officer over in it who said his captain insisted that I come and speak to him. I told him my vessel was a French warship and that I wouldn't go, and that his captain was very lucky to have three ships with him and so many more men than I had, and that if he were alone he wouldn't be so insolent. He replied that his captain was going to attack, and I dared him to try. I said that as long as there was a living soul on my vessel, we would make him pay for his savagery and that he and his captain could go to hell, and I told him to tell that to his captain. The officer returned with my reply, while I prepared myself as best I could, but I could open only four gun ports in the lower battery, because there was water coming in all around, whereas the English batteries were fully exposed and well above the water line. During this time the English commander had signalled one of his 70-gun ships to come up alongside me, within firing range, and had ordered his 40-gun frigate to sail across my bow, within pistol-firing range, while taking the tampions out of her guns. Thinking he meant to ram me (which I would have welcomed since at least that way he would have lost some of his advantage over me in terms of artillery), I called out, "Do you intend to ram me?" and he said for me to come aboard, that those were his orders and that he was not obliged to assume that I was French, that I could have been Spanish. I replied that I would certainly not come aboard, so he said he would see about that, all in good French. I dared him to try something and I had the blessing said for my crew, fully prepared to be beaten and to sink rather than dishonour the king's flag. Finally, having consulted with his comrade on the 70-gun ship who had sent over his boat, he sent me another lieutenant who was better spoken and more polite than the first. He said that his captain sent me his regards and requested that I send an officer aboard his ship. I flatly refused. Without dwelling on the matter, he said he had orders to see my commission. I said he would have to show me his captain's first. "Sir," he said, "that isn't fair; you are not at war with anyone and we are at war with the Spanish. Therefore you should prove that you are French, which you can do only by showing us your commission."

I assembled all my officers and cadets, who all agreed that his request was a fair one, so I decided to show him the letter from the king giving me my command. I asked for the names of his vessels and they were:

The Suffolk, 70 guns*   Capt Knôle commanding the squadron, sail-
The Barford, 70 guns   ing from Antigua and bound for England
The Elthan, 40 guns

When he had given me this information first, I gave him the name of my vessel, my name and my destination, Quebec City. Then he went back to his vessel and I continued on my way.

*My whole crew swears there were 74 guns.

Appendix F
Social Distinctions Between Officers in the French Navy and in the Merchant Marine[1]

Account of a conversation between Mr. Dupierrie Jr and myself, during which he lost his temper for no good reason.

I was coming from a visit to the man-of-war *Mercure*, under the command of Captain Duteillis. As I came aboard my ship, I found my officers to my left and right; they had come out to greet me and I saluted them and was continuing forward when I saw Mr. Dupierrie Jr, so I saluted him as well. He was at the bow of my vessel and had come on board to procure some water.

We struck up a conversation and soon found ourselves discussing women and chaplains. I said that there were chaplains who were as bothersome on board a ship as women. Mr. Dupierrie replied that he would rather have a woman on board than a chaplain, because at least that way he would enjoy himself more and might have some favours from them. I said that not all the officers could enjoy such favours and that a captain had to be discreet in situations prohibited to other officers where punishment was involved, to avoid setting a very bad example. Mr. Dupierrie replied that punishment was fine for those of us who were in the merchant marine but that the officers on men-of-war were never punished.

I said I thought everyone who deserved it was punished in one way or another, but he said that wasn't true. I asked him why and he said that in his crew there were only gentlemen whereas in ours there were only boors. I told him that every rule has an exception and that we had some very honest men from good backgrounds who were forced to sign on for lack of means, to which he replied that they were few and far between. Suddenly he became very angry. He said I was bothering him and that I looked like a lout myself and he used words I cannot put down on paper, so they will have to be left to the imagination. I told him he was mistaken and that, although I was in the merchant fleet, I was a gentleman, like himself. He made no reply other than to say that I looked like a lout. He said he would beat me if he had a stick. I replied that I did not deserve to be treated that way and that no one in my family had ever been treated that way, that he had only to ask around the squadron as to who I was and who my family were to find out that my father was a lieutenant colonel in the Quoaquien regiment and a knight of St. Louis and that my older brother was a captain in the Detrenel regiment, formerly mon conseil. After hearing me out, Mr. Dupierrie calmed down somewhat and told me he had gotten angry because I had not saluted him when I came aboard. I said he was mistaken, that I had had the honour of saluting him, but that perhaps because he had been forward, he had not noticed. I said I was brought up well enough to know that I should salute an honest man when I saw one and that I was always proud to salute any honest man.

I believe Mr. Dupierrie was wrong to have lost his temper and that I should have been the one to get angry, because threatening to beat him is a terrible thing to do to an honest man.

Appendix G
Repairs Made to the Frigate *Néréide*[1]

August 30, 1726

We weighed anchor in the Louisbourg roadstead at eight o'clock this morning and, after making fast, we prepared for careening. I arranged it so we could see the keel of the frigate, and had equipment rigged up for that purpose. We hove her down on mooring posts to which the winding tackle running from the two masts was attached, and we had two anchors on land at a distance of twenty paces from the cannons we were using as mooring posts. Each of these anchors was attached to the two masts, to which were fastened the return blocks. A heavy derrick was then placed in position crossways to the frigate, with guys attached, and all was in readiness.

September 7, 1726

At eight o'clock this morning we careened so we could see the keel, which I found more damaged than I had expected; forty-three feet of the keel was missing in places as far as the rabbet. When I had determined what repairs were needed, I had the ship restored to her normal position. The next day I sent the master carpenter to a place in the woods where I had been told we could find what we needed to make a keelson. This turned out to be true, and I sent a detachment of the crew to bring me the pieces of wood I needed. We had to careen five times to do the repairs. The work was completed on the 20th, after which I prepared to set sail for France.

Appendix H
Damage to the *Comète*, 1753[1]

On Wednesday the ninth of May, seventeen hundred and fifty-three, at six o'clock in the morning, we were located four leagues northwest of North Cape and headed north to clear Rochers aux Oiseaux. The wind was from the east. By noon, judging myself to be east west [sic] of the said rocks, I steered a course between northwest by north and north-north west. We were doing two leagues per hour, the wind was still from the east and there was a thick fog. At three o'clock in the afternoon we came upon an ice floe which we passed in less than three hours, during which time we had a sea which put two feet of water in the hold, punctured my lifeboat, damaged the storeroom and washed two barrels overboard, one full of water and the other of beer. When we went to use the pumps we found them full of corn and, despite the difficulties we were in, I decided to raise them. Once they were in place, we freed the pump, which was taking in a lot of corn. About six o'clock in the evening we came upon another ice floe and the fog from it was so thick that we could see no passage. The wind was still from the east at moderate gale force. The seas were heavy and the ice was very thick. Falling off for the one and coming round for the other, we tore away our foresail and broke the gaff. Then the wind changed direction, coming out of the west. There was a lot of ice and we could see no breaks. I was forced to put about and sail south-southwest using the mainsail and the jib; both reefs were inside all night. On Thursday the tenth of the same month, at eight o'clock in the morning, we sighted Rocher aux Oiseaux four leagues south by southwest. At noon we put about again. The wind was from the north and we headed west; I thought that way we would avoid the ice floe. At that point we sighted and hailed a fishing vessel from Saint Malo under the command of Captain Jacques Cotard who, like us, was sailing for Bonaventure Island. On the fourteenth, we anchored at the island, taking on five inches of water per hour. For the purpose of averages, I am writing this account at the aforesaid Bonaventure Island, where we are anchored beside a fishing vessel from Grandville under the command of Captain Herticot, this fourteenth day of May, seventeen hundred and fifty-three,

Nicolet – marsan gello – Dunoyer.

Appendix I
The library of Captain la Rivière[1]

Louis François de la Rivière: ship's captain. Husband of Marie-Anne Havard and a father, Louis François Merven de la Rivière lives on rue Toulouze in St. Malo. But St. Malo is only a home-port for this ship's captain, who specializes in trans-Atlantic voyages. His presence is noted at Louisbourg on 23 September 1744; he has been living for nearly three months in the home of Sieur Latour on rue d'Orléans. Room and board for two months and 25 days cost him 212 livres. The inventory and sale of his belongings were carried out at the request of his brother Tanguy; the sale yielded a total of 1359 livres, 17 sous. Estate of Louis François Merven de la Rivière, Louisbourg, November 1744:

Item one book entitled *Le petit flambeau de la mer*
Item one book entitled *Traité complet de la navigation*
Item one book entitled *Ordonnance de la Marine*
Item two volumes entitled *Instruction au droit français*
Item two volumes entitled *Oeuvres de Boello*
Item two volumes entitled *Les voyages du royaume de Ciam*
Item one volume entitled *Les mémoires du duc de Villard*
Item one book entitled *Histoires des Seuarembe*
Item one book entitled *Histoire d'Emelei*
Item one volume entitled *Histoire de Maroq* . . .

Sale: books sold to his brother Tanguy Merven for 20 livres.

Appendix J
List of the Personal Effects of Nicolas Certain, a Seaman from the *Vive le Roy* of Dieppe, who Died at Quebec City After Several Days' Illness, 1755[1]

... Two sacks containing his belongings and clothing
Four shirts of various fabrics, half worn out
Four old neckerchiefs
One more neckerchiefs, old and ragged
Five old pairs of three-ply stockings
Two old thick caps
Three cloth bandages
One old coarse-knit jersey
Two old pairs of long cloth pants
Three pairs of breeches: one old and threadbare pair made of blue panne, and the other two pairs of brown and blue material
One pair of old shoes with thin buckles
One fairly new paletot of homespun, lined with a white fabric
One jacket and camisole of a red material, the jacket alone lined with white serge, both almost worn out
One sleeveless waistcoat in poor condition with an old camisole
One old woven garment (buriot) mended with sailcloth
One old overcoat with a hood of a coarse white fabric
One shabby pair of boots, worn right through in places
Two cloth sacks containing these tatters.

Appendix K
Regulations on board ship[1]

The crew and soldiers on board the *Superbe* are ordered to observe the following ordinances, on penalty of being punished as specified below. To wit
1. All officers, petty officers and sailors will be present on time for prayers, on penalty of losing their ration, unless they are sick.
2. Anyone smoking without a lidded claypipe and behind the mainmast will lose his rations.
3. Anyone found urinating along the gangway will lose one day's rations.
4. Anyone defecating between-decks will receive 50 lashes while tied to a cannon.
5. Anyone missing his watch will lose his day's rations, unless he is sick.
6. If a sailor or soldier is in a fight, he will be tied to a cannon and he will be put in irons and fed only bread and water for four days.
7. If there is an exchange of gunshots, all parties will receive 50 lashes while tied to a cannon, after which they will be put in irons for eight days with only bread and water.
8. If anyone steals anything, even from a friend, he will run the gauntlet and will lose his ration for 15 days.
9. If anyone is insulted by his companions, he should lodge a complaint with the officer of the watch, if he is a sailor. If he is a soldier, he should report it to his officers. He will be given justice.
10. Anyone who fails to bring his drinking mug when called for his ration will lose his ration.
11. If anyone, either sailor or soldier, has a complaint about his ration, he should lodge his complaint with the officer of the watch.
12. If anyone smokes his pipe in the between-decks, his bread ration will be denied for four days, then he will be put in irons with only bread and water.

Appendix L
Sailors' song[1]

Along the docks of La Rochelle I spied a captain's daughter;
With a sailor she had fallen into the briny water.
From him I stole this maiden fair, her fichu opened fully;
Hoisting up her skirt I found a fountain edged with wool.
    I freed my trusty pony then and sent him to the well;
Five, six full draughts without a pause he drank, his thirst to quell.
When he returned to me again, his ears they lay flat down.
Whence come you now, my faithful mount?
    Back from the well I come.
Once more, my little pony, drink! Back to the fountain, go!
I wouldn't dare, said he, because I've lost my breath, you know.

Notes

Chapter One:
Maritime Traffic and Outfit of Vessels

The French navy
1. L. Richebourg and A. Boismêlé, *Histoire générale de la Marine* (Amsterdam: 1757), "Code des Armées Navales ou Recueil des édits, déclarations, ordonnances et règlements sur le fait de la marine du Roi depuis le commencement du règne de Louis XIV jusqu'en 1757", 3:24-25 (hereafter cited as *Code des Armées Navales*). In a recent article, Jean Boudriot indicated that the 1670 regulations were modified the following year, so that only vessels carrying over 70 guns were three-deckers. Vessels carrying 64 guns were therefore two-deckers. Jean Boudriot, "Des vaisseaux de 64 canons et général et de l'*Artésien* en particulier" in *Neptunia*, 142 (June 1981).
2. France, AM, Rochefort, 2G2, bundles 2, 5, 7, 8.
3. All the dimensions in Table I and in the remainder of the text are given in French feet. Dimensions in parentheses are in English feet, and come from different sources than those in French feet. (A French foot equals 1.066 English feet.) For sailing vessels in the table which were over 100 French feet in length, the measurement is the perpendicular from stem to stern; for those under 100 feet, it is the length of the keel. The information in Table 1 is drawn from the *Code des Armées Navales*, p. 301, for men-of-war; from France, AN, Marine, B5, vol. 3 for the *Tonnant*, the *Héros*, the *Dauphin Royal*, the *Comète*, and the *Hermione*; from London, P.R.O., Adm. 95, vol. 65, item 21, for the *Alcide*; HCA 32, bundle 175 for the *Chezine*; from F.H. Chapman, *Architectura Navalis Mercatoria*, (London: 1975), pp. 63-65 for the *Chameau* from France, AM, Rochefort, 2G1, bundle 8 for the *Algonquin*; from Robert Gardiner "Les frégates françaises et la Royal Navy" in *Le Petit Perroquet*, 25, (1978) for the *Aréthuse*, the *Comète*, the *Hermione*, and the *Chézine*, pp. 4-27; from AN, Colonies, C11A, vols. 60, 61 and 81 for the *S. Joseph*, the *S. Michel*, the *Triomphant*, the *S. Gilles*, and the *S. Louis*.
4. Pierre Bouguer, *Traité du navire de sa construction et de ses mouvements* (Paris: 1746), pp. 8-9.
5. Gardiner, *op. cit.*, p. 6.
6. Bouguer, *op. cit.*, p. 9.
7. France, AM, Rochefort, 2G2, bundles 1, 2, 3, 4.
8. Jean Boudriot, *Le vaisseau de 74 canons*, 4:264-274.
9. Joseph Dargent, "Relation d'un voyage de Paris à Montréal en Canadas en 1737", in *Rapport des Archives de la Province de Québec* (hereafter cited as *RAPQ*), 1947-1948, p. 15.
10. The information on draughts is drawn from France, AN, Marine, 4JJ, 8-53 and 58; 12-35, 36, 38, 39 and 41.
11. Bouguer, *op. cit.*, p. 11.
12. Canada, PAC, MG2, B4:58. Logbook of the *Entreprenant*, p. 126.
13. Jacques Mathieu, *La construction navale royale à Québec, 1739-1749* (Quebec City: 1971) p. 85.
14. Canada, PAC, MG2, B4:58. Log-book of the *Illustre*, p. 253.

The merchant marine
1. France, Archives communales, Bayonne, series FF: 328; Québec, Archives Nationales, Greffe J.C. Panet, document filed on 10 August 1758. Chénard de la Giraudais commanded the *Machault* in 1760.
2. In all the documentation I consulted, the term "ship" (navire) was reserved for vessels with a tonnage of between 100 and 500. My information in this area is based particularly on the following series: London, PRO, HCA 32, bundles 99 to 242; France, Archives départementales, Charente-

Maritime (hereafter France, AMC) series B, vols 248-259; Archives Maritimes, Rochefort, series 13P8; AN, Colonies, C11A, vols. 36, 60, 61, 71, 74 and 75; and Quebec, AN, series NF 25. These series were also my source of information on the tonnages of brigantines, schooners, and bateaux. For a discussion on tonnage and burden, see Paul Gille, "Jauge et tonnage des navires", in *Le navire et l'économie maritime au XVe au XVIIIe siècle* (Paris: 1957), and Michel Morineau, *Jauges et méthodes de jauge anciennes et modernes*, Cahier des Annales, 24, (Paris: 1966). I should point out that, according to the naval ordinance of 1681, the ton corresponds to a theoretical space of 42 cubic feet and a weight of 2,000 pounds. Montcalm explained in his diary, "In order to understand this manner of speaking which is used when assessing the strength of a merchant vessel, it is necessary to know that the ton is reckoned to be 2,000 pounds in weight; it is worthwhile to note that one never gives more than half the load it could carry in the water, so when reference is made to a vessel of 300 tons burden, this means a ship that could carry and hold 600 tons, but which could never put out to sea" (*Collection des manuscrits du Maréchal de Lévis* (Quebec City: 1895, 6:56). It bears mentioning here that the *Compagnie des Indes*, some of whose vessels would stop over at Louisbourg on their return voyage from the Antilles and Louisiana, used men-of-war for trading purposes. The capacity of these ships ran from 600 to 900 to 1200 tons, or the equivalent of a 26-gun frigate, a 50-gun man-of-war, and a 64-gun man-of-war. Jean Boudriot's article, "Les vaisseaux de la Compagnie des Indes", in *Le Petit Perroquet*, 12 (1973-74), contains details on the structure and the interior installations of these vessels.

3. Daniel Lescallier, *Traité pratique du gréement des vaisseaux et autres bâtiments de mer* (Grenoble: Quatre Seigneurs, 1973), pp. 402-403.
4. *Ibid.*, pp. 410-411.
5. France, AN, Colonies, C11A, 49: 379v-380.
6. Lescallier, *op cit.*, pp. 401-402, 407-408.
7. London, PRO, HCA 32, bundle 175. Appendix C contains a copy of the survey of the *Chezine* as prepared by English ship-builders after the capture of the vessel in early 1760. An examination and comparison of this document with the French construction specifications give a better understanding of the naval architecture of French merchant vessels.

Maritime traffic
1. France, ACM, series B, vols. 251-259.
2. "Lettres de Doreil", 6 July 1755, *RAPQ*, 1944-45, p. 22.
3. Some of the information in Table 4 was gathered and compiled by J.S. Pritchard for his doctoral thesis entitled *Ships, Men and Commerce: A Study of Maritime Activity in New France*, pp. 490-492, (University of Toronto, 1971). Another source of information was France, AD, Gironde, series C, 1638.
4. Pritchard, *op. cit.*, 502.
5. Guy Frégault, *François Bigot administrateur français*, 2:22.
6. Jacques Mathieu, *Le commerce entre le Nouvelle-France et les Antilles au XVIIIe siècle*, p. 148. In contrast to Pritchard, who indicated that the level of trading activity during the Seven Years' War was unprecedented, Jacques Mathieu drew a distinction between maritime activity and the movement of commercial goods. He felt that the impetus came from government rather than private merchants, and that the sea traffic was not for regular trade. This distinction may be necessary in studies of trading activity, but seems less pertinent here, since our main focus is the method of transport.
7. France, ACM, series B, vols. 251-259; AD, Gironde, series 6B, vols. 101-102.
8. France, AD, Gironde, series C, vol. 1638.
9. "Lettre de la chambre de Commerce au Duc de Choiseul: 22-12-1761", *RAPQ*, 1924-1925, p. 223.
10. Pritchard, *op. cit.*, pp. 473-474.
11. France, AD, Gironde, series C, vol. 1638.
12. F.G. Pariset, *Bordeaux au 18e siècle*, p. 225; Jean Cavignac, *Jean Pellet commerçant de gros 1694-1772*, pp. 62-72.
13. Guy Frégault, *François Bigot*, vol. 2; A.G. Reid, "General trade between Quebec and France during the French regime", *CHR*, 34:23 (1953).
14. Paul Butel, *Les négociants bordelais, l'Europe et les Iles au XVIIIe siècle* (Paris: 1974), p. 171.
15. Pritchard, *op. cit.*, p. 501.
16. Butel, *op. cit.*, p. 36, 98.
17. *Ibid.*, p. 248.

Operations of the French royal navy
1. See Appendix B, which lists all the royal vessels scheduled to sail to New France between 1755 and 1760.
2. "Journal de Bougainville", *RAPQ*, 1923-1924, pp. 375-376, 204.
3. A naval force generally consisted of more than 27 vessels armed for war, while a squadron had between 9 and 26 such vessels. Jean Boudriot, *op. cit.*, p. 272.
4. Jean de Maupassant, *Les deux expéditions de Pierre Desclaux au Canada* (Bordeaux: 1915).
5. Appendix A contains a list of all men-of-war and flutes that came to Quebec between 1713 and 1754.
6. Canada, PAC, MG2, B4:59 (d'Anville) and 61 (La Jonquière).
7. France, AN, Marine, G, 49, pp. 47-49.
8. *Ibid.*, pp. 53-54.
9. Gardiner, *op. cit.*, p. 6, 24.
10. France, AN, Colonies, C11A, 99:17-18.

Port activities
1. An account of the careening operations for the *Néréide* is reproduced in Appendix G.
2. "Journal kept by the Chevalier Barbier de Lescoet, second captain on the *Formidable* from April to November, 1757", *Report of Canadian Archives*, 1905, vol. I, pt. 7, pp. 8-11.
3. France, AN, Marine 4 JJ, 13:47, log-book for the frigate *Diane*, 1755.
4. France, AN, Colonies, 80:175-192v; Quebec, AN, NF 25, bundle 1478.
5. France, AN, Marine, 4JJ, 11:7, log-book of the *Chameau*, voyage of 1720. Captain Voutron continued loading until the cargo port was only two inches above the waterline. "As soon as the cargo port was shut – despite the fact that when the last poles were loaded and stored forward the ship rose by two inches, leaving the cargo port four inches above the waterline – the ship having swung stern to wind, the sea came halfway up the cargo port . . ."
6. London, PRO, HCA 32, bundle 132.
7. Quebec, AN, NF 25, bundle 1478.
8. France, AN, Colonies, C11A, 75:336-336v; 93:425-427v.
9. France, AN, Marine, 4JJ; Canada, PAC, MG2, B4, details from the log-books of royal vessels commissioned for Canada and Louisbourg.
10. France, AN, Colonies, B, 108:119, report from the minister to the municipal magistrate of Marseilles, 6 March 1758. The problem became even more acute in time of war.
11. France, AN, series V7, vol. 346, account for fitting out the *Machault* in 1759.
12. France, AN, Colonies, C11A, 78:07-10; 80:168-192v.
13. United States, Cornell University Library, Maurepas papers, "Etat des vaisseaux et autres bâtiments qui sont en état d'être armés et ce qu'il en coûterait pour leur armement pendant six mois de campagne."
14. *Ordonnance de la Marine de 1681*, pp. 169-170.
15. London, PRO, HCA 32, bundles 109, 165, and 219.
16. France, AN, Colonies, C11A, 98:18-19v.

Chapter Two:
The Atlantic Course

Courses and markers
1. Unless otherwise indicated, information on the Atlantic course was extracted from log-books kept in bundles 7 to 13 of series 4JJ in the Marine section of the Archives nationales, France. For the section of this study entitled *Courses and markers*, the following records (name of vessel, captain, year of voyage), and bundles were particularly useful: the *Elisabeth*, Benneville, 1725, 7-27; the *Héros*, La Gallissonière, 1737, 8-50; the *Arc-en-ciel*, Damblimont, 1687, 11-3; the *Chameau*, Voutron, 1720, 11-7; the *Rubis*, Desherbiers de l'Etenduère, 1732, 11-19; the *Rubis*, La Jonquière, 1733, 11-21; the *Rubis*, La Jonquière, 1738, 12-29; the *Rubis*, La Gallissonière, 1739 12-31; the *Rubis*, Rossel, 1743, 12-37; the *Diane*, Froger de l'Eguille, 1755, 13-47. See also vols. 37 to 91 of series MG2, B4, Public Archives of Canada. Volumes 68, 73, 76, and 80 respectively deal with the 1755, 1756, 1757, and 1758 voyages.
2. Jean Talon to the minister, 4 October 1665, in *RAPQ*, 1930-1931, pp. 30-32.

3. E. Espenshade and J. Morrison, *Goode's World Atlas* (14th ed. Chicago: Rand McNally, 1977), pp. 16-17.
4. France, AN, Marine, 4JJ, 11-7.
5. Chabert de Cogolin, *Voyage fait par ordre du Roi en 1750 et 1751 dans l'Amérique septentrionale* (New York: Johnson, 1966), p. 36.
6. F.X. Charlevoix, *Histoire de la Nouvelle-France*, (Montréal: Elysée, 1976). 3:51.
7. France, AN, Marine, 4JJ, 7-27.
8. Pellegrin, "Mémoire sur la navigation du Canada", *Report of Canadian Archives*, 1905, vol. 1, pt. 5, p. 3. For a short biography of G. Pellerin, see the *Dictionnaire biographique du Canada*, 4:671-672.
9. France, AN, Colonies, B, 102:121, the minister to Dubois, Versailles, 1 October 1755.
10. France, AN, Colonies, C11A, 59:151, Beauharnois and Hocquart, Quebec City, 9 October 1733.
11. France, AN, Colonies, B, 108:565, the minister to Ruis, Versailles, July 1758.
12. France, AN, Colonies, C11A, 34:112. For the *Conseil de Marine* (council of admirals), it was necessary to "arrange a sure port of call near the Grand Banks for vessels coming in from the high seas; they would have to sail here anyway to catch the prevailing westerly winds to carry them back to France".
13. Jean Boudriot, *Le vaisseau de 74 canons*, 2:118. Exposure to sun and humidity can also cause a compass needle to rust; this was noted by the captain of the *Arc-en-ciel* in 1688. France, AN, Marine, 4JJ, 11-3.
14. France, AN, Marine, 4JJ, 12-29.
15. M. Daumas, *Les instruments scientifiques aux XVIIe et XVIIIe siècles* (Paris, 1953), p. 241.
16. Jean Boudriot, *Le vaisseau de 74 canons*, 4:320.
17. Samuel de Champlain, *Oeuvres de Champlain* (Montréal: Elysée, 1973) 3:50-53. Cogolin, *op. cit.*, p. 11, gives the same explanations.
18. France, AN, Marine, 4JJ. 12-31.
19. See Appendix D.
20. See Daumas, pp. 17-24, for excellent descriptions of the cross-staff, astrolabe, English quadrant and graphometer. The operation of these instruments is particularly well explained in Charles H. Cotter, *A History of Nautical Astronomy* (London: 1968), and in Jean Boudriot, *Le vaisseau de 74 canons*, vol. 4.
21. The angular distance between the horizon and a star observed at its pole could be measured either directly using the astrolabe, cross-staff and graphometer, or indirectly – and consequently with less eye strain – using the English quadrant and octant. To calculate the latitude from this measurement one must take into account the light refraction due to the Earth's atmosphere and the climate, determine the depression value of the horizon given the observer's position above the surface of the sea, add half the diameter of the star and subtract the parallax that makes the star seem further away than it actually is. These data are contained in nautical almanacs. The final step is to add the declination of the sun (between 0° and 23°30', from the equinoxes to the solstices) for the time at the meridian of origin at the moment of observation. The time is obtained by estimating the longitude and adding or substracting one hour for every 15 degrees of longitude.
22. France, AN, Marine, 4JJ, 11-19.
23. M. Daumas, *op. cit.* p. 240. Because of the sailing vessels' movement, observations of the horizon and the star had to be simultaneous and not successive. The octant made this possible and thus increased the degree of precision. However, observations of angular distances over 90° could not be made with the octant, and this instrument was replaced at the end of the eighteenth century by the sextant, which permitted calculation of angles up to 120°.
24. France, AN, Marine, 4JJ, 8-50.
25. M. Daumas, "Precision Mechanics", *A History of Technology*, 4:410-414.
26. An account is given in Appendix D.
27. F. Marguet, *Histoire générale de la navigation du XVe au XXe siècle*, p. 50.
28. France, AN, Marine, 4JJ, 11-21.
29. France, AN, Marine, 4JJ, 11-7.
30. Pellegrin, *op. cit.*, p. 5.

Speed and distances
1. L.A. Lahontan, *Voyages du baron Lahontan dans l'Amérique septentrionale* (Montréal: Elysée, 1975), 1:17.

2. France, AN, Marine, 4JJ, 7-8, log-book of the *Envieux*, 1695.
3. My figures for crossing times cover the period from Champlain's exploration to the surrender of Montreal in 1760. Data on the king's fleet are taken mainly from France, AN, Marine, 4JJ, 7 to 13; the *RAPQ* for 1923-1924, 1928-1929, and 1930-1931; and the *Report of Canadian Archives* for 1905. The figures for merchant vessels are from: France, AN, Colonies, C11A, vols. 15, 33, 36, 37, 46, and 47; ACM, B, vols. 5747 and 5748; Quebec, AN, NF 25, bundles 768, 1805, and 1810; and Samuel de Champlain, *op. cit.*
4. H.R. Casgrain, *Collection des manuscrits du maréchal de Lévis*, 6:43.
5. Lahontan, *op. cit.*, p. 17.
6. Espenshade and Morrison, *op. cit.*, pp. 14-15.
7. P.G. Roy, "L'intendant Jean Talon", *RAPQ*, 1930-31, p. 1.
8. J.C.B., *Voyage au Canada fait depuis l'an 1751 à 1761* (Quebec City: 1887), pp. 17-29.
9. France, AN, Marine, 4JJ, 11-3, log-book of the *Arc-en-Ciel*, 1687-88.
10. H.R. Casgrain, *Collection des manuscrits du Maréchal de Lévis* (Montreal: 1889), 1:44.
11. France, AN, Marine, 4JJ, 13-46, log-book of the *Actif*, 1755.
12. France, AN, Marine, 4JJ, 11-6, log-book of the *François*, 1716.
13. Jean Talon to the minister, Quebec City, 3 October 1665, *RAPQ*, 1930-1931, pp. 30-32.
14. France, AN, Colonies, C11A, 85:249, Beauharnois to the minister, Quebec City, 13 November 1746.
15. "Journal de Bougainville", *RAPQ*, 1923-1924, p. 314.
16. Charles Daney, "Les cartes routières de la mer", *L'Histoire*, 36, July-August 1981, p. 122.

Climate and averages
1. London, PRO, HCA 32, bundle 163.
2. H. R. Casgrain, *op. cit.*, 6:38.
3. France, AN, Marine, 4JJ, 11-7, log-book of the *Chameau*, 1720.
4. Quebec, AN, NF 25, bundles $441^{1}/_{2}$ and 484, averages of the *Afriquain*, 1710, and the *Amitié*, 1713.
5. France, AN, Marine, 4JJ, 7-4, log-book of the *Aimable*, 1692.
6. France, AN, Colonies, C11A, 25:123-123v, averages of the flute *Hollande*, 1706.
7. France, AN, Marine, 4JJ, 12-43, log-book of the flute *Seine*, 1752.
8. France, AN, Marine, 4JJ, 7-4, log-book of the *Aimable*, 1692.
9. Charlevoix, *op. cit.*, p. 52.
10. Gabriel Sagard, *Le grand voyage au pays des Hurons 1632* (Paris: Editions B. Guégan, 1929), p. 71.
11. Charlevoix, *op. cit.*, p. 50.
12. *Aventures du Sr C Lebeau ou Voyage curieux et nouveau parmi les sauvages de l'Amérique septentrionale* (New York: 1966), p. 44. Hereafter cited as *Aventures du Sr C. Lebeau*.
13. France, AN, Colonies, C11A, 67:209, Hocquart to the minister, Quebec City, 2 September 1737.
14. France, AN, Marine, 4JJ, 11-31, log-book of the *Rubis*, 1739.
15. France, ACM, B, vol. 5733. Petition of B. Paris, captain of the *Trois-Maries*, 12 May 1745.
16. France, AN, Marine, 4JJ, 9-80, log-book of the flute *Rhinocéros*, 1756; Colonies, C11A, 85:38-41, averages of the schooner *Marie*.
17. France, AN, Marine, 4JJ, 7-13, log-book of the *Atalante*, 1716; 4JJ, 11-21, the *Rubis*, 1732; and 4JJ, 11-32, the *Rubis*, 1740.
18. J.P. Aulneau to his mother, Quebec City, 10 October 1734, *RAPQ*, 1926-1927, p. 263.

Dangers and safety measures on the Atlantic
1. France, AN, Marine, 4JJ, 7-16, 23, log-books of the *François*, 1716, and the *Victoire*, 1723; London, PRO, HCA 32, bundle 97-5, log-book of the *Atalante*.
2. This conclusion is drawn from the reports from interrogations of high-ranking officers of captured vessels. See London, PRO, HCA 32.
3. J. Godechot, *Histoire de l'Atlantique*, (Bordas: 1947), pp. 147-150, and 165.
4. France, AN, Colonies, B, 104:109-112, circular sent to the judges and consul of port cities in France, Versailles, 28 January 1756.
5. France, Archives of the La Rochelle chamber of commerce, bundle 5843.

6. Canada, Public Archives, MG2, B4, 96:3, seizures by men-of-war and other vessels in the king's fleet since the beginning of the war.
7. France, Bibliothèque du Service Historique de la Marine, manuscript 188A (8107), document containing a brief account of the war between England and France.
8. Guy Frégault, *La guerre de la conquête* (Montréal: Fides, 1955), p. 205.
9. London, PRO, HCA 32, bundles 163-256. Most of the 45 vessels were headed for Louisbourg.
10. J.S. McLennan, *Louisbourg from its foundation to its fall* (Sydney: 1969), p. 308.
11. Papers seized aboard the *S. Martin*, sailing vessel captured on 9 January, 1757.
12. France, AN, Colonies, F2B, 2:150-160. The *Robuste* was transporting troops to Quebec City but was obliged to return to France after the encounter, having lost almost all its masts.
13. London, PRO, HCA 32, bundle 181. Proceedings arising from the capture of the *Dauphin*.
14. France, AN, Marine, 4JJ, 9-14. Log-book of the *Brillant*, a ship belonging to the French East India Company, 1744.
15. For additional information on these two expeditions, see France, AN, Marine, 4JJ, 8-59, log-book of the *Mars*, 1746; and "Un combat naval raconté par un missionnaire", *Neptunia* 123 (1976), pp. 1-5.
16. London, PRO, HCA 32, bundle 198. Among the papers seized aboard the *Hermione* in 1757 was a detailed description of the various signals agreed upon for use by the squadron bound for Louisbourg.

Travelling up the St. Lawrence
1. Benjamin Sulte, "Un voyage à la Nouvelle-France", *Revue canadienne* 6:22, (1886), p. 23.
2. "Journal de Bougainville", *RAPQ*, 1923-24, p. 310.
3. Unless otherwise indicated, information on navigation in the St. Lawrence was obtained from logbooks. See France, AN, Marine, 4JJ, 11-7, (the *Chameau*, 1720); 13 (the *Elephant*, 1727); 15 (the *Elephant*, 1729); 19 (the *Rubis*, 1732); and 21 (the *Rubis*, 1733); 4JJ, 12-29, 31, 32, 34, 35, and 37 (the *Rubis*, voyages of 1738, 1739, 1740, 1741, 1742, and 1743).
4. Lahontan, *op. cit.*, p. 5.
5. Pellegrin, *op. cit.*, p. 5.
6. *Aventures du Sr C Lebeau, op. cit.*, p. 47.
7. France, AN, Marine, 4JJ, 11-6, log-book of the *François*, 1716.
8. In 1756, Parscau DuPlessis, the vessel's ensign, disembarked to hunt hare on Bic Island, but came back empty-handed. The hare that were normally so plentiful on the island had been completely eliminated the year before by the crews of the many vessels that moored nearby. L.G. Parscau DuPlessis, "Journal d'une campagne au Canada à bord de la Sauvage", *RAPQ*, 1928-9, p. 216.
9. Clément Pagès, "Relation d'un voyage de Paris en Canada", *RAPQ*, 1947-1948, p. 26.
10. *Aventures du Sr C Lebeau, op. cit.*, p. 49; Comte de Quinsonas, *Monseigneur de Laubérivière* (Paris: 1936), p. 91.
11. France, AN, Colonies, C11A, 44:72-74, ordinance issued by Vaudreuil and Begon, Quebec City, 20 October 1721.
12. L.G. Parscau DuPlessis, *op. cit.*, p. 217.
13. France, AN, Colonies, C11A, 7:55-56v, Denonville to the minister, Quebec City, 20 August 1685. Information on the exploration of the St. Lawrence River and the gulf between 1727 and 1740 was obtained primarily from France, AN, Colonies, C11A, 49:435-437; 54:174-176v; 58:58v; 59:151v-154v; 63:119-121v; 65:15-16; 69:201-202; 72:71-71v; and 75:73.
14. France, AN, Marine, 4JJ, 12-31.
15. France, AN, Colonies, C11A, 2:153v, Talon to the minister, Quebec City, October 1665.
16. France, AN, Colonies, C11A, 98:441-444v, document discussing lands bordering the St. Lawrence, 1752. Pellegrin, *op. cit.* Pilots could also consult a report written by Sieur Deshaies in 1739. Jacques Mathieu used this report extensively to describe river navigation in his study of trade between New France and the Caribbean, because it gives a good overview of the knowledge of the St. Lawrence acquired to that point. J. Mathieu, *op. cit.*, pp. 80-82.
17. Jean-Claude Hébert, ed., *Le siège de Québec en 1759 par trois témoins* (Quebec City: 1972), p. 66.
18. France, AN, Colonies, C11A, 104:03-04, Vandreuil and Bigot to the minister, Quebec City, 22 October 1759.
19. France, AN, Marine, 4JJ, 11-7.

20. Casgrain, *op. cit.*, 6:51.
21. France, AN, Marine, 4JJ, 11-6, log-book of the *François*, 1716.
22. A list of these shipwrecks does not fall within the scope of this study, and at this stage in my research my list would be incomplete. Nevertheless, it is apparent that most shipwrecks at the entrance to the river resulted from storms, whereas the closer the wrecks occurred to Quebec City, the more likely they were caused by human error.
23. France, AN, Marine, 4JJ, 11-19, log-book of the *Rubis*, 1732.

Chapter Three:
The People and their Occupations

The crew
1. France, AN, Marine, 4JJ, 9-64, log-book of the *Triton*, 1751.
2. The data in table 11 applies almost exclusively to eighteenth-century vessels and were drawn mainly from the following documents: France, AN, Marine, 4JJ, 7 to 13; Marine, (G49); and Rochefort, AM, 6P22, and 13P8; United States, Cornell University Library, Maurepas papers; London, PRO, HCA 32, bundles 94 to 254; and *RAPQ*, 1923-1924 and 1931-1932. For information regarding the crews sailing between New France and the Carribean, see J. Mathieu, *Le commerce entre la France et les Antilles*, pp. 94-101.
3. They are the *Machault* and the *Maréchal de Senneterre*, vessels built in Bayonne and bought by Joseph Cadet in 1758. France, AM, Rochefort, 13P8, 26:72-73; 112:20.
4. France, Bibliothèque du Service Historique de la Marine, manuscript 118.
5. "Papiers de la Pause", *RAPQ*, 1931-1932, p. 4.
6. The source for all the crew lists studied is London, PRO, HCA 32, bundles 94-254. The Archives nationales de France, Marine, C6, contain the crew lists for the King's vessels in the eighteenth century. The crew lists for the fishing boats from St. Malo are in the Archives maritimes de Brest.
7. *Code des Armées Navales*, 3: 121.
8. France, AN, Colonies, B, 108:209, the minister to Rostan, Versailles, 10 April 1758.
9. France, AN, Colonies, C11A, 36:57, Vaudreuil to the minister, Quebec City, 19 July 1716; and France, AN, Colonies, C11A, 45:223v, Bégon to the minister, Quebec City, 14 October 1723.
10. France, AN, Colonies, C11A, 42:88-88v. Ordinance of 26 October 1720. When necessary, captains of the King's vessels could also requisition seamen from merchant vessels to carry out such tasks as the filling of hogsheads with fresh water.
11. The figures for the ages and wages of sailors on merchant vessels are drawn from crew lists examined in London, PRO, HCA 32, bundles 94-254. Information on wages paid to crews of king's vessels is drawn from France, AN, Marine, G, 138, piece 3.
12. *Ordonnance de la Marine de 1681*, p. 217.
13. London, PRO, HCA 32, Bundle 184. The monthly salaries of the captain (L. Houin), the first mate and the lieutenant were 150, 80 and 45 livres respectively. The surgeon's salary was not indicated. Captains of king's vessels were sometimes given permission to carry goods for private sale. The captain of the *Rubis* had such goods on board in 1741, as did the captain of the *Chariot Royal* in 1757. France, AN, Colonies, C11A, 76:05 and London, PRO, HCA 32, bundle 178. However, these vessels were not fitted out for fighting, and the income from the sale of private goods was used to improve the quality of the food at the captain's table. It was probably a question of prestige.
14. All crew lists examined indicated this advance payment. The *Ordonnance de la Marine de 1681*, pp. 225-228 and the *Code des Armées Navales*, pp. 145-152 provide the regulations on wages.
15. Gilles Proulx, "Soldat à Québec", 1748-1759, manuscript report no. 242 (Ottawa: Parks Canada, 1977), pp. 97-101.
16. London, PRO, HCA 32, bundle 234. Bill of lading for the *Port-au-Prince*. The prices were those in France. In peacetime, prices in Canada were generally two times higher because of the shipping and insurance costs. Jacques Mathieu, *Le commerce entre la Nouvelle-France et les Antilles au XVIIIe siècle* (Fides: 1981), p. 189. In 1757, Canadian prices were at least five times higher than those in France. Canada, PAC, MG5, B2, vol 11, pp. 85-86. Prices of goods in Canada.
17. France, AN, Colonies, F2B, 2:159-160, La Rochelle chamber of commerce, 18 April 1757.
18. L.A. Lahontan, *op. cit.*, 1:6; L.U. Fontaine, *Voyage du Sieur de Diéréville en Acadie* (Quebec: 1885), pp. 15-16.

19. Chabert de Cogolin, *op. cit.*, p. 36.
20. Quebec, AN, NF 25, bundle 1206. Duchesny was testifying at the proceedings regarding the slaying of the sailor Pierre Guillebert, Quebec City, 24 October 1739. In another case, a ship's captain claimed that he lacked his adversaries' moderation and politeness because living with his seamen had made him more rustic (NF 25, bundle 1295). A. Araby vs. Havy and Lefebvre, Quebec City, 21 November 1742.
21. France, AN, Colonies, C11A, vol. 69:47-50, Beauharnois and Hocquart to the minister, Quebec City, 6 October 1738.
22. Canada, PAC, MG6, B17, series B40, Bayonne chamber of commerce.
23. The presence of mind of Vaudreuil in 1729 (France, AN, Colonies, C11A, 51:398), the strength of character of l'Etenduère (C11A, 81:427-432v), and the daring of Voutron (C11A, 98:18-19) were admired. They all commanded king's vessels. Captains of merchant vessels, however, were not forgotten. "This navigator of 55 to 60 years has the reputation of being a wise and able man, a sea dog, if you'll pardon the expression", wrote Hocquart with regard to a certain Harismendy, a Basque captain. (C11A, 80:157-164).
24. London, PRO, HCA 32, bundle 256. *The Dictionnaire biographique du Canada* (Quebec City: 1974) contains a biography of Poulin de Courval. It should be noted that he remained in the merchant marine until at least 1760. In the early years of the Seven Years' War, he commanded merchant ships chartered by the king.

The passengers
1. The passengers' reasons for travelling are found mainly in this series of letters: France, AN, Colonies, C11A.
2. France, AN, Colonies, C11E, 11:41, Varin to the minister. Quebec City, 1 September 1749. In a chapter devoted to French emigration to Canada, Jean Hamelin estimated that 1,130 persons with a trade came to Canada between 1630 and 1760. They were volunteers. Jean Hamelin, *Economie et Société en Nouvelle France*, (Quebec City), pp. 75-100.
3. Quebec, AN, NF 25, bundle 1707; France, AN, Colonies, B, 104:420, Versailles, 13 December 1756; Charles Bréard, *Journal du corsaire Jean Doublet* (Paris: 1887), p. 28; Canada, PAC, MG2, B4, 43:137, voyage of the *Héros*.
4. France, AN, Colonies, C11A, 48:68, Dupuy to the minister, Quebec City, 20 October 1726.
5. Hamelin, *op. cit.*, p. 78.
6. France, AN, Colonies, B, 108:363, the minister to Rostan at Versailles, 30 October 1758.
7. The source of my information is France, AN, Colonies, C11A, vols. 5:53, 54, 58, 59, 60, 63, 64, 66, 67, 68, 70, 71, and 72.
8. France, AN, Marine, 4JJ, 8-51, log-book of the *Jason*, 1738; Joseph Dargent, *op. cit.*, p. 13.
9. France, AM, Rochefort, 10, vol. 78. Those in question were Nicolas Goulet and Antoine Hallé in 1730, and André Lagorre in 1733. The prisoners were Antoine Coiffier, Joseph Bertet and Jacques, a Pawnee Indian.
10. Gilles Proulx, *Soldat à Québec*, pp. 7-10.
11. France, AN, Colonies, B, 104:469-470, the minister to de Ruis, Versailles, 13 January 1756.
12. France, AD, Gironde, 6B, 52:36-110.
13. Hamelin, *op. cit.*, p. 77.
14. France, AD, Gironde, 6B, 52:38-40; 101:133, 1755.
15. France, AN, Colonies, B, 102:202v, the minister to de Ruis, Versailles, 22 March 1755.
16. "Journal de Bougainville", *RAPQ*, 1923-1924, p. 382.
17. Claude Martin, *La vie de la Vénérable Mère Marie de l'Incarnation* (Paris: 1677), p. 394. Similarly, Intendant Jean Talon did everything in his power to prevent the "demoiselles" who arrived in Canada in 1667 from writing to France to complain about the poor treatment they received during the crossing. These negative comments might have prompted women planning to emigrate to change their minds. *RAPQ*, 1930-1, p. 86. Jean Talon, Quebec City, 27 October 1667.
18. France, AN, Colonies, B, 104:469-470. The idea was somewhat unrealistic, since it is difficult to resist very long with rifles against sailing ships that were generally well armed with cannons.
19. Fontaine, *op. cit.*, p. 7.
20. Charlevoix, *op. cit.*, p. 69.
21. France, AN, Colonies, C11A, 80:157-164, Hocquart to the minister, Quebec City, 25 October 1743.
22. Dargent, *op. cit.*, p. 13. Duquesnel seems to have been an unpleasant character. This description of him was written in 1745, after his death: "He was a poor bloke to whom we felt very little

allegiance. He was a temperamental and unpredictable man who was prone to drink, and who demonstrated neither moderation nor manners in taking wine. He shocked nearly all the officers at Louisbourg and compromised them in the eyes of their soldiers." *Lettre d'un Habitant de Louisbourg*, edited by G.M. Wrong (Toronto: 1897), pp. 15-16.
23. Rev. Father Nau to Rev. Father Richard, Quebec City, 20 October 1734, *RAPQ*, 1926-1927, p. 267.
24. France, AN, Colonies, C11A, 55:213v-214, Hocquart to the minister, Quebec City, 15 October 1731.
25. Sulte, *op. cit.*, p. 22.

Crew members' duties
1. Quebec, AN, NF 25, bundle 4071. Pierre Hévé took legal action in April 1755.
2. London, PRO, HCA 32, bundle 132. Papers seized from the *Marguerite*, one of the ships in the Duc D'Anville squadron. Appendix F relates a quarrel between a ship's captain and an officer from a man-of-war, as recalled by the captain. This argument gives some indication of the conflicts that frequently arose between the royal navy and the merchant marine, and of the social backgrounds of officers in the two fleets. Some nobles did work in the merchant marine. The reader can easily imagine the reception given officers of the merchant marine in some cases when they joined the king's service.
3. These data on books belonging to ships' captains are from my study entitled *Les bibliothèques de Louisbourg*, manuscript report no. 271 (Ottawa: Parks Canada, 1974). Although my sample group is quite small because I was able to consult only three lists of captains' belongings, books were mentioned in all three cases. These figures must be considered in the context of colonial Louisbourg: in the 85 post-mortem inventories that I studied, only 25 indicated books; there were some 120 titles and 640 books. The three captains owned around 30 books. Appendix I gives the list of the volumes from the inventory of Captain Louis François Merven de la Rivière. The ten or so inventories of sailors' belongings that I examined in Quebec City and Louisbourg indicate only three or four religious books in all.
4. France, AM, Rochefort, 1R, vol. 46, Career of Jacques Chaviteau.
5. France, AM, Rochefort, 1E, 162:503. A master carpenter drowned after diving to inspect the hull of a ship in the port of Louisbourg.
6. London, PRO, HCA 32, bundle 234. Instructions from the outfitter to the captain of the *Pénélope*, La Rochelle, 10 June 1757: "be sure to carry lumber to have your coopers make enough barrels during the crossing for the transfer in Santo Domingo".
7. Lescallier, *op. cit.*, p. 289.
8. France, AN, Colonies, C11A, 30:40-40v, Vaudreuil to the minister, Quebec City, 1 October 1709; F3, 15:272-272v. Vaudreuil to the minister, Quebec City, 5 October 1709. Moreover, the authorities indicated that the seamen were much more familiar with artillery than were the Canadians.

Chapter Four:
Life Aboard Ship

Routine and sleeping quarters
1. *Aventures du Sr. C. Lebeau*, p. 14.
2. London, PRO, HCA 32, bundle 97-5, log-book of the *Atalante*, 1740.
3. *Code des Armées navales*, p. 213. "The King's vessel the *Téméraire* passed nearby and the crew shouted that it was taking on thirty-six inches of water per watch; in other words, every four hours." This is excerpted from the log of the *Aimable, en route* for Newfoundland in 1692. France, AN, Marine, 4JJ 7, bundle 4. Watches were not necessarily of a standard length, as this excerpt from Appendix D seems to indicate: "I verified with a good watch that our timer gained 8 minutes over 24 hours." Hourglasses were at the mercy of the seamen, who sometimes turned them over before the sand had run through completely!
4. France, AD, Vendée, memoirs of André Collinet, history of Les Sables d'Olonnes narrated by a local shipowner, pt. 8.
5. London, PRO, HCA 32, bundle 97-2, log-book of the *Argonaute*, 1742-1744.
6. *Aventures du Sr. C. Lebeau*, p. 25.
7. Canada, PAC, MG6, A5, Nantes chamber of commerce, vol. 744.

8. Quebec, AN, NF 25, bundle 768, sale of the brigantine *Madeleine*, 27 August 1727. *Code des Armées Navales*, pp. 28-29.
9. Gabriel Gravier, ed. *Relation d'un voyage à la Nouvelle-Orléans à bord du vaisseau la Gironde de la Compagnie des Indes* (Paris: 1872).
10. Rev. Father Nau to Rev. Father Richard, Quebec City, 20 October 1734, *RAPQ*, 1926-1927, p. 267.
11. France, AN, Colonies, C11A, 7:31-32v, Denonville to the minister, La Rochelle, 25 May 1685.
12. France, AN, Marine, 4JJ, 11-7.
13. *Ordonnance de la Marine de 1681*, p. 131.
14. Quebec, AN, NF 25, bundle 1478, Bernard Paris, captain of the *Saint-Ursin*, Quebec City, 2 August 1747.
15. *Code des Armées navales*, p. 252.
16. Quebec City, AN, NF 25, bundles 13, 14, 15, 480, 553$^{1}/_{2}$, 1808, 1844, and 1871. In the words of Robert Challes, "It is true that these inventories are not long; indeed, a sailor can consider himself well-off if, on his return from an ocean voyage, he has two shirts to his name: one on his back and the other on the shrouds or in tow." A. Augustin-Thierry, *Voyage aux Indes d'une escadre française (1690-1691) par Robert Challes* (Paris: Plon, 1933), p. 232.
17. France, AN, Colonies, C11A, 12:110-111, D'Iberville to the minister, Saint-Martin, 16 December 1692.
18. France, AN, Marine, G, 138:14.
19. *Code des Armées Navales*, pp. 66, 165 and 241.
20. "Journal de Bougainville", *RAPQ*, 1923-1924, p. 385.

Diet

1. Food and Agriculture Organization, *Calorie Requirements*, Report of the Second Committee on Calorie Requirements of the United Nations Food and Agriculture Organization (Rome: 1957), pp. 10-11.
2. London, PRO, HCA 32, bundle 198, instruction to Sieur Le Tourneur purser's clerk, 1757. In calculating the number of calories yielded by the various ration components, I relied on the studies of Charlotte Chatfield, *Table de composition des aliments* (Rome: 1954); and M. Cépède and M. Lengelle, *Economie alimentaire du globe* (Paris: 1953).
3. *Code des Armées Navales*, p. 58.
4. Quebec, AN, NF 25, bundle 481$^{1}/_{2}$. The flour was that salvaged from a shipwreck in 1710.
5. France, AD, Gironde, C, vol. 4392, memoir on the manufacture of biscuits for sea voyages.
6. London, PRO, HCA 32, bundle 144-1, papers seized from the *Pénélope*, 1746.
7. France, AM, Rochefort, 6E2, observations on the storage of provisions, 1749.
8. France, AN, Colonies, B, 108:363, the minister to Rostan, Versailles, 30 October 1758.
9. France, AM, Rochefort, 6E2, observations on the storage of provisions, 1749; and London, PRO, HCA 32, bundle 179-1, list of provisions laid in aboard the *Catherine* at Louisbourg in 1757.
10. Rev. Father J.P. Aulneau to his mother, Quebec City, 10 October 1734, *RAPQ*, 1926-1927, p. 261.
11. France, AM, Rochefort, 6E2, note on provisions aboard the *Héros*, 20 May 1730. When a ship called into port, food was prepared on shore rather than on the vessel. This eliminated the need to make a fire on board, and it was probably more practical to purchase food on land. Quebec, AN, NF 25, bundle 651.
12. Louis Crespel, *Voyages du RPE Crespel dans le Canada et son naufrage en revenant en France* reprinted by A. Côté (Quebec City: 1884), p. 34.
13. Fontaine, *op. cit.*, p. 12.
14. For additional details on the vitamin content of the sailor's rations and an interpretation of its effects, refer to Charlotte Chatfield, *op. cit.*, and Jean Boudriot, *Le vaisseau de 74 canons* (Grenoble: 1977), 4:179-181.
15. Numerous examples are to be found in London, PRO, HCA 32, bundles 132 (the *Marguerite*), 179 (the *Catherine*), 191 (the *Fils Unique*) and 201 (the *Jolie Galère*).
16. London, PRO, HCA 32, bundle 219, Capture of the *Mercure*, 17 March 1758.
17. France, AM, Rochefort, 6E2, provisions of the *Héros* in 1730.
18. P.G. Roy, *Inventaire des Ordonnances des Intendants de la Nouvelle-France* (Beauceville: 1919), 3:191-192, ordinance of 12 June 1755.

19. France, AN, Colonies, B, 104:195-197, memoir from the king to the Chevalier de Bellinguant, Versailles, 26 March 1756.
20. France, AN, Colonies, C11A, 105:139. Vaudreuil to the minister, Quebec City, October 1760. An article published by historian Léon Vignols on meat from Ireland imported to France and re-exported to the colonies gives reason to believe that the quality of food supplies on the vessels was often less than first-rate. Léon Vignols, "L'importation en France au 18e siècle de boeuf salé d'Irlande" *Revue historique*, 49, (1928), p. 87.
21. London, PRO. HCA 32, bundle 198. Papers from the *Hermione*, captured on 22 November 1757.
22. At least, this is the opinion of the writer Diéréville; L.U. Fontaine, *op. cit.*, p. 230.
23. Alain Gheerhant, *Voyages du père Labat aux Iles de l'Amérique* (Club des Libraires de France), pp. 23-24.
24. France, AN, Colonies, F2B, 2:110-111, food and utensils brought aboard the *Topaze*, 1756.
25. Fontaine, *op. cit.*, p. 21.
26. Richard Lick, "Les intérieurs domestiques dans la seconde moitié du XVIIIe siècle d'après les inventaires après décès de Coutances", *Annales de Normandie* 20(4), (December 1970).
27. Gheerhant, *op. cit.*, p. 23.

Illness and medical treatment
1. Montcalm to the Marquise de Montcalm at Montpellier, Quebec City, 11 May 1756, *Report of the Public Archives*, 1929, pp. 39-40; and France, AN, Marine, 4JJ, 7-4, log-book of the *Aimable*, 1692.
2. France, AN, Marine, 4JJ, 11-3, log-book of the *Arc-en-ciel*, 1687-1688.
3. Augustin-Thierry, *op. cit.*, p. 181.
4. Boudriot, *op. cit.*, 4:181. Scurvy is described very well by the author.
5. France, AN, Marine, 4JJ, 7-4, log-book of the *Aimable*, 1692.
6. France, AN, Colonies, C11A, 15:132, Champigny to the minister, Quebec City, 13 October 1697.
7. France, AN, Colonies, C11A, 101:39-40v, Vaudreuil to the minister, 26 June 1756.
8. Boudriot, *op. cit.*, 4:156.
9. France, AN, Colonies, C11A, 46:117-122v, Vaudreuil to the minister, Quebec City, 29 October 1724; and C11A, 73:05-08, record of deaths and cases of illness aboard the *Rubis*, 1740.
10. France, AN, Colonies, C11A, 40:52, Vaudreuil to the minister, Quebec City, 26 October 1719.
11. France, AN, Marine, 4JJ, 12-27, log-book of the *Jason*, 1737.
12. France, AN, Marine, 4JJ, 12-34, log-book of the *Rubis*, 1741.
13. Father Nau to Father Richard, Quebec City, 20 October, 1734, *RAPQ*, 1926-27, p. 267.
14. Augustin-Thierry, *op. cit.*, p. 204.
15. Parscau DuPlessis, *op. cit.*, p. 217. In defence of the officers of the *Léopard*, metropolitan authorities ordered the destruction of the vessel when it arrived in Quebec City because of its poor condition. This was no doubt partly responsible for the officers' attitude. France, AN, Colonies, B, 103:141, the minister to Bigot, 15 March, 1756.
16. France, AN, Marine, 4JJ, 8-59, log-book of the *Mars*, 1746.
17. Sulte, *op. cit.*, pp. 27-28; France, AN, Marine, 4JJ, 11-7, log-book of the *Chameau*, 1720.
18. France, AN, Colonies, B, 107:242-242v, the minister to Bart and De Lalanne, 15 November 1758.
19. Quebec, Archives of the Monastère de l'Hôtel-Dieu de Quebec. The information in table 15 is drawn from hospital records from 1755 to 1759.
20. "Lettres de Doreil", *RAPQ*, 1944-45, pp. 81 and 113; and France, AN, Marine, 4JJ, 13-46, log-book of the *Actif*, 1755.
21. France, AN, Colonies, B, 107:367, the minister to Drucourt and Prevost, Versailles, 18 February 1758; and Vincent Brun, *Guerres maritimes de France, Port de Toulon* (Paris: 1861), 1:394. In a recent article on scurvy, the author stated that the decisive factor in the loss of Canada was the devastation of the squadron of Dubois de la Mothe in 1757 due to a typhus epidemic that killed 10,000 seamen and thus destroyed the French naval forces in the Atlantic. Marie-Martine Acerra, "Le scorbut: la peste du marin" *L'Histoire* No. 36 (July-August 1981), pp. 74-75. Although illness did not help the Canadian cause, the French policy of not defending the maritime routes was much more crucial. The political strategy preceded the epidemic of 1757-58.
22. France, AN, Colonies, C11A, 7:62v, Denonville to the minister, Quebec City, 20 August 1685.
23. Comte de Quinsonas, *op. cit.*, p. 91. Father Paris was aboard the *Rubis* in 1740. Canada, PAC, MG2, B4, 91:68, voyage of the *Aigle*, 1758.
24. Canada, PAC, MG2, B4, 43:114-117.

25. Augustin-Thierry, *op. cit.*, pp. 49-50.
26. Louis Auguste Rossel, "Journal de ma campagne à l'Île Royale (1757)", *RAPQ*, 1931-1932, p. 376.
27. Sylvio Leblond et al. *Trois siècles de médecine québécoise* cahier d'Histoire, no. 22 (Société historique de Québec, 1970), p. 24.
28. Quebec AN, NF 25, bundle 1358, proceedings against Jean Lacoste, 1744.
29. France, ACM, Series B, vol. 6040. File on Pierre Capdeville. This document lists the detailed contents of the chest of a surgeon who came to Quebec City and Isle Royale in 1733.
30. France, AN, Colonies, C11A, 49:381-388, Dupuy to the minister, Quebec City, 15 October 1727.
31. Augustin-Thierry, *op. cit.*, p. 233.

Religious practice
1. *Ordonnance de la Marine de 1681*, p. 150.
2. Quebec, AN, NF 25, bundle 606$^{1}/_{2}$. Louisbourg, 10 October, 1707. Fitted out by E. Dulong, the *Marie Anne* was leaving for Quebec City.
3. Quebec, AN, NF 25, bundle 1807. Quebec City, 24 June 1753. The *Renommée* was on its way from Bordeaux to Quebec City when the storm hit.
4. France, AN, Colonies, C11A, 87:314-362. In 1746, Beaujeu was on his way to Acadia with Canadian volunteers. They would participate in the activities of the Duc d'Anville.
5. Sulte, *op. cit.*, pp. 31-32. Abbé Navières wrote that the church of Sainte-Anne was huge and that it was decorated with paintings donated to fulfill vows made when various vessels were in peril during the crossing to Canada.
6. Canada, PAC, MG 18, J14, "Relation d'un voyage intéressant au Canada".
7. France, AN, Marine, 4JJ, 12-36, log-book of the *Canada*, 1742.
8. Casgrain, *op. cit.*, 6:42.
9. "Le Journal de Monsieur de Bougainville", *RAPQ*, 1923-1924, p. 384.
10. Augustin-Thierry, *op. cit.*, pp. 52-59.
11. "Naufrage de l'*Eléphant*", *Nova Francia* (1930), p. 384.
12. France, AN, Marine, 4JJ, 7-19, log-book of the frigate *Paon*, 1722.
13. France, AN, Marine, 4JJ, 7-17, log-book of the *Portefaix*, 1721.
14. France, AN, Marine, G 137:5, discussion on naval discipline.
15. For more details on bishops crossing to New France see Mgr. de Saint-Vallier, *Etat présent de l'Eglise canadienne*; Naufrage de l'*Eléphant*", *Nova Francia*, (1930), Comte de Quinsonas, *op. cit.*, and Clement Pagès, "Relation d'un voyage de Paris en Canada", *RAPQ*, 1947-1948, pp. 20-28.
16. "Naufrage de l'*Eléphant*", *Nova Francia*, (1930), pp. 377-378. "But we had the consolation of seeing them do, in front of soldiers, sailors, all manner of blackguards, of their own free will, with no concern for what the rest might think and without being subjected to scorn, what among decent men is done furtively and in secret."
17. Crespel, *op. cit.*, pp. 80-81.

Insubordination and discipline
1. London, PRO, HCA 32, Bundle 199, crew list of the *Hasard*, 1757.
2. London, PRO, HCA 32, bundle 97-4, crew list of the *Atalante*, 1744.
3. France, AN, Colonies, B, 108:426, the minister to Rostan, Versailles, 22 October 1758.
4. France, AN, Marine, 4JJ, 9-64, log-book of the *Triton*, 1751. In 1685, Isaac Salomon, a sailor aboard the *Aigle Noir*, jumped ship because of his captain's brutality. The captain "takes pleasure in doing so, because he knows a sailor would not dare take revenge for fear of grave punishment, and that is why the said Pruneau enjoys beating sailors excessively merely for the sport of it". Quebec City, AN, NF 25, bundle 172, trial of Isaac Salomon, 15 October 1685.
5. *Ordonnance de la marine de 1681*, pp. 172-173.
6. *Code des Armées Navales*, p. 159.
7. *Ibid.*, p. 242.
8. Fontaine, *op. cit.*, p. 16.
9. France, ACM, series B, vol. 5748. Quebec City, 9 November 1758. Incident aboard the *Prince de Condé* on 17 July 1758 between seaman R. Augard, on the one hand, and Captain Bigrel and first mate Collinet, on the other.

10. France, AN, Colonies, C11A, 54:323-326, Hocquart to the minister, Quebec City, 11 November 1731.
11. Quebec, AN, NF 25, bundle 1810. Average of the *Saint-Antoine*, Quebec City, 13 September 1755.
12. Quebec, AN, NF 25, bundle 586, trial of Pierre Faucher, Quebec City, October 1718; 656, trial of Michel Duzant, Quebec City, July 1723; 1206, trial of J.F. Duchesny, Quebec City, October 1739.
13. Augustin-Thierry, *op. cit.*, p. 119.
14. *Ordonnance de la marine de 1681*, pp. 172-173; *code des Armées navales*, pp. 66, 237, and 242. Father Labat described running the gauntlet as follows: "One end of a rope was tied to the forecastle and the other to the poop. The soldier was stripped of his jerkin and tied around the waist to a metal ring that ran along the rope. All the crew members stationed themselves along both sides of the rope with gaskets; these are small, flat, braided ropes used in furling the sails. He had to run the length of the vessel seven times while the others hit him with gaskets. After three lengths, we asked for mercy for the man, and our captain consented." Alain Gheerhant, *op. cit.*, p. 29.

Recreation
1. L.A. Lahontan, *op. cit.*, 1:30.
2. Gilles Proulx, "Aubergistes et Cabaretiers de Louisbourg, 1713-1758", Manuscript report no. 136 (Ottawa: Parks Canada, 1972), pp. 9-10.
3. Quebec, AN, NF 25, bundle 1206, trial of J.F. Duchêny, Quebec City, October 1739.
4. Lahontan, *op. cit.*, 1:5. Most passengers who kept a diary of their trans-Atlantic crossing described this ceremony in detail.
5. Joseph Dargent, *op. cit.*, p. 14. Irene Frain Le Pohon, "Les superstitions des gens de mer", *L'Histoire*, 36 (July-August 1981), pp. 55-56. Some authors feel that the primary purpose of baptism was to dispel fear. In my opinion, the financial benefits to the seamen must also be taken into account.
6. Charlevoix, *op. cit.*, p. 61.
7. France, AN, Colonies, C11A, 52:42-49v. Account of the Quebec City festivities in September-October 1730 to celebrate the birth of the Dauphin.
8. John Clarence Webster, ed. *Relation of the voyage to Port Royal in Acadia or New France by the Sieur de Diéréville* (Toronto: 1933), p. 308.
9. Parscau DuPlessis, *op. cit.*, p. 214.
10. Fontaine, *op. cit.*, p. 6.
11. Casgrain, *op. cit.*, 6:38.
12. France, AN, Marine, G, 138:14.

Conclusion
1. France, AN, Marine, 4JJ, 11-6, log-book of the *François*, 1716.

Appendix A
1. The information in this appendix is taken from the document series France, AN, Colonies, series B, 35 to 112 and Marine, series 4 JJ, cartons 7 to 13, bundles 2 to 76; and from J. Vichot, *Répertoire des navires de guerre français* [catalogue of French warships], for the places and dates of construction.

Appendix B
1. *Ibid.*; France, AN, Marine, G 49; AM, Rochefort, 2G1 and 2G2; London, PRO, HCA 32, bundles 167, 168, 178; Parscau DuPlessis's journal, *RAPQ*, 1928-1929; the La Pause papers, *RAPQ*, 1931-1932; and the Doreil letters, *RAPQ*, 1944-1945.

Appendix C
1. Greenwich, National Maritime Museum, ADM, B, vol. 164. Dimensions in this survey are in English feet. Papers seized on board the *Chézine* indicate that she was a 450-ton ship fitted with 24 guns and that the captain at the time of capture in 1760 was Pierre Nicolas Duclos. London, PRO, HCA 32, bundle 175. The *Chézine* came to Quebec City in 1759; it was one of the ships fitted out in Bordeaux by Pierre Desclaux to go to the rescue of New France. According to the records

of departures of ships from Bordeaux in 1759, the *Chézine* was of 420 tons burden and carried 22 guns. J. de Maupassant, *Les deux expéditions de Pierre-Desclaux* (Bordeaux: 1915), p. 12.

Appendix D
1. Canada, PAC, MG2, B4, 38:249-259. Excerpt from the ship's log kept by Sieur de Radouays, first mate on the *Eclatant*, which sailed over the Grand Banks in 1722.

Appendix E
1. France, AN, Marine, 4JJ, 12-37. This describes an encounter between the *Rubis* and three English ships while she was sailing to Quebec City in 1743. French merchant ships could not have much freedom or security on the seas if king's vessels had to endure confrontations such as this with the English.

Appendix F
1. London, PRO, HCA 32, bundle 132. This tells of an incident that took place on board the schooner *Marguerite* which belonged to Leneuf de Beaubassin from Louisbourg. The schooner had been fitted out by the king and was being used as a storeship in the Duc d'Anville squadron in 1746. Pierre Robin was captain.

Appendix G
1. France, AN, Marine, 4JJ, 7-29. This is an excerpt from the log-book of the frigate *Néréide*. Upon the command of De Chaon, she hit rocks upon entering the Louisbourg harbour in 1726. The careening work described in this excerpt gives some idea of the type of operation that could be required to refit a vessel.

Appendix H
1. Quebec, AN, NF 25, bundle, 1706. This document filed with the provost marshall's office in Quebec City shows the difficulties – ice, fog, gales – facing ships crossing the North Atlantic.

Appendix I
1. Information from France, AN, Outremer, G1, vol. 407, G2, vol. 199, file 192: ACM, B, vol. 274.

Appendix J
1. Quebec, AN, NF 25, bundle 1808.

Appendix K
1. London, PRO, HCA 32, bundle 238-2. Excerpts from documents seized aboard the *Renommée* in 1757.

Appendix L
1. London, PRO, HCA 32, bundle 242. This is an excerpt from the documents seized on the *Surprise*, a merchant ship out of La Rochelle that was captured on its way to Louisbourg from Rochefort in 1757. The song was likely a favourite of some of the seamen.

Bibliography

Acerra, Marie-Martine. "Le scorbut; la peste du marin". *L'Histoire* 36, Paris: Le Seuil/La Recherche, July-August 1981.
Aman, Jacques. *Les officiers bleus dans la marine française au XVIIIe siècle*. Genève: Droz, 1976.
Asselin, J.P. "L'ex-voto de Monsieur Roger". *Revue de Sainte-Anne de Beaupré* 56:10. October 1958.
Augustin-Thierry, A. *Voyage aux Indes d'une escadre française (1690-1691)* by Robert Challes. Paris: Plon, 1933.
Aventures du Sr. C. Lebeau ou Voyage curieux et nouveau parmi les sauvages de l'Amerique Septentrionale. New York: Johnson Reprint Corporation, 1966.
Bellin, Jacques-Nicolas. *Petit Atlas Maritime*: vol. 5: *l'Amérique septentrionale*. Paris: 1764.
Boudriot, Jean. *Le vaisseau de 74 canons*. 4 vols. Grenoble: Edition des Quatre Seigneurs, 1973-1977.
———. "Les vaisseaux de la Compagnie des Indes". *Le Petit Perroquet* 12. Grenoble: Edition des Quatre Seigneurs, 1973-1974.
———. "Des vaisseaux de 64 canons en général et de l'*Artésien* en particulier". *Neptunia* 142. Paris: Association des Amis des Musées de la Marine, June 1981.
Bouguer, Pierre. *Traité du navire de sa construction et de ses mouvements*. Paris: Jombert, 1746.
Braudel, Fernand. *Civilisation matérielle et capitalisme*. Paris: A. Colin, 1967.
Bréard, Charles. *Journal du corsaire Jean Doublet*. Paris: Perrin, 1887.
Brière, Jean-François. "Le trafic terre-neuvier malouin dans la première moitié du XVIIIe siècle, 1713-1755". *Histoire Sociale* 2:22. Ottawa: Université d'Ottawa, November 1978.
Brun, Vincent. *Guerres maritimes de la France, Port de Toulon*. Paris: H. Plon, 1861.
Butel, Paul. *Les négociants bordelais l'Europe et les Iles au XVIIIe siècle*. Paris: Aubier, 1974.
Canada. Public Archives. Map Collection: A1-3000 (1734), HJ-10000 (1680), H3-900 (1744).
    Prints: Vue de Québec (1761).
    MG1, F2B, vol. 2.
    MG2, B4, vols. 7-98, voyages, 1676-1760.
    MG6, A5, series C, bundle 774, Nantes Chamber of Commerce
    MG6, B17, series B40, Bayonne Chamber of Commerce
    MG18, J14, Relation d'un voyage intéressant au Canada.
Casgrain, H.R. *Collection des manuscrits du Maréchal de Lévis*. 12 vols. Québec: J.L. Demers, 1889-1895.
Cavignac, Jean. *Jean Pellet commerçant de gros, 1694-1772*. Paris: S.E.V.P.E.N., 1967.
Champlain, S. de. *Oeuvres de Champlain*. Vol. 3. Montréal: réédition Elysée, 1976.
Chapman, F.H. *Architectura Navalis Mercatoria*. London: Adlard Coles, 1979.
Charlevoix, F.X. *Histoire de la Nouvelle-France*. Vol. 3. Montréal: réédition Elysée, 1976.
Chatfield, Charlotte. *Table de composition des aliments*. Rome: F.A.O., 1954.
Cepède, M. and Lengellé, M. *Economie alimentaire du globe*. Paris: Génin, 1953.
Cogolin, Chabert de. *Voyage fait par ordre du Roi en 1750 et 1751 dans l'Amérique septentrionale*. New York: Johnson Reprint Corporation, 1966.
Cotter, Charles H. *A History of Nautical Astronomy*. London: Hollis & Carter, 1968.
Crespel, Louis. *Voyages du R.P.E. Crespel dans le Canada et son naufrage en revenant en France*. Québec: rééditions A. Côté, 1884.
Daney, Charles. "Les cartes routières de la mer". *L'Histoire* 36, Paris: Le Seuil/La Recherche, July-August 1981.
Daumas, Maurice. *Les instruments scientifiques au XVIIe et XVIIIe siècles*. Paris: P.U.F., 1953.
———. "Precision Mechanics". *The History of Technology*. Vol. 5. Charles Singer. London: Oxford University Press, 1975.
Delumeau, Jean. *La peur en Occident*. Paris: Fayard, 1978.
Dictionnaire biographique du Canada. Vols. 3 and 4. Québec: P.U.L., 1974, 1980.

Espenshade, E. and Morrison, J. *Goode's World Atlas*. Chicago: Rand McNally, 1977.

Fontaine, L.U. *Voyage du Sieur de Diéréville en Acadie*. Québec: A. Côté, 1885.

Forfait, M. *Traité élémentaire de la mâture des vaisseaux*. Paris: rééditions des Quatre Seigneurs, 1979.

France. Archives communales.
  Bayonne, séries FF, bundle 328.

France. Archives départementales.
  Charente-Maritime, séries B, vols. 248-259, 5747, 5748, and 6040.
  Gironde, série 6B, vols. 52 and séries C, bundle 4392.
  Vendée, André Collinet memoirs.

France. Archives maritimes.
  Rochefort, series 6E2, 2G1, 2G2, 6P23, 13P8. France. Archives nationales.
  Fonds Colonies, series C^{11}A, vols. 1-126; series B, vols. 35 - 112, series C^{11}E, vol. II, series F2B, vol. 2, series F3, vol. 15; series D.F.C. bundle IV.
  Fonds Français, series V7, vol. 346; series 62AQ, vol. 44.
  Fonds Marine, series 4JJ, bundles 7-13, series G, bundles 49, 137, 138.

France. Bibiliothèque Nationale, Dépôt des cartes et plans.
  GeC 5019.

France. Bibliothèque du Service historique de la Marine, man.-
  118, 140 and 188A.

France. Paris, Musée de la marine.
  Paintings by Joseph Vernet and Nicolas Ozanne.

Frégault, Guy. *La guerre de la conquête, 1754-1760*. Montréal: Fides, 1955.

———. *François Bigot administrateur français*. 2 vols. Montréal: Etudes de l'Institut d'Histoire Française, 1948.

Furetière, Antoine de. *Le Dictionnaire universel*. Paris: Rééditions le Robert, 1978.

Gardiner, Robert. "Les frégates françaises et la Royal Navy". *Le Petit Perroquet* 24. Paris: Editions des Quatre Seigneurs, 1978.

Gheerhant, Alain. *Voyages du père Labat aux Iles de l'Amérique*. Paris: Club des Libraires de France, 1956.

Gille, Paul. "Jauge et tonnage des navires". *Le navire et l'économie maritime du XVe au XVIIIe siècle*. Paris: S.E.V.P.E.N., 1957.

Godechot, Jacques. *Histoire de l'Atlantique*. Paris: Bordas, 1947.

Great Britain. Public Record Office. High Court of Admiralty 32, bundles 94-256. Documents seized aboard French vessels during the war of Austrian Sucession and the Seven Years' War.

Great Britain. National Maritime Museum, Ships plans collection. Public visual Index. Adm. B, vols. 134-166.

Groulx, Lionel. *Histoire du Canada français*. Vol. 1. Montréal: Fides, 1960.

Gutton, Jean-Pierre. *La société et les pauvres en Europe*. Paris: P.U.F., 1974.

Hamelin, Jean. *Economie et société en Nouvelle-France*. Québec: Cahier de l'Institut d'Histoire, P.U.L., 1960.

Lahontan, L.A. *Voyages du baron Lahontan dans l'Amérique septentrionale*. Montréal: rééditions Elysée, 1975.

Leblond, Sylvio et al. *Trois siècles de médecine québécoise*. Québec: Société historique de Québec, cahier d'Histoire 22, 1970.

LePohon, Irène Frain. "Les superstitions des gens de mer". *L'Histoire* 36. Paris: Le Seuil/La Recherche, July-August 1981.

Lescallier, Daniel. *Traité pratique du gréement des vaisseaux et autres bâtiments de mer*. Grenoble: rééditions des Quatre Seigneurs, 1973.

Le siège de Québec en 1759 par trois témoins. Ed. by J.C. Hébert. Québec: Ministère des Affaires culturelles, 1972.

Lettre d'un habitant de Louisbourg. Ed. by G.M. Wrong. Toronto: Williams Briggs, 1897.

Lick, Richard. "Les intérieurs domestiques dans la seconde moitié du XVIIIe siècle d'après les inventaires après décès de Coutances". *Annales de Normandie* 20:4, December 1970.

Marguet, F. *Histoire générale de la navigation du XVe au XXe siècle*. Paris: Société d'édition géographique, maritime et coloniale, 1931.

Martin, Claude. *La vie de la vénérable Mère Marie de l'Incarnation*. Paris: chez Louis Billaine, 1677.

Mathieu, Jacques. *La construction navale royale à Québec, 1739-1759*. Québec: Société historique de Québec, cahier d'Histoire 23, 1971.

―――― . *Le commerce entre la Nouvelle-France et les Antilles au XVIIIe siècle*. Montréal: Fides, 1981.

Maupassant, Jean de. *Les deux expéditions de Pierre Desclaux au Canada*. Bordeaux: Imprimerie Gounouilhou, 1915.

Maurepas papers. Ithaca, New York: Cornell University.

McLennan, John S. *Louisbourg From Its Foundation To Its Fall*. Sydney: Fortress Press, 1969.

Merllié, Louis. "Un combat naval raconté par un missionnaire". *Neptunia* 123. Paris: Association des Amis des Musées de la Marine, 1976.

Merrien, Jean. *La vie quotidienne des marins au temps du roi soleil*. Paris: Hachette, 1964.

Morineau, Michel. *Jauge et méthodes de jauge anciennes et modernes*. Cahier des Annales 24. Paris: S.E.V.P.E.N., 1966.

"Naufrage de l'Eléphant". *Nova Francia*. Paris: Société d'Histoire du Canada, 1930.

Ordonnance de la Marine de 1681. Paris: chez Guillaume Cavelier, 1681.

Pariset, F.G. *Bordeaux au XVIIIe siècle*. Bordeaux: Société historique du Sud-Ouest, 1968.

Pritchard, J.S. "Ships, Men and Commerce: study of maritime activity in New France". Doctoral thesis. Toronto: University of Toronto, 1971.

Proulx, Gilles. *Aubergiste et Cabaretiers de Louisbourg*, 1713-1758, manuscript report, 136. Ottawa: Parks Canada, 1972.

―――― . *Soldat à Québec 1748-1759*, manuscript report, 242. Ottawa: Parks Canada, 1977.

―――― . *Tribunaux et lois de Louisbourg*, manuscript report, 303. Ottawa: Parks Canada, 1975.

―――― . *Les bibliothèques de Louisbourg*, manuscript report, 271. Ottawa: Parks Canada, 1974.

Quebec. Archives nationales. Fonds J.-C. Panet, 10 August 1758.

NF 25, Collection of legal and notarial documents, bundles 13, 14, 15, 172, 441$^1/_2$, 480, 481$^1/_2$, 484, 553$^1/_2$, 606$^1/_2$, 651, 656, 768, 1206, 1358, 1478, 1706, 1707, 1805, 1807, 1808, 1810, 1844, 1871, 4071.

Quebec. Archives du monastère de l'Hôtel Dieu.

Record of patients.

Quinsonas, Comte de. *Monseigneur de Laubérivière*. Paris: Librairie Orientale et Américaine, 1936.

Rapport des Archives Canadiennes, vols. 1886, 1887, 1899, 1904, 1905 and 1929. Ottawa.

Rapport des Archives de la Province de Québec, vols. 1923-1924, 1924-1925, 1926-1927, 1928-1929, 1930-1931, 1931-1932, 1944-1945, 1947-1948.

Rapport du 2e Comité des besoins en calories de l'Organisation des Nations Unies pour l'alimentation et l'agriculture. *Les besoins en calories*. Rome: F.A.O., 1957.

Reid, Allena G. "General Trade between Quebec and France during the French Regime". *Canadian Historical Review* 34, 1953.

Relation d'un voyage à la Nouvelle Orleans à bord du vaisseau la Gironde de la Compagnie des Indes. Edited by Gabriel Gravier. Paris: 1872.

Richebourg, L. and Boismêlé, A. *Histoire générale de la marine*. Vol. 3. Amsterdam: 1758.

Roy, Pierre-George. *Inventaire des Ordonnances des Intendants de la Nouvelle-France*. Vol. 3. Beauceville: L'Eclaireur Limitée, 1919.

Sagard, Gabriel-Théodat. *Le grand voyage au pays des Hurons*. Edited by B. Guégan. Paris: Editions du Carrefour, 1929.

Saint-Vallier, Mgr. Jean-Baptiste de la Croix Chevrières de. *Etat présent de l'Eglise et de la colonie française dans la Nouvelle-France*. Paris: Pépie, 1688.

Short, Robert. *Spoils of War: Portrait of the French and Spanish Ships taken by Lord Anson, Captain Buckle, and Sir E. Hawke in the year 1747*. Lympne Castle: Harry Margary, 1977.

Sulte, Benjamin. "Un voyage à la Nouvelle-France". *Revue canadienne* 6:22. Montréal: Prendergast and Co, 1886.

Vichot, Jacques. *Répertoire des navires de guerre français*. Paris: Association des Amis des Musées de la Marine, 1967.

Vignols, Léon. "L'importation en France au 18e siècle de boeuf salé d'Irlande", *Revue historique* 49. Paris: P.U.F., 1928.

Voyage au Canada fait depuis l'an 1751 à 1761, by J.C.B., Québec: Léger Brousseau, 1887.

Webster, John Clarence. *Relation of the voyage to Port Royal in Acadia or New France by the Sieur de Diéréville*. Toronto: The Champlain Society, 1933.

Wismes, Armel de. *Ainsi vivaient les marins*. Paris: France-Empire, 1971.

Index of Tables

1. Dimensions of royal vessels and merchantmen 18
2. Draughts 20
3. Merchantmen sailing between La Rochelle and New France, 1748–1759 26
4. Commercial traffic between France and New France, 1749–1754 . 27
5. Commercial traffic between France and Canada, 1755–1760 27
6. Commercial traffic between La Rochelle-Bordeaux and New France, 1755–1760 32
7. King's vessels in New France, 1755–1760 33
8. Cost of fitting out kings' vessels in 1743, for six months 44
9. Crossing times 57
10. Daily distances of the *Actif* 58
11. Complements in the French navy and merchant marine 82
12. Ages and wages of sailors in the French navy between 1745 and 1755 86
13. Daily rations for a petty officer and a seaman, for a six-month journey 108
14. Daily rations for the sick 109
15. Seamen hospitalized at the Hôtel-Dieu in Quebec City, 1755–1759 114

Index of Names

Abel, *see* Olivier
Abénaquise, the 37, 135
Achille, the 135
Actif, the 57, 114, 135
Afriquain, the 133
Aigle, the 51, 64, 83, 115, 135
Aimable, the 59, 112, 135
Aix, Isle of 43
Alcide, the 16, 22, 56, 135
Alcyon, the 134
Algonquin, the 16, 37, 135
Amphion, the 135
Anglesea, the 134
Anticosti, Isle of 54, 64, 77
Anville, Duke of, *see* La Rochefoucauld
Appollon, the 135
Aquilon, the 135
Arce, *see* Lom
Arc en ciel, the 53, 57, 112, 135
Ardent, the 17
Ardillières, *see* Le Moyne
Aréthuse, the 23, 135
Argonaute, the 101
Arismeinge, Jean 123
Astrée, the 133
Atalante, the 36, 123, 135
Aulneaux, Jean-Pierre 71
Aurora, *see Abénaquise*, the
Avenant, the 128
Avène, *see* Renaud

Badford, the 144
Baron of La Galissonnière, Roland-Michel., Marquis de La Galissonnière 52, 78, 130, 133
Bart, Jean 71
Bayonnais, the 123
Bayonne 26, 85, 133
Beauchêne 134
Beauharnois de Beaumont and de Villechauve, Claude de 133
Beaujeu, *see* Liénard
Beaumont, *see* Beauharnois
Beauville, de 133
Belle-Isle 47
Belle-Isle, Strait of 49, 51, 64, 78, 115
Bellin, Nicolas 54, 60, 62, 63, 78
Belliqueux, the 135
Berri, battallion of 114
Biche, the 135
Bienfaisant, the 40, 135
Bigot, François 29, 90, 134
Bizarre, the 135
Bon, the 112
Bonaventure, *see* Denys
Bonaventure, Island 148
Bordeaux 27, 28, 29, 32, 59, 70, 73, 90, 102, 107, 123

Boscawen, Edward 73
Boscawen of Exeter, the 73
Boucher, Madame François 127
Bougainville, Louis-Antoine de, Count of Bougainville 59, 92, 121
Bourgogne, regiment of 73
Bréard, Jacques-Michel
Brest 37, 42, 57, 90, 112, 114, 133, 135, 136, 140
Brillant, the 64
Brisay de Denonville, Catherine de, Marquis of Denonville, *see* Courtin of Tangeux
Brisay de Denonville, Jacques-René de, Marquis of Denonville 78, 115
Brittany 29
Brune, the 135
Buade, Louis de, Count of Frontenac and of Palluau 13

Cadet, Joseph 29, 36
Cabideuc, Emmanuel-August de, Count Dubois de La Motte 51, 80, 92, 114
Caméléon, the 134
Canada, the 20
Cape Breton, Island 49, 54, 89, 112
Capricieux, the 135
Cartier, Jacques 13
Cavagnial, *see* Rigaud
Célèbre, the 135
Certain, Nicolas 150
Chabert de Cogolin 85, 130
Chabosseau 80
Chaleur Bay 36
Challes, Robert 113, 121, 125
Chameau, the 16, 30, 43, 49, 54, 61, 64, 79, 103, 112, 113, 133
Champlain, Samuel de 52
Chaon, de 133
Charent, river 43
Chariot Royal, the 57, 134, 135
Charlevoix, Pierre-François-Xavier de 61, 92, 127, 133
Charron de La Barre, François 112
Chaussegros de Léry, Marie-Madeleine-Régis (Legardeur de Repentigny) 90
Chavagnac, Knight of 128
Chaviteau, Jacques 54, 78, 97
Cherbourg 125
Chèvre, the 135
Chevrières, *see* La Croix
Chézine, the 16, 20, 25, 137
Cogolin, *see* Chabert
Colbert, Jean-Baptiste 72, 83
Comète, the 135, 148
Concorde, the 135

Conteneuil 133
Cosse 134
Cotard, Jacques 148
Cotentin, Anne-Hilarion de, Count of Tourville 72
Coudres, Islands of 59, 71, 77, 78, 79, 125, 133
Courval, *see* Poulin
Crespel, Emmanuel 123
Cul-de-Sac 127
Cumberland, the 73

Damblimont 53
Dardanelles, Strait of 127
Dargent, Joseph 92
Daubigny 134
Dauphin, the 44, 56, 73
Dauphin Royal, the 16, 135
Défenseur, the 135
Denys de Bonaventure, Simon-Pierre 54
Denys de Vitré, Théodose-Mathieu 80
Desclaux, Pierre 70
Desgouttes 133
Deshaies 78
Desherbiers, Henri-François, Marquis de l'Étendrière 52
Des Méloizes, *see* Renaud
Desrosiers, Cape 77
Diadème, the 135
Diamant, the 19
Diane, the 42, 48, 49, 51, 54, 79, 134
Dièreville 85, 92, 109, 111, 128
Dizé (Dizet), Pierre 78
Doreil, André (Jean-Baptiste) 114
Dosquet, Pierre-Herman 121
Dragon, the 135
Driade, the 44
Dubois de La Motte, Count, *see* Cabideuc
Dubreil de Pontbriand, Henri-Marie 78, 121, 133
Duc d'Anville, the 134
Duc de Bourgogne, the 135
Duchêny, Jean-François 85
Duguay-Trouin, René 71
Dunkerque 133
Dupierre 145, 146
Du Plessis, *see* Parscau
Duquesnel, *see* Le Prévost
Duteillis 145
Du Vigneau 134

East India Company 113
Echo, the 136
Éclatant, the 52
Éléphant, the 64, 107, 133
Élisabeth, the 49
Elthan, the 144

171

Émeraude, the 134
Entreprenant, the 20, 136
Espérance, the 37, 135
Étenduère, Marquis de 80, 133
Éveillé, the 136

Fauvette, the 136
Fidèle, the 90, 135
Finisterre, Cape 22
Flambeau de la Mer, the 54
Fleur de lys, the 136
Flore, the 44
Fontenu, de 128
Forant, Isaac-Louis de 133
Formidable, the 136
Fortune, the 136
Fossecave, Joseph 90
Foucault 134
Fouchy 52
Fournier, Father 53
François, the 133
Frédéric, gate (Louisbourg) 62
Friponne, the 134
Froger de l'éguille 79
Froment, Joseph 123
Frontenac, Count of, *see* Buade

Garnier, Jean-Baptiste 78
Gibraltar, Strait of 127
Gironde, the 112, 133, 134
Glorieux, the 136
Gomain 134
Goos, Pieter 53, 54
Gradis, Abraham 70, 89, 110
Gradis, family 29, 32
Grand Banks, the 49, 51, 53, 54, 71, 76, 103, 109, 127, 140, 141, 143
Green Banks 54
Guernsey, Isle of 73
Guyart, Marie 92
Guyana 26, 29

Hadley 52
Hardy, the 136
Harrison, John 53
Hasard, the 123
Havard, Marie-Anne (Merven de La Rivière) 149
Hector, the 136
Hermione, the 16, 136
Héros, the 16, 93, 116, 133, 136
Herticot 148
Heureux Moine, the 117
Hévé, Pierre 95
Hocquart, Commander 113
Hocquart, Gilles 64, 93, 133
Hôpital Général of Québec 114
Hôtel-Dieu of Québec 114, 117
Hougue, La (Battle of) 72
Houin, Jacques 84
Houin, Louis 84
Huault, Joseph 59

Iberville, *see* Le Moyne
Illustre, the 136
Imbert, Jacques 90
Inflexible, the 136

Jason, the 19, 64, 90, 92, 113, 116, 133
Jauge 70
Joly, Julien 78

Kamouraska 77, 79
Kersalaun, de 141
Keulen, *see* Van Keulen
Knowles, Sir Charles 144

La Barre, *see* Charron
Labat, Father 110
La Chassée, de 117
La Clue, Knight of 81, 123
La Corne, Maurice de 90
Lacoste, Jean 117
La Croix de Chevrières de Saint-Vallier, Jean-Baptiste de 121
La Filière 134
La Galissonnière, Marquis de, *see* Baron
La Giraudais, *see* Chénard
Lahontan, Baron of, *see* Lom d'Arce
La Jonquière, the 133
La Jonquière, Marquis de, *see* Taffanel
La Maraudière, Abbé 121
Lamirande 133
La Motte, *see* Cabideuc
Languedoc, regiment of 57
La Richardière, *see* Testu
La Rivière, *see* Merven
La Rochefoucauld de Roye, Jean-Baptiste-Louis-Frédéric de, Marquis de Roucy, Duke of Anville 76, 113
La Rochelle 25, 26, 27, 28, 32, 37, 43, 47, 54, 69, 70, 90, 93, 123, 152
La Sarre, regiment of 114
La Saussaye 115, 133
Latache, Marie 90
La Touche, *see* Aulneau
Latouche Macarty, Charles *see* Latouche
Latour, Lord 149
Lauberivière, *see* Pourroy
La Villéon 134
Leblanc 118
Le Cordier 53
Legardeur de Repentigny, Louis 133
Legardeur de Repentigny, Marie-Madeleine-Régis, *see* Chaussegros de Léry
Legardeur de Tilly 134
Légère, the 136
Léguille, *see* Froger

Le Havre 26, 37, 133, 134, 135
Lemaire, family 51
Le Mercier, François-Marc-Antoine 90
Le Moyne d'Iberville and D'Ardillières, Pierre 103
Léopard, the 32, 112, 113, 134, 136
Lepage de Saint-Barnabé, Pierre 77
Le Prévost Duquesnel, Jean-Baptiste-Louis 92, 133
Léry, *see* Chaussegros
Lévis, François de, Duke of Lévis 57
Licorne, the 57, 136
Liénard de Beaujeu, Daniel-Hyacinthe-Marie 118
Lièvres, Islands of 77
Lilleronde 125
Loire, the 77
Lom d'Arce, Louis-Armand de, Baron of Labontan 54, 77, 85, 125
London 72
Louis XV 72
Louisbourg 26, 29, 32, 33, 36, 40, 42, 49, 52, 54, 57, 62, 65, 73, 76, 77, 81, 90, 101, 106, 110, 114, 119, 121, 127, 149
Lys, the 56, 136

Machault, the 21, 35, 36, 38, 39, 44, 96, 120, 122
Macreuse, the 136
Madeleine, the 101
Magnifique, the 136
Manicouagan 77
Maréchal de Senneterre, the 36
Marie de l'Incarnation, *see* Guyart
Marie-Anne, the 118
Marie-Élisabeth, the 81
Mars, the 44, 113
Marseilles 26, 78, 89
Martinique 28
Matane 79
Maurepas, Count of, *see* Phélypeau
Méchin 133
Menneville, *see* Duquesne
Mercure, the 110, 145
Merven, Tanguy 149
Merven de La Rivière, Louis-François 149
Merven de La Rivière, Marie-Anne, *see* Havard
Messager, the 136
Métis 77
Montcalm, Louis-Joseph de, Marquis de Montcalm 57, 80, 92, 112, 121, 128
Montlouet, de 140
Montréal 36

172

Nantes 26, 137
Nau, Luc-François 93, 113
Navières, Joseph 77, 93
Navy Board 22
Nepveu 134
Neptune, the 54
Néréide, the 42, 65, 147
Northumberland, the 134
Nouvelle Victoire, the 90

Observatory of Paris 54
Oies, Cape 77
Olivier, Abel 80
Olivier, François 90
Opiniâtre, the 136
Orléans, Isle 77, 79, 80
Orléans, street 149
Outarde, the 51, 83, 136
Ozanne, Nicolas 88

Palluau, Count of, *see* **Buade**
Paön, the 121
Paris, city 54, 93, 140
Paris, Abbé 115
Parscau Du Plessis, L.G. 128
Péan, Angélique (Lilie), *see* Renaud d'Avène Des Méloizes
Péan, Michel-Jean-Hugues 90
Pèlerins, the 77
Pellegrin, Gabriel 49, 54, 77, 78, 79
Périer de Salvert, Antoine-Alexis 134
Phélypeau, Jean-Frédéric, Count of Maurepas 52
Phélypeaux, Louis, Count of Pontchartrain 52, 72
Plymouth 134, 137
Point-Lévy 66, 77
Poli, the 103
Pomone, the 36, 136
Pontbriand, *see* Dubreil 121
Pontchartrain, Count of, *see* Phélypeaux
Portefaix, the 121
Port Royal 128
Poulin de Courval, François-Louis 87
Pourroy de Lauberivière, François-Louis de 112, 121, 133
Prudent, the 40, 136

Québec 21, 26, 27, 29, 32, 33, 36, 37, 44, 49, 54, 57, 59, 66, 71, 73, 77, 78, 79, 80, 85, 89, 90, 99, 100, 106, 107, 112, 113, 114, 115, 118, 124, 125, 127, 135, 140, 144, 150
Querquelin 133
Quincampoix, Isle of 64

Raby, Augustin 80
Radouays, Lord of 53
Race, Cape 140, 141
Raisonnable, the 136
Raudot 103
Renaud D'Avène Des Méloizes, Angélique (Lilie), (Péan) 90
Renommée, the 64, 107, 118, 123, 124
Repentigny, *see* Legardeur
Rhinocéros, the 64, 136
Ricoeur 127
Rigaud de Vaudreuil, Louis-Philippe de, Marquis de Vaudreuil 79, 133
Rimouski 77, 115
Rioux, Nicolas 77
Ristigouche River 148
Robin, Pierre 125
Robuste, the 73
Rochefort 37, 42, 43, 47, 51, 68, 133, 135, 136
Rochers Aux Oiseaux 127, 148
Rossel (Commander) 79, 133
Rossel (Ensigne) 115
Roucy, Marquis de, *see* La Rochefoucauld
Rouge, Isle 77
Roy 80
Royale, Isle 30, 62, 64, 76, 84, 133
Royal Navy (French) 72
Royal-Roussillon, regiment of 114
Roye, *see* La Rochefoucauld
Rozier 118
Ruaux, Islands of 77
Rubis, the 16, 19, 44, 51, 52, 64, 77, 78, 79, 80, 112, 113, 114, 115, 116, 133

Sables-d'Olonne, the 84
Sagard, Gabriel 61
Sage, the 136
Sainte-Anne-de-Beaupré 78, 118, 119

Saint-Antoine, the 125
Saint-Barnabé, *see* Lepage 21
Saint-Clair 133
Saint-Domingue 28
Saint-Gilles, the 16
Saint-James 133
Saint-Joseph, the 16
Saint-Laurent, the 20
Saint-Louis, the 16
Saint-Malo 49, 73, 148, 149
Saint-Martin-de-Ré
Saint-Michel, the 16
Saint-Paul, Isle of 49
Saint-Pierre, Isle of 49, 54
Saint-Sébastien, the 57
Saint-Vallier, *see* La Croix
Salé 71
Salvert, *see* Périer
Samson, the 123

Samsom, Michel 123
Sarrazin, Michel 112
Sauvage, the 57, 136
Savard 80
Scatarie, Isle of 49
Seine, river 77
Seine, the 37, 61, 134
Sept-Îles 77
Seven Years' War 26, 28, 36, 51, 70, 72, 73, 76, 83, 84, 89, 90, 105, 110
Sirène, the 136
Sphinx, the 136
Suffolk, the 144
Superb, the 136, 151
Sybille, the 44

Taffanel de la Jonquière, Jacques-Pierre de, Marquis de Jonquière 36, 53, 54, 74, 78, 130, 133
Talon, Jean 47, 57, 79
Tangeux, *see* Courtin
Tartar, the 73
Téméraire, the 61, 112
Ténériffe 54, 140
Testu de la Richardière, Richard 78, 79
Tigre, the 44, 134, 136
Tilly 78
Tonnant, the 16, 42, 65, 136
Torbay, the 73
Toulon 37, 81, 88, 91, 134, 135, 136
Toulouse, street 149
Tourville, Count of, *see* Cotentin
Tremblay 80
Triomphant, the 16
Triton, the 81, 123
Trois Maries, the 64

Vaillant, the 136
Valeur, the 136
Van Keulen, Gerard 53, 54
Vaudreuil, Marquis de, *see* Rigaud
Vauquelin, Jean 23
Voutron 133
Vernet, Joseph 70
Verrier, Claude-Joseph 62
Verrier, Étienne 62
Verte, Isle 77, 79
Verville, Jean-François de 121
Victoire, the 133
Vienne, river 77
Vierge de Grace, the 124
Villechauve, *see* Beauharnois
Vitré, *see* Denys
Vive le Roy, the 150
Voutron 134

West Indies, the 26, 29, 51, 110

Zephyr, the 44, 134, 136